PROVERBS
A DEVOTIONAL COMMENTARY

WILLIAM MACDONALD

PROVERBS
A DEVOTIONAL COMMENTARY

WILLIAM MACDONALD

PROVERBS
By William MacDonald
Copyright © 2009

Published by
GOSPEL FOLIO PRESS
304 Killaly St. W.
Port Colborne, ON, Canada L3K 6A6
1-800-952-2382
www.gospelfolio.com

Scripture taken from the New King James Version unless otherwise noted.

Hard Cover ISBN: 9781897117668
Paper Back ISBN: 9781926765037

Cover design by Rachel Brooks

Printed in the United States of America.

Contents

Proverbs
Introduction

Let's get right to the point. The key word of this book is wisdom. It is found 54 times. As the book progresses, it becomes clear that wisdom is not only an attribute; it is also a person. And still closer study reveals that wisdom is the Lord Jesus Christ, the Son of God.

That means that whenever you come to the word wisdom, used of a person, you can substitute the name Christ. This makes the book glow with unexpected splendor.

There are several verses in the New Testament that justify identifying wisdom with our Lord Jesus Christ.

In 1 Corinthians 1:24, the Lord Jesus is called *"the wisdom of God."*

Colossians 2:3 says distinctly that *"all the treasures of wisdom and knowledge"* are found in Him.

In 1 Corinthians 1:30 we read that *"Christ Jesus, who became for us wisdom from God—and righteousness and sanctification and redemption."*

There are other times when our Lord is identified as the wisdom of God. In Luke 11:49, the Pharisees and lawyers had mounted a furious attack on Him. He replied by saying, *"Therefore the wisdom of God also said, 'I will send them prophets and apostles, and some of them they will kill and persecute.'"* Here the Lord identifies Himself as the wisdom of God. He had predicted the savagery of his foes in Matthew 23:34-36.

When the Savior found the Jewish people to be utterly unpleasable, He said, *"The Son of Man came eating and drinking, and they say, 'Look, a glutton and a winebibber, a friend of tax collectors and sinners!' But wisdom is justified by her children"* (Matt. 11:19). Here wisdom refers to the Lord Himself. His children are the disciples and all who received Him. They reckoned the Lord to be the promised Messiah.

But there is a problem. The person named wisdom in Proverbs is a woman. Take 9:1-6, for instance. It is a lady who invites men and women to her feast. How then can wisdom be applied to the Lord?

The answer is that in both the Hebrew and Greek languages, the noun wisdom is feminine. Matthew, Luke, and the others we have quoted would have committed a colossal blunder if they had translated it in the male gender.

Centuries after Solomon penned the book of Proverbs, our Lord was walking with two disciples to a place called Emmaus. On the way, *"He expounded to them in all the Scriptures the things concerning Himself"* (Luke 24:27). When He came to Proverbs, He found a treasure trove in the many references concerning wisdom. He applied them to Himself. We can do the same thing today. We can find the Lord Jesus throughout the book.

The key verse is 1:7, *"The fear of the LORD is the beginning of knowledge, but fools despise wisdom and instruction."* It is also found in 9:10: *"The fear of the LORD is the beginning of wisdom, and the knowledge of the Holy One is understanding."* The subject of the fear of the Lord or the lack thereof is also mentioned in the following verses in Proverbs: 1:29; 2:5; 8:13; 10:27; 14:26; 14:27; 15:16; 15:33; 16:6; 19:23 and 23:17.

The Book of Proverbs deals largely with two characters: the wise man and the fool. The wise person is one who trusts the Lord. In New Testament parlance he is a born again believer. It does not mean that he perfectly displays every virtue that is found in the book. It does mean that he characteristically chooses what is holy. For instance, he obeys his parents, chooses decent companions, and avoids the global sin, immorality.

The fool is a person who has not believed in the Lord. Today we would say that he has never been born again. This does not mean that he has committed every sin that is ascribed to fools. Rather it means that his life is characterized by sin.

It may sound harsh to call unbelievers fools, but consider the following. God offers salvation as a free gift. There is absolutely nothing to pay. There is no meritorious work that must be done.

8

There is no risk. There is everything to gain and nothing to lose. What should we call someone who rejects a gift like that?

You will meet other interesting people here. There is the loving father, imparting sound advice to his son. There are two prominent women—the ideal wife and the immoral woman. There are good companions and the kind to avoid. There are good rulers and some who are forgettable. The book is a composite of human life in every age.

Many of the proverbs about the fool end with death. It may sound as if a fool always dies promptly. That, of course, is not the case. What it means is that a fool's life does not tend to longevity and it ends in eternal separation from God if he does not repent of his sins and trust the Savior.

Many of the proverbs are statements of general truth, but you must allow for exceptions.

Many proverbs are repeated in the book. This is doubtless repetition for emphasis.

Moral behavior in the Book of Proverbs does not rise to the heights found in the New Testament. The Old Testament teaches that we should not steal (Ex. 20:15). The New Testament goes beyond this: *"Let him who stole steal no longer, but rather let him labor, working with his hands what is good, that he may have something to give him who has need"* (Eph. 4:28).

In Proverbs you will not find many of the great spiritual truths that are revealed in the New Testament. Here are some of the major ones: the church composed of all believing Jews and Gentiles; Christ the Head of the church; all believers are members; the Church as the body and bride of Christ; new ministries of the Holy Spirit; new nearness to God the Father; new truth concerning the after-life; the Rapture of the Church; the believer's position in Christ, not the law, as the believer's rule of life. These truths were not revealed until the apostles and prophets of the New Testament era.

Some words in the Hebrew manuscripts are obscure and difficult to translate. This explains the difference in the way some verses read in different translations, and the difficulty in explaining a few of the verses.

With all this in mind, let us turn to the text of Proverbs.

Proverbs 1

1 *The proverbs of Solomon the son of David, king of Israel:*

2 *To know wisdom and instruction,*
To perceive the words of understanding,

3 *To receive the instruction of wisdom,*
Justice, judgment, and equity;

4 *To give prudence to the simple,*
To the young man knowledge and discretion—

5 *A wise man will hear and increase learning,*
And a man of understanding will attain wise counsel,

6 *To understand a proverb and an enigma,*
The words of the wise and their riddles.

7 *The fear of the LORD is the beginning of knowledge,*
But fools despise wisdom and instruction.

8 *My son, hear the instruction of your father,*
And do not forsake the law of your mother;

9 *For they will be a graceful ornament on your head,*
And chains about your neck.

10 *My son, if sinners entice you,*
Do not consent.

11 *If they say, "Come with us,*
Let us lie in wait to shed blood;
Let us lurk secretly for the innocent without cause;

12 *Let us swallow them alive like Sheol,*
And whole, like those who go down to the Pit;

13 *We shall find all kinds of precious possessions,*
We shall fill our houses with spoil;

14 *Cast in your lot among us,*
Let us all have one purse"—

15 My son, do not walk in the way with them,
Keep your foot from their path;

16 For their feet run to evil,
And they make haste to shed blood.

17 Surely, in vain the net is spread
In the sight of any bird;

18 But they lie in wait for their own blood,
They lurk secretly for their own lives.

19 So are the ways of everyone who is greedy for gain;
It takes away the life of its owners.

20 Wisdom calls aloud outside;
She raises her voice in the open squares.

21 She cries out in the chief concourses,
At the openings of the gates in the city
She speaks her words:

22 "How long, you simple ones, will you love simplicity?
For scorners delight in their scorning,
And fools hate knowledge.

23 Turn at my rebuke;
Surely I will pour out my spirit on you;
I will make my words known to you.

24 Because I have called and you refused,
I have stretched out my hand and no one regarded,

25 Because you disdained all my counsel,
And would have none of my rebuke,

26 I also will laugh at your calamity;
I will mock when your terror comes,

27 When your terror comes like a storm,
And your destruction comes like a whirlwind,
When distress and anguish come upon you.

28 Then they will call on me, but I will not answer;
They will seek me diligently, but they will not find me.

29 Because they hated knowledge
And did not choose the fear of the LORD,

30 They would have none of my counsel
And despised my every rebuke.

31 Therefore they shall eat the fruit of their own way,
And be filled to the full with their own fancies.

32 For the turning away of the simple will slay them,
And the complacency of fools will destroy them;

33 But whoever listens to me will dwell safely,
And will be secure, without fear of evil."

Chapter 1

The "Purpose" of the Proverbs (1:1-6)

1:1 The author of most of the book was Solomon, the only son of David to reign as king in Jerusalem. He was one of the wisest men in God's creation. Chapter 30 is ascribed to Agur, and 31 to King Lemuel. That's all we know about these latter two persons.

1:2. At the beginning of this verse it helps to supply the words "The purpose of this book is." The king devotes five verses here to his reasons for writing.

He strikes the keynote at the very outset. The word wisdom, as used here, means the ability to make sound decisions and take action that best promotes the glory of God, the blessing of others, and one's own good. Wisdom teaches people the virtues to cultivate and the sins to avoid.

1:3. The word instruction presupposes that there is a teacher. The Christian's teacher is the Holy Spirit. He uses Solomon, Agur (Prov. 30) and Lemuel (Prov. 31) to give instruction that calls for obedience.

This book is designed to instruct its readers about what is just, true, and proper, and what is free from bias or favoritism.

1:4. It teaches simple-minded people to be prudent, that is, how to act with skill and good judgment. Young men receive knowledge that will help them make good decisions.

1:5. You can tell a wise man by his willingness to receive instruction and thus grow in wisdom and knowledge.

1:6. Solomon's proverbs contain riddles and enigmas. Chapter 11:24 is an example of an enigma: *"There is that scattereth, and yet increaseth; and there is that withholdeth more than is meet, but it tendeth to poverty."* This is hard to understand by people who think you get rich by accumulating treasure.

The Key

1:7. This (and its counterpart in 9:10) is the key verse of the book of Proverbs. Usually when we think of the fear of the Lord we think of being punished by Him. But that is not the beginning of wisdom. Here the fear of the Lord is:

- Trusting in Him for eternal salvation.
- Surrendering one's life to Him for whatever He wishes to do with it.
- Obeying His word.
- Worshiping Him.
- Praying to Him.
- Walking in holiness.
- Fearing to displease Him.

In brief, the fear of the Lord means living in reverent fellowship with Him.

Fools despise a life of wisdom.

Shun evil companions (1:8-19)

1:8. Verses 8-19 are addressed to *"my son."* They reveal the heartbeat of parents who are anxious that their son should enjoy the good life and bring credit to his father and mother. There is an ocean of emotion in the simple words *"my son."* They are full of love, aspiration, joy, and parental pride. They are the whispered exclamation when a father holds his baby boy for the first time. They are the words of admiration when he sees his son's first step and hears his first word. The father breathes it as he follows his boy through the early seasons of life. His satisfaction grows when his firstborn confesses Christ, is baptized, and takes his place in the fellowship of the church. His joy knows no bounds when his son makes decisions that he has been taught from the Word of God. The son fears the Lord, committing himself to Jesus in a life of devotion.

H.A. Ironside gives the reason for the Proverbs:

> "God would save all who heed what is there recorded from the heart breaking experiences of the man who was chosen to write them."

1:9 If young people follow the wise teachings of their parents, they will develop a character of moral beauty (ornaments) and honor (chains of gold). A man of wisdom is a man of honor.

1:10 In the following verses, Solomon warns against the terrible mistake of choosing bad friends. Many are tempted to admire and imitate the wicked because of their apparent success and superficial happiness (see Pss. 37 and 73). Solomon is not saying that it is just one great step from rebellion at home to death as a gangster. Rather he is picturing a possible progression that begins with disobedience at home, goes on to unwise choice of friends, then to a life of wickedness, culminating in death. Note that concern for wisdom in choosing friends is at the very beginning of the father's advice. This shows how important the subject is.

Here is a modern scenario that illustrates where the wrong crowd can lead a fellow.

Steve's parents noticed that he was hanging around with friends who were questionable to say the least. He adopted their clothing style, their haircut, and their vocabulary.

His grades at school began to slip. Then he frequently missed classes.

When he was home, he spent most of the time in his room with the door closed. He became increasingly withdrawn and disturbed.

His parents tried to win him back to family life, but he was uncooperative. When they showed kindness, he showed no gratitude; he was unpleasable. No matter how they counseled or warned him he didn't care, and it even showed on his face.

His mother and dad were distraught. They didn't want to believe what they suspected.

Then one day when his mother was cleaning his room, she found a glass pipe and other drug paraphernalia. Now she understood. Her son was on drugs.

Steve supported his drug habit by stealing. When this proved insufficient, he began pushing drugs.

It all ended abruptly with a call from the police. Their son had overdosed. His body was at the local morgue.

1:11. The father again zeros in on the choice of companions. The wrong crowd invites a young fellow to join them. Their timing is perfect because he has reached the age where he wants to belong, to be accepted by his peers. So he feels enormous pressure to join them in spite of parental warnings. The offered bait is the excitement of violence, the lure of secrecy, and the thrill of power.

1:12. The gang doesn't hide the fact that murder is part of the package. He knows in advance that he may be a killer.

Their innocent victims will go down to Sheol and the Pit. Sheol may mean the grave or the disembodied state. The Pit is the place of the dead. Both words express the obscurity in the minds of the people at that time. They had dim and indistinct views of what happens at the time of death. It is clear to us, because Christ *"brought life and immortality to light through the gospel"* (2 Tim. 1:10).

1:13. There is the promise of making money easily and quickly. The gang speaks confidently of all kinds of treasures – houses full of them.

1:14. The desire of the young man to belong is heightened when the gang promises to share a common purse. But notice, still there is no word about arrest, trial, conviction, imprisonment, and possible capital punishment.

1:15. The father advises his son to stay away from these thugs and their murderous intentions. It is important for young people to be wise in their choice of friends and companions.

1:16. As soon as he joins them, he will quickly be involved in crimes and the shedding of innocent blood. Notice the words run and haste. It is urgent. There is no time to think of the consequences.

1:17. Those evil doers have no time to weigh the matter carefully. Even a bird will not fly into a net if it sees the danger ahead.

1:18. But these men plunge forward in their lust for easy money, careless of the fact that their crimes may land them in the penitentiary or the cemetery.

A stupid person is sometimes called a birdbrain. That is an insult to birds. Birds will not willingly fly into a visible net that may cost them their life. They are not as stupid as these law-breakers, who know the danger ahead but show no restraint. "I'm not afraid," they say. But they should be!

1:19. This is the typical behavior of sinners who are after unrighteous gain; it not only destroys the life of the innocent but their own lives as well.

When young men refuse parental teaching and wind up as common criminals, and when you ask the parents, "How did that ever happen?" the common reply is, "He got in with the wrong crowd." But that is not a sufficient explanation. He knew it was wrong. He knew it was risky. Why didn't he have a little backbone and say, "No thanks, I'm not interested in your offer." Why didn't he have the gumption to say in the words of an old hymn:

> I will not go with you to hell.
> I choose with Jesus Christ to dwell.
> – Anonymous

Wisdom's call to the vulnerable (1:20-33)

1:20. In verses 20-33 we see Wisdom personified as a wom-an of excellence. She is ubiquitous, calling out her urgent mes-sage at every public square.

1:21. Because her call is so publicly proclaimed, there is no excuse for anyone. No one can say he didn't know. Wisdom's banquet is available to all.

1:22. To the naïve, the scorners, and the fools who despise being told anything, she has a word of rebuke (see v. 29), even if she knows beforehand that they are unteachable.

1:23. If they would just do an about-face, that is, repent, she would give them a new frame of mind and teach them the right way.

1:24. It is clear that this is not her first attempt to reach them. She has been calling repeatedly. She has been stretching out her hand to them. She did not wait for them to ask for her advice; she took the initiative, calling them to listen.

1:25. They rejected her counsel, and utterly refused her correction.

1:26. As a result, she will laugh at their calamity and mock at their distress. It seems strange that wisdom would do this. Would that not be vengeful and mean spirited?

One explanation is that laughing and mocking are figures of speech in which human traits and emotions are ascribed to Wisdom. It does not mean that any laughing and mocking are actually involved. For example, when we say, "That clever man had the last laugh," it does not mean than any laugh was involved. The simple meaning is that by his convincing argument, he was able to have the last, winning word. He settled the matter. Here is another idiomatic expression, "She now had to laugh on the other side of her face." It means that she got a taste of her own medicine.

Another explanation is that when God laughs it is never sinful, but righteous, as in Psalm 2:4 where the LORD laughs and holds the unrighteous in derision. Spurgeon commented on this as being the divine reaction to the absurd, irrational and futile attempts of man to dislodge His government.

And so it is in verse 26. When wisdom is said to laugh and mock, it means that she is thinking of the calamity that comes to fools who reject her counsel. Obedience would have averted the distress and anguish. Whatever else this means, it cannot mean that God laughs unrighteously or cruelly at the fool's calamity. The words are simply idioms that express wisdom's regret over the fool's inevitable retribution. It is a literary device attributing human behavior to God. That is true also in Psalm 2:4. It would be unworthy of God to find humor in man's downfall.

George Williams explains:

> Verse 26 does not mean that wisdom will actually deride her rejecters. It is the language of idiomatic argument. The rejecters laughed and mocked at wisdom; when therefore the calamities came upon them

which wisdom predicted, their laughter and mock-
ery turned on themselves, and so wisdom might be
justly said to deride their calamity.[1]

In similar language, Psalm 2:4 describes the Lord's reaction to man's futile defiance, and His righteous pleasure in His
final vindication.

1:27. The fool's downfall will come with the fury of a storm
and the destruction of a tornado. It will be a time of desperate
trouble and suffering.

1:28. The cries for help will go unanswered and the search
for wisdom will prove futile. It will be too late (cf. Jer. 11:11).

1:29. They had consciously decided to hate knowledge and
the fear of God. Now payday has come.

1:30. They had stubbornly rejected wisdom's advice and
correction. That explains their hopeless condition.

1:31. They must suffer the consequences. They sowed their
wild oats; now they must reap the harvest. They chose to do things
their own way; but now they can't choose the consequences.

1:32. Their destiny is an inescapable result of their devil-
may-care attitude and stubborn refusal.

1:33. If only they had chosen the way of wisdom, they
would now be enjoying peace and security.

There is a striking parallel between this passage picturing
Wisdom's message (v. 20-33) and Christ's gospel invitation to
lost humanity. Note the following:

Christ is everywhere. The world can hear His message
through missionaries, the Bible, radio, television, and the Internet. The Bible can be purchased at the local drug store, and
found even in hotel rooms.

His name is banned in many places. It is not politically correct to talk about Him. We must not use the word Christmas or
sing Christmas carols in school. Prayer to Him in the schools is
forbidden. Efforts are made to remove the name of God from
the pledge of allegiance—and from coins.

But He is the inescapable Christ. In unexpected ways and

---

1 *The Student's Commentary on the Holy Scriptures*, Grand Rapids,
MI, Kregel Publications, 1926, p.417.

at unrehearsed times, some famous person will testify for Him. An athlete will confess Him publicly. A government official will tell of Christ's power to save. A singer will choose one of the old hymns of the faith. A child will get in a word of praise for Jesus. A secular crowd will sing "Amazing Grace." The Lord loves to use people with little formal education to confound the skeptics with a few well-chosen verses of Scripture. Jesus cannot be hidden.

His message is for all mankind. Some are simple. Others are scorners. Still others are fools. But all are sinners who need a Savior.

He calls on all to turn, that is, to repent, and promises to pour out His Spirit on them if they do. In other words, their sins will be forgiven and they will be made fit for heaven. Then He will teach them the great truths of the Christian faith.

Christ has been calling people for a long time. In sunshine and rain He has patiently waited for entrance. Paul quotes Him as saying, *"All day long I have stretched out My hands to a disobedient and contrary people"* (Rom. 10:21).

His invitation is rejected by the majority. People refuse the gospel even though it offers eternal salvation without cost and without price. They despise their Creator God.

People who refuse the gospel will experience calamity, terror, destruction, distress, and anguish. The Lord will laugh and mock, not in a vindictive way, but in righteous indignation, frustration and sorrow, thinking what they might have enjoyed. "Of all sad words of tongue or pen, the saddest of these are: 'It might have been'" (John Greenleaf Whittier).

Christ will not always strive with men. The day of grace will end. Then it will be too late to be saved. He will not be there to answer sinners' call or to reveal Himself to them in salvation.

Their doom is their own fault. They hated the knowledge of God, did not choose to fear Him, refused His advice, and despised His correction (cf. 2 Thess. 2:10-12). Now they must reap the awful results of their unbelief. Their rejection of Christ will doom them. Their smugness and self-satisfaction seals their fate.

Only those who believe in the Lord Jesus Christ will find safety and security.

Proverbs 2

1 *My son, if you receive my words,*
And treasure my commands within you,

2 *So that you incline your ear to wisdom,*
And apply your heart to understanding;

3 *Yes, if you cry out for discernment,*
And lift up your voice for understanding,

4 *If you seek her as silver,*
And search for her as for hidden treasures;

5 *Then you will understand the fear of the LORD,*
And find the knowledge of God.

6 *For the LORD gives wisdom;*
From His mouth come knowledge and understanding;

7 *He stores up sound wisdom for the upright;*
He is a shield to those who walk uprightly;

8 *He guards the paths of justice,*
And preserves the way of His saints.

9 *Then you will understand righteousness and justice,*
Equity and every good path.

10 *When wisdom enters your heart,*
And knowledge is pleasant to your soul,

11 *Discretion will preserve you;*
Understanding will keep you,

12 *To deliver you from the way of evil,*
From the man who speaks perverse things,

13 *From those who leave the paths of uprightness*
To walk in the ways of darkness;

14 *Who rejoice in doing evil,*
And delight in the perversity of the wicked;

15 *Whose ways are crooked,*
And who are devious in their paths;

16 *To deliver you from the immoral woman,*
From the seductress who flatters with her words,

17 *Who forsakes the companion of her youth,*
And forgets the covenant of her God.

18 *For her house leads down to death,*
And her paths to the dead;

19 *None who go to her return,*
Nor do they regain the paths of life—

20 *So you may walk in the way of goodness,*
And keep to the paths of righteousness.

21 *For the upright will dwell in the land,*
And the blameless will remain in it;

22 *But the wicked will be cut off from the earth,*
And the unfaithful will be uprooted from it.

Chapter 2

Conditions for receiving
the knowledge of God (2:1-5)

2:1. This chapter is in praise of wisdom. It is directed to Solomon's son, but it is suitable for all his children. It is a heart-to-heart talk from a parent's heart to theirs.

2:2. The main point is that children should set their hearts on wisdom, which is another way of saying, Give first place to the Lord. Having done that, they should devote themselves to gaining a deep understanding of the Word of God.

This verse pictures what should take place in every Christian home where the parents urge their young ones to come to the Savior.

2:3. Another goal should be to develop discernment in the things of God by testing everything by the Scriptures. And the children should pray earnestly for understanding of the great doctrines of the faith.

2:4. They should search for wisdom as they would for silver, for other precious metals, and for precious stones hidden in the earth.

Someone may object that all we need for salvation is faith in Christ. That is true, but there is a certain mysterious, non-meritorious action that we must take. Consider the following: *"Seek the LORD while He may be found"* (Isa. 55:6). *"And ye shall seek me, and find me, when ye shall search for me with all your heart"* (Jer. 29:13). *"Strive to enter through the narrow gate"* (Luke 13:24). The prodigal son said, *"I will arise and go to my father"* (Luke 15:18). *"If anyone hears My voice and opens the door"* (Rev. 3:20). There is an inertia to be overcome.

The Bible is our most precious earthly possession. It will be our Book in eternity. What we learn about it here determines our capacity to enjoy the glories of heaven. This should motivate each of us to study it and meditate on it more.

These verses teach that a person should desire wisdom with such intensity that he is willing to expend his finest efforts to obtain it.

2:5. If he is that serious about gaining divine wisdom, he will never fail to find it. He will come to know God and to give Him the place of preeminence in his life.

It is as people find the Person called Wisdom that they understand what faith in Him means, and learn about the knowledge of God. The blinders are removed from their eyes and the Sacred Word glows with sublime light.

The wisdom from above (2:6-22)

2:6. The Lord is wisdom and He gives wisdom. It is through Him that we learn the answers to the problems of life. He reveals salvation's plan. He divulges God's plan of the ages.

2:7. He provides all that is necessary for life and godliness (1 Pet. 1:3). He provides spiritual armor to shield us from the enemy.

2:8. His words promote justice, thus preserving His people from lawlessness. His words protect them from the enemy like spiritual armor.

2:9. When a person comes to know Christ as Lord and Savior, he has a whole new way of thinking. He thinks God's thoughts after Him. He strives to be fair in all his dealings and to treat everyone without favoritism. It becomes his way of life.

In the following 13 verses, Solomon again lists some of the benefits that wisdom brings to a life: preservation by acting discreetly (v. 11); protection through understanding what God's will is (v. 11); deliverance from evil men (vv. 12-15); and deliverance from the evil woman (vv. 16-19). This latter section (vv. 16-19) is the first of several warnings against immoral women.

2:10. A person must seriously desire wisdom and knowledge with heart and soul. His search will never be disappointed.

2:11. Then good sense and wise thinking will save him from falling into the traps of sin.

2:12. It will save him from evil ways, and from the rebellious type whose conversation is perverse and vulgar, and who jokes about lawbreaking and tells how to beat the system.

2:13. Here the warning is about those who turn away, abandon the right road, and leave decent society to live in the shady back alleys of lawlessness.

2:14. They find their happiness in breaking the law and in partnering with others who do. A New Testament counterpart of this is Romans 1:32. In today's society they may be guilty of hacking into computers, running scams, trafficking in illegal copies of CDs, DVDs, music, games and programs, possessing and trafficking in drugs, of stealing cars, and of breaking into homes.

2:15. Their plans and behavior are alike crooked. In spirit, soul, and body, they are depraved.

2:16. In verses 10 to 15, Solomon has been thinking how a life of wisdom would save his son from walking with evil men. Now he thinks of another great deliverance—that is from the evil woman. It is not without significance that nine passages and individual verses are devoted to the seductress (2:16-2:25; 5:1-20; 6:24-35; 7:6-27; 9:13-19; 22:14; 23:26-28; 30:20; 31:3). She is also known as an immoral woman, an evil woman, a harlot, a foolish woman, and an adulteress. Another version calls her a wayward woman.

She appeals to a man's pride by flattering him with honeyed words.

2:17. She leaves her husband to sleep with other men. She forgets the marriage covenant by which she vowed before witnesses to remain faithful "till death do us part." In Malachi 2:14 the Lord rebukes unfaithful men who break their marriage vows.

2:18. Having sex with a morally loose woman leads in only one direction—that is, to death. It is a sin unlike any other. *"But he who commits sexual immorality sins against his own body"* (1 Cor. 6:18). The person may repent and be forgiven but there are consequences that persist.

This is one of many verses warning that various forms of evil behavior lead to death. What is meant by death here? Does it mean the separation of spirit, soul, and body that occurs at the end of life? No, that comes to everyone, if the Lord doesn't come first. Does it mean premature death? It could mean that, but that is not as usual as the verses suggest. What then is meant by death in Proverbs? It means the eternal separation from God that comes at the end of a life of sin that has never been repented of and forgiven. In other words, it is what happens at the end of the road when a person's behavior has shown that he was never born again.

2:19. Those who go in to the immoral woman lose something they never regain. The sin haunts them. They have lost their innocence and their clean conscience. Those who practice this sin and do not repent will not inherit the kingdom of God (1 Cor. 6:9; Gal. 5:19-21).

2:20. Solomon has issued these solemn warnings to his son so that he will walk in the way of the good and just, so that he will maintain his purity and confine his sexual activity to the married state.

2:21. It is people of righteousness and integrity who are promised a good life in a good land. It is those who are blameless, especially in regard to this sin, who will continually enjoy the more abundant life. Obedience is still the pathway to blessing.

2:22. The eventual doom of the wicked, liars and unfaithful is to be cut off from the realm of peace and prosperity. Psalm 1:6 says, *"the way of the ungodly shall perish."*

Proverbs 3

1 My son, do not forget my law,
But let your heart keep my commands;

2 For length of days and long life
And peace they will add to you.

3 Let not mercy and truth forsake you;
Bind them around your neck,
Write them on the tablet of your heart,

4 And so find favor and high esteem
In the sight of God and man.

5 Trust in the LORD with all your heart,
And lean not on your own understanding;

6 In all your ways acknowledge Him,
And He shall direct your paths.

7 Do not be wise in your own eyes;
Fear the LORD and depart from evil.

8 It will be health to your flesh,
And strength to your bones.

9 Honor the LORD with your possessions,
And with the firstfruits of all your increase;

10 So your barns will be filled with plenty,
And your vats will overflow with new wine.

11 My son, do not despise the chastening of the LORD,
Nor detest His correction;

12 For whom the LORD loves He corrects,
Just as a father the son in whom he delights.

13 Happy is the man who finds wisdom,
And the man who gains understanding;

14 For her proceeds are better than the profits of silver,
And her gain than fine gold.

15 She is more precious than rubies,
And all the things you may desire cannot compare with her.

16 Length of days is in her right hand,
In her left hand riches and honor.

17 Her ways are ways of pleasantness,
And all her paths are peace.

18 She is a tree of life to those who take hold of her,
And happy are all who retain her.

19 The LORD by wisdom founded the earth;
By understanding He established the heavens;

20 By His knowledge the depths were broken up,
And clouds drop down the dew.

21 My son, let them not depart from your eyes—
Keep sound wisdom and discretion;

22 So they will be life to your soul
And grace to your neck.

23 Then you will walk safely in your way,
And your foot will not stumble.

24 When you lie down, you will not be afraid;
Yes, you will lie down and your sleep will be sweet.

25 Do not be afraid of sudden terror,
Nor of trouble from the wicked when it comes;

26 For the LORD will be your confidence,
And will keep your foot from being caught.

27 Do not withhold good from those to whom it is due,
When it is in the power of your hand to do so.

28 Do not say to your neighbor,
" Go, and come back,
And tomorrow I will give it,"
When you have it with you.

29 Do not devise evil against your neighbor,
For he dwells by you for safety's sake.

30 Do not strive with a man without cause,
If he has done you no harm.

31 Do not envy the oppressor,
And choose none of his ways;

32 For the perverse person is an abomination to the LORD,
But His secret counsel is with the upright.

33 The curse of the LORD is on the house of the wicked,
But He blesses the home of the just.

34 Surely He scorns the scornful,
But gives grace to the humble.

35 The wise shall inherit glory,
But shame shall be the legacy of fools.

Chapter 3

It pays to obey (3:1-10)

3:1. The wise king continues to plead with his son for a life of obedience to parental advice. He should not only remember the instructions but obey them. The Rechabites in Jeremiah 35 are an example of this kind of faithful behavior.

The father's role in the home is to provide, protect, lead, and teach. Here is a list of desirable traits any father might include in his training program. They are part of a U. S. Marine's training. But two are missing and these should be at the head of the list, as shown:

Faith	Personal purity
Justice	Judgment
Decisiveness	Initiative
Dependability	Tact
Integrity	Enthusiasm
Bearing	Unselfishness
Courage	Knowledge
Leadership	Encouragement

3:2. It is a general truth that a clean life and a life of obedience lead to a long life. This person is spared from an untimely death caused by drugs, alcohol, sexually transmitted diseases, and violence. However, as we have said before, many of the proverbs allow for exceptions.

3:3. In beautiful, figurative language, Solomon covets for his son a life of loving kindness toward others and honesty in all his ways. He wants his son to bind these virtues around his neck where he will always see them, and write them on his mind where he will always remember them.

3:4. Obedience is the sure way to find favor with God and a good reputation with man.

3:5. Here is also a sure way to know God's will. First, believe with all your heart that He knows what is best and will do the best for those who leave the choice with Him (cf. 28:25b). Second, confess that you do not know the right way to go. Say with Jeremiah, *"O LORD, I know the way of man is not in himself; It is not in man who walks to direct his own steps"* (Jer. 10:23).

3:6. In every decision, acknowledge Him as Lord of your life (cf. 16:3). Give Him first place. Do this and He promises to make His will so clear that to refuse would be positive sin.

Here are some additional suggestions on obtaining guidance.

1. The most important thing in discerning the will of God is a close walk with Him (Ps. 25:9).

2. Since the Lord most often reveals His will through His Word, spend much time in the Bible.

3. Persevere in prayer.

4. Seek the advice of godly Christians, such as the elders in your church.

5. Ask the Lord to confirm the guidance in the mouths of two or three witnesses.

6. If no guidance comes, God's guidance is to wait patiently. Darkness about action is light about waiting.

7. Wait until the guidance is so clear that to refuse would be positive disobedience. God speaks through His Word, through wise counsel, through the marvelous converging of circumstances, and through the influence of the Holy Spirit on a person's intellect, emotions, and will.

3:7. There is danger in being wise in your own conceit (Job 37:24; Rom.12:3). You don't have anything that wasn't given to you (1 Cor. 4:7). You can't do anything unless the ability is given to you from heaven (John 3:27). Jesus said, *"without Me you can do nothing"* (John 15:5c). *"Neither he who plants is anything, nor he who waters, but God who gives the increase"* (1 Cor. 3:7). Remember that *"God is in heaven, and you on earth"* (Eccl. 5:2). This fact alone should reduce us all to size. Our responsibility is to walk softly before the Lord and to wear the white flower of a blameless life. It's good for our physical health as well as for our spiritual vitality.

3:8. Here we are introduced to what is known as psychosomatics, a branch of medicine that deals with the relationship between spirit and body. *The Journal of the British Medical Society* once said, "There is not a cell in the human body that is totally removed from the spirit." A clean life tends toward a healthy life, and a healthy life tends toward longevity.

> A definite link exists between emotions and inner changes in the physical system. Anger, rage, and fear, to name a few, can cause the heart to beat faster, the face to flush, breathing rate to increase, and blood pressure to rise. A person's blood supply goes to the muscles, and the adrenal glands pour their secretions into the blood stream. If the emotions last longer than a few moments, the thyroid gland speeds up its secretions and the digestive system can slow down and even stop.
> High emotional levels can harm the body. A state of continual anxiety or worry upsets the digestive system, and stomach ulcers can develop {although not all ulcer conditions are due to emotional highs).[2]

3:9. Now Solomon turns to the subject of sound financial management. We should give God his portion. He is the global Owner (1 Chron. 29:14) and we are here to manage his possessions. We are expected to honor Him by the way we give, but not all giving does that. We should give Him a percentage of our income and of any raise in wages—the first fruits means off the top, not the left-overs. In the Old Testament the people of Israel were instructed under law to give tithes (a tenth) and offerings. In the New Testament the rule under grace is to give as the Lord has prospered us (1 Cor. 16:2b).

3:10. God promised the people of Israel that if they were faithful in giving, they would have super-harvests of grain and grapes. The blessings emphasized in the Old Testament were material blessing in earthly places. That is not true in the New

---

2 Louis Goldberg, *The Practical Wisdom of Proverbs*, Grand Rapids, MI.: Kregel Publications, 1990. pp. 141-2.

Testament. Here the emphasis is on spiritual blessings in heavenly places (Eph. 1:3).

Here are some of the "all spiritual blessings that are ours in Christ Jesus":

Eternal life; forgiveness; redemption; reconciliation; salvation; acceptance in the Beloved; being complete in Christ; loved by God as Christ is loved; being justified; sanctified; glorified; having Christ as our High Priest, Intercessor, Advocate, and Helper; being indwelt by the Spirit; baptized by the Spirit into the body of Christ; given the seal and earnest of the Spirit; anointed by the Spirit; having a new citizenship; being a child of God; son of God; heir of God; a holy and royal priest; more than conqueror; being conformed to His image; having joy; peace; hope; rest; freedom; a purpose in life; and satisfaction.

Wealth in our day is more of a test than an index of God's blessing. That is why the disciples were shocked when Jesus said it was hard for a rich man to enter the kingdom. Their thinking was based on the Old Covenant teaching. Now they had to adapt their thinking to the New Testament.

Here are some insights from the New Testament about giving:

- We should first give ourselves to the Lord (2 Cor. 8:5).
- We should be open at times to give more than could be expected. The Macedonians gave *"beyond their ability"* (2 Cor. 8:3). So did the widow in Mark 12:42-44.
- Our giving should be systematic: *"on the first day of the week"* (1 Cor. 16:2a).
- It should be purposeful, not haphazard or random (2 Cor. 9:7)
- It should be generous (2 Cor. 8:2). The Lord Jesus is our example in this (2 Cor. 8:9).
- We should give willingly and cheerfully, not grudgingly or by obligation (2 Cor. 8:3; 9:7).
- It should be private. We should not give to be seen by others. Don't let your right hand know what your left hand is doing (Matt. 6:2-4; Luke 18:12).
- We cannot outgive God (Luke 6:38).

- What we give is only a token that all we have belongs to God (Ps. 50:12)
- Giving is an act of priestly worship (Heb. 13:16).

No matter how much we give, it can never be an adequate sacrifice for what He has done for us.

The value of wisdom (3:11-18)

3:11. Whenever we see the word chastening, we invariably think of corporal punishment. It means much more than this. In the Bible chastening includes everything that is involved in training a child—counsel, correction, motivation, encouragement, teaching, and rebuke.

Sensible people do not despise this training by the Lord. They know it is for their own good. They know it is proof of their Father's love. They know it means that He accepts the one being trained as His own son. It is a proof of sonship.

This passage is quoted and enlarged on in Hebrews 12:5-11. If we respect parental discipline, even though it is sometimes faulty, how much more should we submit to God's perfect discipline. Training by parents may be imperfect, even when they do the best they can. God's training is always loving and fair, designed to produce holiness in us. Child training may not seem pleasant at the time, but it brings lasting fruit to those who are exercised by it, that is, to those who accept it gladly for their lasting benefit.

3:12. Left to ourselves we would be like wild donkeys' colts. We all learn to say no before we ever say yes. A loving father wants his child to be godly, spiritually minded, lawful, civil, courteous, wise, knowledgeable, responsible and obedient. This comes only through patient and prolonged training. A son should realize this, and he should appreciate parents who love him enough to chasten him.

Dale Martin Stone captures the process of chastening in his poem "The Making of a Disciple."

When God wants to drill a man,

And thrill a man, and skill a man,
When God wants to mold a man
To play for Him the noblest part,
When He yearns with all His heart
To build so great and bold a man
That all the world shall be amazed,
Then watch God's methods,
Watch His ways!

How He ruthlessly perfects
Whom He royally elects,
How He hammers him and hurts him,
And with mighty blows converts him,
Making shapes and forms which only
God Himself can understand,
Even when His man is crying,
Lifting a beseeching hand.

Yet God bends but never breaks
When man's good He undertakes,
When He uses whom He chooses,
And with every purpose fuses
Man to act, and act as man,
As it was when He began.
When God tries His splendor out,
Man will know what He's about.
—Dale Stone

3:13. The son who becomes wise and obtains understanding gains happiness in the bargain and benefits that are better than gold and silver.

3:14. Personified here as a woman, wisdom is more valuable than silver and gold. But remember that it is speaking about our Lord. Paul spoke of gaining Christ in Philippians 3:8.

3:15. He is more precious than priceless gems. No matter how long your wish list may be, it cannot compare with the worth of wisdom and the knowledge of our Lord and Savior Jesus Christ (2 Pet. 3:17). To grow in the knowledge of Him a person must

38

seek Him and learn of Him in His Word instead of spending his life pursuing entertainment and passing pleasure.

Dave Branon lists the fantastic possibilities that lie ahead for the young person who chooses God's way:

- Long life and peace (v. 2).
- Favor in the sight of God and man (v. 4).
- Direction from God (v. 6).
- Health and strength (v. 8).
- Abundance (v. 10).
- Happiness (v. 13).
- Wisdom – an incomparable prize (v. 15).[3]

3:16. His right hand is loaded with long life, his left with riches and honor. Here Solomon is speaking of spiritual riches and the honor that comes only from God.

3:17. Apply this verse to the Savior and read, "[His] ways are ways of pleasantness and all [His] paths drop peace." This is the confession of every believer who has tasted and seen that the Lord is good.

> His ways are ways of pleasantness,
> And all His paths are peace.
> His words are words of graciousness,
> And love which ne'er shall cease.
> His works are works of holiness
> And victory over sin.
> His wounds are wounds of tenderness:
> He only wounds to win.
>   —F. H. Oakley

3:18. Wisdom is like a tree that yields blessings for those who eat its fruit. Those who cling to Him know what true happiness is.

God's wisdom in creation (3:19-20)

3:19. Creation is one gigantic display of God's wisdom.

---

3 *Our Daily Bread*, October 12, 2003.

"Nature with open volume stands to spread her Maker's praise abroad" (Isaac Watts). Psalms 8 and 104, for example, extol the Lord's wisdom and majesty displayed in His creation.

3:20. It can be seen, whether in topography, astronomy, oceanography, nephology (the study of clouds), or any other science. Each one bears the finger print of Him who is incarnate wisdom. This is grace indeed that the wisdom that created and sustains the universe, and that distils the vapor from the sea and distributes it as dew on the land should be the same wisdom that delights to order and prosper the smallest details of a man's private and public life.[4]

3:21. Solomon does not tire of repeating his appeal to his son. Christian parents should follow his example. He reminds him to remember and to keep the counsel he has received. Forgetfulness and unfaithfulness are worse than ignorance. He should ever behave with sound wisdom and discretion. Only in this way will he be able to make responsible decisions.

3:22. Right decisions in turn will result in a life of inward peace and satisfaction and outward respect and honor.

3:23. The godly life is one of safety; He keeps us in the hollow of His hand. He ensures freedom from stumbling; *"When you run, you will not stumble"* (Prov. 4:12b).

3:24. He will deliver from fitful sleep and fears of loss and harm. Those who trust Him will need no pill to be sure of a good night's rest (cf. Pss. 3:5; 4:8; Hos. 2:18). Peter was able to sleep even though he faced possible death the next day (Acts 12:6).

3:25. Even if a terror attack should come as a result of some evil plot, he need not fear.

3:26. The Lord is there as his protector, security, and confidence, keeping his foot from getting caught in the trap. Fellowship with God is ideal.

3:27. Here are four verses that begin with the words *"Do not."* Do not refuse any inward prompting to do good. It came from the Lord. You miss a great blessing when you fail to act.

3:28. Don't put off until tomorrow what you can do for your neighbor today. Tomorrow may be too late. A soul may be lost,

---

4 Williams, George, *The Student's Commentary on the Holy Scriptures*, Grand Rapids, MI:Kregels' Publications, 1981, p.419.

a heart may be broken, or a life may be ruined.

Jan Palach publicly protested the occupation of Czechoslovakia by Warsaw Pact troops. One day a Christian in Prague spoke to him about the Savior. When he learned that Jan did not have a New Testament, he promised to send one. But he delayed—delayed—delayed. On July 16, 1969, Jan doused himself with gasoline in St. Wenceslas Square and set himself aflame. The Christian was too late—too late—too late.

3:29. Don't plot against your neighbor. There is something very valuable about the tie between neighbors. They are there for our safety. They call the police, the fire department, or the ambulance for help when we need it. They warn us of dangers. In many ways, they serve us faithfully. We should never do anything to weaken or sever that relationship.

3:30. Don't strive with a man who hasn't done anything wrong to you. As much as possible, live at peace with all men (Rom. 12:18). There's enough trouble in the world already without starting more.

In the last four verses of this chapter, the writer contrasts four types of people in whom the Lord finds no delight and four who please Him.

3:31. Don't envy an oppressor (23:17; 24:1). This perverse person scorns what is right and proper. He is disgusting in the eyes of the Lord.

3:32. A righteous person, on the other hand, lives in sweet communion with Him and receives special messages of guidance, comfort, and instruction from Him.

3:33. God pronounces a curse on the house of the wicked and its occupants. His favor is on the righteous household.

The wicked Haman plotted to destroy Mordecai and his fellow Jews, but he died on the gallows that he had built for Mordecai (Est. 7:10).

3:34. Those who treat the Word of the Lord with scorn and contempt are subject to divine contempt. But He showers humble people with His favor.

3:35. God will honor those who show their wisdom by trusting and obeying Him. Fools will inherit nothing better than shame and disgrace. We all reap what we sow.

Proverbs 4

1 Hear, my children, the instruction of a father,
And give attention to know understanding;

2 For I give you good doctrine:
Do not forsake my law.

3 When I was my father's son,
Tender and the only one in the sight of my mother,

4 He also taught me, and said to me:
" Let your heart retain my words;
Keep my commands, and live.

5 Get wisdom! Get understanding!
Do not forget, nor turn away from the words of my mouth.

6 Do not forsake her, and she will preserve you;
Love her, and she will keep you.

7 Wisdom is the principal thing;
Therefore get wisdom.
And in all your getting, get understanding.

8 Exalt her, and she will promote you;
She will bring you honor, when you embrace her.

9 She will place on your head an ornament of grace;
A crown of glory she will deliver to you."

10 Hear, my son, and receive my sayings,
And the years of your life will be many.

11 I have taught you in the way of wisdom;
I have led you in right paths.

12 When you walk, your steps will not be hindered,
And when you run, you will not stumble.

13 Take firm hold of instruction, do not let go;
Keep her, for she is your life.

14 Do not enter the path of the wicked,
And do not walk in the way of evil.

15 Avoid it, do not travel on it;
Turn away from it and pass on.

16 For they do not sleep unless they have done evil;
And their sleep is taken away unless they make someone fall.

17 For they eat the bread of wickedness,
And drink the wine of violence.

18 But the path of the just is like the shining sun,
That shines ever brighter unto the perfect day.

19 The way of the wicked is like darkness;
They do not know what makes them stumble.

20 My son, give attention to my words;
Incline your ear to my sayings.

21 Do not let them depart from your eyes;
Keep them in the midst of your heart;

22 For they are life to those who find them,
And health to all their flesh.

23 Keep your heart with all diligence,
For out of it spring the issues of life.

24 Put away from you a deceitful mouth,
And put perverse lips far from you.

25 Let your eyes look straight ahead,
And your eyelids look right before you.

26 Ponder the path of your feet,
And let all your ways be established.

27 Do not turn to the right or the left;
Remove your foot from evil.

Chapter 4

Examples of wisdom (4:1-13)

4:1. As Solomon thinks of his boyhood and of the way his parents had instructed him, he seeks to pass that legacy on to all his children, not to just one son. He urges them to listen attentively and understand fully.

4:2. He gives them quality instruction that they should never abandon. A French saying is *noblesse oblige*. It means that people of noble rank or birth are obligated to live accordingly. Solomon's children were members of the royal family. As such they were expected to behave as nobility should. He sought to groom them for their responsibilities. This included their dress, personal appearance, courtesy, and adherence to the laws and traditions of the realm.

Christian parents should train their children in preparation for the time when they will become children of the King Eternal by faith in Jesus Christ. They will be members of the Royal Family. The world will expect them to be different and it should not be disappointed. Their behavior should be above reproach in holiness, love, and purity.

4:3. Solomon looks back to his boyhood when his parents made every effort to bring him up in a godly way. He meant so much to them that they spared no effort in training him for the throne.

4:4. He clearly remembers how his father had taught him and emphasized the importance of wisdom in going through life. By listening carefully, remembering faithfully, and obeying consistently, he would be assured of a meaningful and productive life.

4:5. It all comes down to getting wisdom which by transference means getting Christ. He should learn to make good decisions and to get the best possible results in the best possible way. He should always do what is right. If he never forgets this nor turns away from his father's words, he will do well.

4:6. In Revelation 2:4 the church left her first love. The danger here is leaving wisdom. It indicates carelessness, neglect and bad choices. Parents may teach children, but if the children do not cling to what they have learned, they will not profit from it. If wisdom is their loved companion, she will save them from making shipwreck. So if we walk with the Lord, He will keep us from disgrace.

4:7. Wisdom is the principal thing. Since the Lord Jesus is our wisdom, we can say that knowing Him as Lord and Savior is the most important thing in life. Man should let nothing keep him from trusting Jesus or from understanding His precious word.

4:8. As we embrace Him by giving Him the place of preeminence, He will promote us to new spiritual heights and honor us. Ken was not doing well as an auto salesman because he would not engage in unethical sales tactics. The boss called him and said, "Ken, when you work for this company, this company must come first in your life."

Ken replied, "Sir, this company doesn't come first in my life. The Lord comes first. My family comes second, and this company comes third."

Ken lost his job but he got a better one in which he didn't have to compromise his faith. The Lord honored him because he honored the Lord.

4:9. In this life, faithfulness to Jesus results in moral beauty and nobility of character. In heaven, the rewards will be crowns of glory and of life.

4:10. Having finished a summary of his father's advice, Solomon now reinforces it with his own counsel. If his son is teachable, God will reward him with a good, long life (or something better).

4:11. The father has fulfilled his obligation in training his son in the right paths of wisdom. This is the privilege and responsibility of parents – to give their children a good foundation and to get them onto the right path in life from the beginning.

4:12. If the son practices what he has heard, he will not stumble or be hindered in walking or running.

4:13. If he never forsakes wisdom, if at all cost he diligently holds onto the counsel he has received, he will find that it brings the fulfilled life—the life worth living.

The neighborhood gang (4:14-19)

4:14. Again the call goes out for separation from evil companions. Young believers must have the commitment to say "No" and to value God's approval more than men's. It is right to share the gospel with this class of men, as with all sinners who need the Savior. But that will usually cause the wicked to drop association with the believer like a hot iron.

Scripture gives clear principles to guide us in our association with others. First of all, we should love all mankind: friends and foes, saints and sinners. We should pray for them and do good to them. Jesus was the Friend of publicans and sinners, and we should be too.

However, in His contacts with these people, He was always faithful to His Father and to the word of God. He never stooped to their level of speech or behavior.

This is the key distinction that we must observe—friendship without compromising the truth, love without partnership, witness without waffling. This applies to social life, to marriage, to business, and to the church.

In social life, we must look on others as precious, never-dying souls to whom we are obligated to witness, but we must never condone their sinful lifestyle. Instead we rebuke it. In marriage, it is an unequal yoke when a believer marries an unbeliever. God forbids this union (2 Cor. 6:14).

In business, the same is true. A partnership between a believer and unbelievers violates divine wisdom and common sense.

And what shall we say of churches with mixed membership, and of others who support the ecumenical movement, aiming to unite all religions in one world church? God's Word is clear: *"Come out of her, my people, lest you share in her sins, and lest you receive of her plagues"* (Rev. 18:4).

Sometimes when a son or daughter becomes wild and rebellious, parents might have to ask themselves some questions.

- Did we discipline the son or daughter when he or she misbehaved or did we subscribe to the current doctrine of permissiveness?

- Did we make wise decisions for the child when he was too young to make them?
- Did we constantly watch the friendships he was making and exercise our parental authority?
- Did we instill in him the courage to swim against the tide, to stand for what is right? Did we raise him for the kingdom or for the world?

4:15. The highway of the wicked should be avoided, no matter what the cost may be. The believer should make a detour if sin looms ahead. God is a God of separation. He wants His people to practice separation. Paul makes this clear in 2 Corinthians:

> *"Do not be unequally yoked together with unbelievers. For what fellowship has righteousness with lawlessness? And what communion has light with darkness? And what accord has Christ with Belial? Or what part has a believer with an unbeliever? And what agreement has the temple of God with idols? For you are the temple of the living God....Therefore 'Come out from among them and be separate,' says the Lord. 'Do not touch what is unclean, And I will receive you. I will be a Father to you, And you shall be My sons and daughters, Says the LORD Almighty'" (1 Cor. 6:14-18).*

4:16. The reason for this strong counsel is clear. Wicked men suffer insomnia unless they have pulled off some evil job. They can't have a good night's rest unless they have caused someone to crash morally.

4:17. They cultivate wickedness as if it were their daily food; they choose it like a special menu or diet, and delight in violence as if it were wine.

4:18. The contrast is like the difference between night and day. The life of the righteous person is like the dawning light; it grows ever brighter until it reaches the full splendor of noontime.

4:19. The path of the wicked is so dark that he stumbles from one sin to another, but he doesn't understand why he trips so often.

Advice from a father's heart (4:20-27)

4:20. Again Solomon uses a familiar formula to arrest the attention of his son. He calls for careful consideration of his counsel.

4:21. A father's advice should always be before the son's eyes for guidance and ever in his heart as treasure.

4:22. Obedience to words of wisdom brings life and health. It is another reminder that what's good for us spiritually is good for us physically. This is accepted as fact today in the field of psychosomatic medicine.

4:23. When Solomon says to keep your heart with all diligence, he is not referring to the organ that pumps blood, but to the citadel of our being, the faculty that makes the decisions. The heart is the spring from which our actions flow (cf. Prov. 23:26). The stream is the kind of life that results. A mind that feeds on pornography will result in a life of sin and shame. If we think about a sin long enough, eventually we will commit it.

4:24. Solomon continues a swift succession of imperatives that all say the same thing—be done with evil and choose the way of godliness. He names various members of our body in a way that reminds us of Romans 6:13, *"present your members as instruments of righteousness to God."* First he deals with speech. His son is to put away dishonest and crooked speech (contrast this with the evil speech in 6:12-19).

4:25. The eyes are next. Keep your eyes fixed on the highway of holiness. Be careful what you read in magazines and what you look at on television and the Internet. Much defilement is acquired through the eyes, and modern technology has made the sin of looking easier than ever before.

4:26. As for your feet, stay away from places that feed the old nature. Don't let anything lure you from the path of purity and decency.

4:27. Prayerfully ponder your conduct. The world is like a mined field. Walk circumspectly (Eph. 5:15), avoiding any evil perils. Be careful where your feet take you. Don't get sidetracked off of the path of godliness and wisdom. Don't take spiritual detours and shortcuts. Use only routes that you know are safe. Don't turn aside to even sample what is doubtful. If it's evil, have the will power to say no.

Proverbs 5

1 *My son, pay attention to my wisdom;*
Lend your ear to my understanding,

2 *That you may preserve discretion,*
And your lips may keep knowledge.

3 *For the lips of an immoral woman drip honey,*
And her mouth is smoother than oil;

4 *But in the end she is bitter as wormwood,*
Sharp as a two-edged sword.

5 *Her feet go down to death,*
Her steps lay hold of hell.

6 *Lest you ponder her path of life—*
Her ways are unstable;
You do not know them.

7 *Therefore hear me now, my children,*
And do not depart from the words of my mouth.

8 *Remove your way far from her,*
And do not go near the door of her house,

9 *Lest you give your honor to others,*
And your years to the cruel one;

10 *Lest aliens be filled with your wealth,*
And your labors go to the house of a foreigner;

11 *And you mourn at last,*
When your flesh and your body are consumed,

12 *And say:*
" How I have hated instruction,
And my heart despised correction!

13 *I have not obeyed the voice of my teachers,*
Nor inclined my ear to those who instructed me!

14 I was on the verge of total ruin,
In the midst of the assembly and congregation."

15 Drink water from your own cistern,
And running water from your own well.

16 Should your fountains be dispersed abroad,
Streams of water in the streets?

17 Let them be only your own,
And not for strangers with you.

18 Let your fountain be blessed,
And rejoice with the wife of your youth.

19 As a loving deer and a graceful doe,
Let her breasts satisfy you at all times;
And always be enraptured with her love.

20 For why should you, my son, be enraptured by an immoral woman,
And be embraced in the arms of a seductress?

21 For the ways of man are before the eyes of the LORD,
And He ponders all his paths.

22 His own iniquities entrap the wicked man,
And he is caught in the cords of his sin.

23 He shall die for lack of instruction,
And in the greatness of his folly he shall go astray.

Chapter 5

Avoid the sexual trap (5:1-23)

5:1. We have suggested that wisdom represents the Lord Jesus Christ. It is equally true that the immoral woman represents the world of man without God. She caters to the lust of the eyes, the lust of the flesh, and the pride of life.

5:2. As we have seen, young men are warned against this ungodly woman nine times in the book of Proverbs. But why this repeated emphasis? It is because sexual sin is one of the greatest dangers in a person's life. It is the cause of the fall of many mighty men, whether in business, politics, entertainment, or religion. Although the world maintains that there are no moral absolutes, the media still delights in splashing headlines exposing the rich and famous and their scandals. They know instinctively that sex outside of marriage is wrong.

It is helpful to think of the immoral woman as representing not only the world but also all forms of illicit sex: fornication, adultery, prostitution, bigamy, polygamy, pedophilia, lesbianism, homosexuality, transvestism, and same-sex marriage.

As we read these repeated warnings against immorality, we should remember that not one of us is safe until we reach heaven. The counsel applies to us as much as to Solomon's son. We too should keep our ears open to godly advice and keep our lips from speaking carelessly about sexual sin. The more we talk glibly about it, the less serious it becomes in our mind. A person who is always talking about sex reveals what is central in his thoughts and perhaps in his behavior.

5:2. Refined and genteel people often feel uncomfortable reading about this woman. But this is the Word of God and it is not to be passed over. Young people should be frankly forewarned by their parents, and thus fore-armed.

We must balance our disgust at this woman and her profession with the fact that the Lord Jesus died for her sins as well as for ours. And she can be saved just as we are. Heaven will have many like her who were made spotlessly clean through Christ's precious blood.

Our Lord said that tax collectors and harlots enter the kingdom of God before self-righteous religious hypocrites (Matt. 21:31-32).

5:3. The first impression of a harlot may be favorable. Her come-on is sweet and smooth. It is pleasing and winsome.

5:4. But contact with her proves to be the ultimate bitterness. A man may sell his birthright for a moment of selfish passion with a woman like this. Hebrews 11:25 reminds us that the pleasures of sin are only temporary. The pleasure is the bait that covers the cruel hook.

5:5. When she has succeeded in seducing her victim, he finds it is an experience that tears him apart with guilt and remorse. Those who patronize her are on a slippery path that leads eventually to disease, dishonor, and death.

5:6. Be warned that her ways are unstable, that is, tricky and shifty. Her strategy is beyond prediction.

5:7. Here again as in 4:1 he uses the plural, *"children."* You can feel a father's emotion when Solomon pleads with his children to listen carefully and to obey consistently as he warns them about the great danger of immorality.

5:8. Contact with a prostitute, even nearness to her house, should be avoided. The exception, of course, is an attempt to reach her with the gospel. In that case, a woman should do the evangelising.

5:9. In sex outside of marriage, a person shares his procreative powers with an unworthy stranger, a woman with the morals of an alley cat.

5:10. His masculinity is squandered on a stranger, his God-given strength on a foreigner. Any woman who is not your wife is a stranger in this sense.

5:11. He wallows in regret when his body is wracked by sexually transmitted disease. Many of these diseases are incurable although they can be controlled.

5:12. Too late the son who wouldn't listen realizes his folly in selling his purity for a moment of pleasure.

One of the brilliant writers of the nineteenth century fell to the temptation of unnatural sex. Hear him crying out in remorse:

> The gods have given me almost everything. But I let myself be lured into long spells of senseless and sensual ease....Tired of being on the heights, I deliberately went to the depths in search for new sensation....I grew careless of the lives of others. I took pleasure where it pleased me and passed on. I forgot that every little action of the common day makes or unmakes character, and that therefore what one has done in the secret chamber, one has some day to cry aloud from the house-tops. I ceased to be lord over myself. I was no longer the captain of my soul, and did not know it. I allowed pleasure to dominate me. I ended in horrible disgrace.[5]

5:13. The disobedient son of the previous verse refused godly instruction and insisted on having his own way.

5:14. What was done in secret is now shouted from the housetops. The man's reputation is ruined. His fall is the subject of talk among his acquaintances. There is a public blot on his life, written in indelible ink.

5:15. To avoid this catastrophe, the son should confine the pleasures of married life to his own wife. God instituted marriage for this purpose as well as for procreation (vv. 15-17), purity (1 Cor. 7:2), and a picture of Christ and the church (Eph. 5:32).

5:16. It is shameful and doesn't make sense for a man to waste his procreative powers as if he were spilling good water in the streets.

5:17. The intimate joys of married life belong to a man and his wife, and not to others.

5:18. He should rejoice in his own children and in the sweetheart of his youth who is now his wife.

5:19. She should ravish him, give herself unreservedly to him, expressing her love, and be to him like a loving deer and

---

5 Oscar Wilde, *The Portable Oscar Wilde*, New York: Penguin Group, 1981, pp. 580-1.

a graceful doe, the one whose love enraptures him. He should enjoy her love and feel incomplete without her.

5:20. It doesn't make sense for him to be satisfied with a whore, or be hugged by a wicked woman.

5:21. Perhaps the young man thought that he could sin and no one would see. But God sees everything we do and everywhere we go.

5:22. The Lord has established certain laws or principles in the world. One is that we can't sin and get away with it. The one who goes in to an immoral woman is heading for a trap. His sin will bind him like a stout rope.

E. Stanley Jones wrote:

> You cannot "get away with it," for it registers itself in inner deterioration, in the inner hell of not being able to respect yourself, in compelling you to live underground in blind labyrinths.[6]

5:23. Life for him will become a living death, and he will wander aimlessly in shame and remorse.

---

6 E. Stanley Jones, *The Christ of the Mount*, Nashville: Abingdon Cokesbury Press, 1931, p. 43.

Proverbs 6

1 My son, if you become surety for your friend,
If you have shaken hands in pledge for a stranger,

2 You are snared by the words of your mouth;
You are taken by the words of your mouth.

3 So do this, my son, and deliver yourself;
For you have come into the hand of your friend:
Go and humble yourself;
Plead with your friend.

4 Give no sleep to your eyes,
Nor slumber to your eyelids.

5 Deliver yourself like a gazelle from the hand of the hunter,
And like a bird from the hand of the fowler.

6 Go to the ant, you sluggard!
Consider her ways and be wise,

7 Which, having no captain,
Overseer or ruler,

8 Provides her supplies in the summer,
And gathers her food in the harvest.

9 How long will you slumber, O sluggard?
When will you rise from your sleep?

10 A little sleep, a little slumber,
A little folding of the hands to sleep—

11 So shall your poverty come on you like a prowler,
And your need like an armed man.

12 A worthless person, a wicked man,
Walks with a perverse mouth;

13 He winks with his eyes,
He shuffles his feet,
He points with his fingers;

14 Perversity is in his heart,
He devises evil continually,
He sows discord.

15 Therefore his calamity shall come suddenly;
Suddenly he shall be broken without remedy.

16 These six things the LORD hates,
Yes, seven are an abomination to Him:

17 A proud look,
A lying tongue,
Hands that shed innocent blood,

18 A heart that devises wicked plans,
Feet that are swift in running to evil,

19 A false witness who speaks lies,
And one who sows discord among brethren.

20 My son, keep your father's command,
And do not forsake the law of your mother.

21 Bind them continually upon your heart;
Tie them around your neck.

22 When you roam, they will lead you;
When you sleep, they will keep you;
And when you awake, they will speak with you.

23 For the commandment is a lamp,
And the law a light;
Reproofs of instruction are the way of life,

24 To keep you from the evil woman,
From the flattering tongue of a seductress.

25 Do not lust after her beauty in your heart,
Nor let her allure you with her eyelids.

26 For by means of a harlot
A man is reduced to a crust of bread;
And an adulteress will prey upon his precious life.

27 Can a man take fire to his bosom,
And his clothes not be burned?

28 Can one walk on hot coals,
And his feet not be seared?

29 So is he who goes in to his neighbor's wife;
Whoever touches her shall not be innocent.

30 People do not despise a thief
If he steals to satisfy himself when he is starving.

31 Yet when he is found, he must restore sevenfold;
He may have to give up all the substance of his house.

32 Whoever commits adultery with a woman lacks understanding;
He who does so destroys his own soul.

33 Wounds and dishonor he will get,
And his reproach will not be wiped away.

34 For jealousy is a husband's fury;
Therefore he will not spare in the day of vengeance.

35 He will accept no recompense,
Nor will he be appeased though you give many gifts.

Chapter 6

Avoid the co-signing trap (6:1-5)

6:1. The good king turns his attention to the subject of suretyship. That means assuming liability for someone else's debt in case of default. Solomon's six references to this business transaction (11:15; 17:18; 20:16; 22:26; 27:13) may indicate that it was a common practice in those days. And perhaps it is a more common practice today than we realize.

In all references, the advice is the same: Don't act as a surety guaranteeing someone else's debt, whether it be a stranger or a friend. It's a reminder that when money comes in the door, friendship goes out the window. It also means that those who borrow money without credit or collateral cannot be trusted.

In spite of this warning against it, the Lord Jesus became our Surety on the Cross of Calvary. He paid the debt that we owed but couldn't pay.

> Worthy of death, O Lord we were;
> That vengeance was our due;
> In grace the spotless Lamb did bear
> Himself our sins and guilt and shame;
> Justice our Surety slew.
> With Him our Surety we have died,
> With Him we there were crucified.
> —James G. Deck

6:2. Even an oral pledge is binding in some courts of law. Once you have made a promise, you are responsible to pay if the debtor does not.

6:3. If his son ever makes this mistake, Solomon urges him to find some honorable way to get free from the legal power of his friend. Even if it means humiliation, he should plead with his friend to release him.

6:4. It is so urgent, that he should do it before he goes to bed. It is more important than sleep.

6:5. Driven by fear, he should use the skill, speed, and the cleverness of a gazelle in fleeing from the hunter, or a bird in escaping from a fowler.

Avoid the Laziness Trap (6:6-11)

6:6. Now Solomon moves from unwise business contracts to laziness. Just as Jesus later drew spiritual lessons from nature, so the king uses ants as examples of industry.

> "The ant is put before us as an example of industry and energy. Don't lie in bed and dream or fold your hands and mourn that you don't have much brains. Neither does the ant, but what brain it has is all gray matter, and not putty. Get up and go to work. Make the most of what you have. What you need is the formic acid of a persistent effort. No matter if you are very small and black and live in an ant hill, if you have only grit. The ant is famous for industry, energy, ingenuity, economy; for division and combination of labor. Whether as masons, agriculturists, carpenters, or carvers of wood, they furnish examples for admiration and imitation."[7]

6:7. They have no visible chain of command, no overseer or ruler, yet they do not rush around aimlessly. Their activity is guided and efficient.

6:8. They work hard in the summer to provide food for the winter. This does not teach that all ants hibernate, but that they provide food for the time when they can't work. As believers we don't have to provide for our future. God promises us that if we diligently put Him and His righteousness first, we will never lack the necessities of life (Matt. 6:33).

6:9. The sluggard is allergic to work. He needs an alarm

---

7 A. T. Pierson, *Knowing the Scriptures*, N.Y.: Gospel Publishing House, 1910, p. 439.

clock to wake up in the morning. Then he needs enormous energy to extricate himself from under the bedclothes and onto the floor.

6:10. But no! He wants just a little more sleep. In this he resembles elephant seals. They spend most of their lives sleeping.

6:11. Then he wonders why bills accumulate, why the refrigerator is empty, and why the landlord is knocking at the door for the rent. His anthem, is:

> It's nice to get up in the morning, aye,
> But it's nicer to lie in bed.

Beware of the shyster (6:12-15)

6:12. Next is a portrait of a worthless, wicked man. He appears to be incorrigible. His mouth is as filthy as a garbage dump.

6:13. He uses different kinds of body language, working mischief with his eyes, feet, fingers, all with a sinful, corrupt meaning.

6:14. His perverse heart is forever planning some evil scheme. If his thoughts were visible to the public they would be rated unsuitable for viewing. Wherever he goes, quarrels follow, because he has a knack for starting them.

6:15. Does he get away with it? No, eventually his sins catch up with him and he learns that the way of the transgressor is hard. Here is an example:

When a water main burst, it flooded not only the street but some of the neighboring houses. The police arrived to check the houses, and found a healthy crop of marijuana growing in one of them. The owner thought that no one would ever know that he was cultivating and selling an illicit drug. God has many novel ways of bringing to light the hidden things of darkness. Who would have expected a water main to expose a drug dealer? Life is full of "water mains."

Things that God hates (6:16-19)

6:16. Yes, although God is love, that is not the sum total of what He is. As hard as it is for some to accept, there are things that the Lord hates (Ps. 45:7). And there are people who make

Him angry (Ps. 7:11). If He hates the following things, we should hate them too. The words *"six...yes, seven"* are a formula used in connection with a series (cf. Job 5:19), but here it is not meant to be exhaustive.

6:17. God hates a proud look. If the perfect Man was not proud, how can we claim that distinction?

> Was my Saviour meek and lowly
> And shall such a worm as I,
> Weak, and earthly, and unholy,
> Dare to lift my head on high?
> —Henry Francis Lyte

God hates a lying tongue. Satan is a liar. He has been a liar from the beginning. When we lie, we are acting like him. God cannot lie, and He never gives us permission to lie.

Murder is another sin that the Lord despises. It started with Cain at the dawn of civilization.

6:18. One who plots evil comes under the divine displeasure.

And He hates people who are human dynamos when it comes to committing misdemeanors and felonies.

6:19. It is not surprising that the Lord abominates a false witness. In all the history of false witnesses, one case stands above the rest in shame and infamy. At the trial of Jesus, sinful man brought false testimony against the Lord of life and glory. Inveterate liars charged their Creator-God with crimes He did not do. Needless to say, their testimonies did not agree, but they helped to tilt the scales of justice against Him.

The sixth type of person whom the Lord loathes is one who causes strife among brethren. There are numerous ways to do this, not the least of which are doctrinal fads, gossip and secret criticism.

Beware of the prostitute (6:20-35)

6:20. It is no coincidence that the wisdom taught to a son in this book is couched in the words of a father and mother. A godly home is the place where young people are trained to live exemplary lives. It is parents who have the wisdom that is from above who are able to raise wise children. The decline of emphasis on family values produces a generation of losers.

6:21. A young person should make good parental advice a constant part of his thinking and should translate it into honorable action.

6:22. When he goes away on a trip, it will guide him. When he sleeps, it will keep him from sinful fantasies. When he wakes up, it will teach him.

6:23. What he learned at home will be like a bright lamp, illuminating the way he should go and the decisions he should make. His training will serve to rebuke sin and will deliver him from immorality.

Again the subject of immorality appears and for good reason. Who can measure the crushing sorrow of a woman when the man she loves deserts her for another woman? Or the grief when a military man gets a Dear John letter from his wife who had promised to be true to him while he was overseas? Think of all the legal wrangling and harassment over alimony and child support. Or the terrible loss of security that children feel when a parent walks out on them. Only God knows all the jealousy, violence, and even murder that unfaithfulness brings. Reputations are shattered. Lips are sealed. Life is never the same. And too often a remorseful parent lives to see his sin repeated by his son or daughter. That is the sting of the scorpion.

6:24. The mention of immorality introduces the evil woman, here also called a seductress and adulteress. One of her favorite ploys is flattery. It appeals to a man who does not feel he is appreciated at home.

6:25. Her beauty, provocative appearance and bold, alluring eyes further weaken his resistance. It is widely known that women who gaze steadily at men are giving an invitation with their eyes. Better to look down or away than to look into those eyes.

6:26. In his passionate lust, he forgets that she can reduce him to poverty by extortion and blackmail. He forgets that she may cost him his life through disease or the rage of her husband. In today's world he forgets that she may be a police woman, playing the role in a prostitution sting.

6:27. He thinks that he can sin without suffering its consequences, forgetful that he can't take fire into his chest without burning his clothes.

6:28. Adultery without consequences is as impossible as walking on hot coals without burning his feet.

6:29. Anyone who commits adultery with his neighbor's wife will be exposed eventually. His sin will come to light.

6:30. Even a starving thief who steals does not get off with the crime. How much more an adulterer.

6:31. The thief must restore seven times the amount that he stole. It may cost him all that is in his house. Under the law of Moses, he had to restore the cost plus one fifth (Lev. 6:5). When it says sevenfold in this verse, that may be a figurative expression for full compensation as required by the law. Seven is the number of completeness.

Mention of the trespass offering in Leviticus 6:5 makes us think of Christ as this offering. When sin entered the world, God was robbed of glory, honor, worship, service, and obedience. Man was robbed of fellowship with the Lord and eternal life. By Christ's work at Calvary, God has received more glory than if Adam had never fallen. And we are better off in Christ than if sin had never entered; He restored what He never took away (Ps. 69:4b).

> Aside He threw His most divine array
> And veiled His Godhead in a garb of clay;
> And in that garb did wondrous love display,
> Restoring what He never took away.
> —Anonymous

6:32. It is much more serious to commit adultery than to steal a loaf of bread. Both the crime and the penalty are immensely greater. For one thing, the man ruins his life (1 Cor. 6:18).

6:33. He suffers physical wounds and lasting shame. The memory cannot be eradicated.

6:34. When the jealous husband learns what has happened, his rage is furious. It may lead him to murder the guilty one.

6:35. He won't accept any payoff. No payment or gift will appease him. No person with a right mind commits adultery. It is simply stupid, in today's language, a no-brainer.

Proverbs 7

1 *My son, keep my words,*
And treasure my commands within you.

2 *Keep my commands and live,*
And my law as the apple of your eye.

3 *Bind them on your fingers;*
Write them on the tablet of your heart.

4 *Say to wisdom, "You are my sister,"*
And call understanding your nearest kin,

5 *That they may keep you from the immoral woman,*
From the seductress who flatters with her words.

6 *For at the window of my house*
I looked through my lattice,

7 *And saw among the simple,*
I perceived among the youths,
A young man devoid of understanding,

8 *Passing along the street near her corner;*
And he took the path to her house

9 *In the twilight, in the evening,*
In the black and dark night.

10 *And there a woman met him,*
With the attire of a harlot, and a crafty heart.

11 *She was loud and rebellious,*
Her feet would not stay at home.

12 *At times she was outside, at times in the open square,*
Lurking at every corner.

13 *So she caught him and kissed him;*
With an impudent face she said to him:

14 *" I have peace offerings with me;*
Today I have paid my vows.

15 *So I came out to meet you,*
Diligently to seek your face,
And I have found you.

16 *I have spread my bed with tapestry,*
Colored coverings of Egyptian linen.

17 *I have perfumed my bed*
With myrrh, aloes, and cinnamon.

18 *Come, let us take our fill of love until morning;*
Let us delight ourselves with love.

19 *For my husband is not at home;*
He has gone on a long journey;

20 *He has taken a bag of money with him,*
And will come home on the appointed day."

21 With her enticing speech she caused him to yield,
With her flattering lips she seduced him.

22 Immediately he went after her, as an ox goes to the slaughter,
Or as a fool to the correction of the stocks,

23 Till an arrow struck his liver.
As a bird hastens to the snare,
He did not know it would cost his life.

24 Now therefore, listen to me, my children;
Pay attention to the words of my mouth:

25 Do not let your heart turn aside to her ways,
Do not stray into her paths;

26 For she has cast down many wounded,
And all who were slain by her were strong men.

27 Her house is the way to hell,
Descending to the chambers of death.

Chapter 7

A primary peril – immorality (7:1-27)

7:1. Once again Solomon urges his son to accept and keep his advice as a priceless treasure. Unfortunately, not all young people view their parent's advice this way. Often they give in to the desire to be independent and to do as they please.

7:2. The godly father's counsel is the way to a good life, and should be guarded as the apple of the eye, one of the most sensitive external parts of the body.

7:3. A wise son will bind the instructions on his fingers, so as to guide him in all that he does. And he should write them on the tablet of his mind for lasting memory.

7:4. He should treat his father's words with the respect and love he has for his sister and nearest relative.

7:5. Again when Solomon thinks of his son's future and the dangers along the way, he continues with the subject of the immoral woman (cf. 5:3). He considers this as one of the greatest dangers that a young man faces. It is the great global peril.

7:6. The king saw a portrayal of the scenario in living color one day as he was looking out the window.

7:7. He saw a young fellow, perhaps naïve and with little knowledge of what the world is like. You might say that he didn't have common sense.

7:8. Nearby was the house of a prostitute, a "lady of the night." He took the path toward her front door.

7:9. The last rays of daylight were slipping over the horizon and darkness was falling. Sad to say, it was not only the night that was dark. It was the young fellow's mind.

7:10. How strange that right at that moment, she should meet him. Outwardly she was dressed provocatively, drawing attention to her body (contrast 1 Tim. 2:9), and inwardly she was cunning.

7:11. She was no quiet, gracious homebody, but a loud-mouthed, aggressive, assertive woman who did not stay at home where she belonged. She was always out in public, shifting from place to place.

7:12. Our friend didn't have to search for her. She made herself highly visible and readily available: in the streets, in the squares, at every corner. It is not surprising that they met. Maybe he foolishly took this favorable circumstantial timing as proof that what he was doing was all right.

7:13. She immediately took the initiative, embracing him, brazenly kissing him, speaking with shameless audacity.

7:14. She professes to be religious. She has just been to the synagogue with a peace offering. Now she is going home with some of the meat that she is permitted to take home (Lev. 7:11-18). She has fulfilled her religious obligations.

7:15. She lies saying that he, a total stranger, is the very one she has been looking for, inflating his ego.

7:16. Any question as to her goal is dispelled by her sensuous description of her bedroom. She points to the tapestry on her bed and the sheets of finest linen.

7:17. As if just for him, she went to the expense of spraying the bed with costly fragrances. Is it a coincidence that many modern perfumes have suggestive names such as Sin?

7:18. In case he still doesn't perceive her objective, she flat-footedly invites him to go to bed with her. She calls it love, which of course is also a lie. The Bible calls it lust. She calls it living. The Bible calls it the way to death and hell.

7:19. Suppose her husband should come home unexpectedly? Not to worry. He has gone on a long trip.

7:20. He had taken plenty of money with him and wouldn't be home till the full moon (NASB), which would be a long time, judging by the darkness of the sky.

7:21. To keep our friend from changing his mind, she pressures him with a barrage of flattery.

7:22. The fateful moment arrives. It is like an ox going to the slaughterhouse or a fool to a house of correction.

7:23. He lay there, as if shot in a vital organ. He went after the evil woman like a bird hastening to the trap, not knowing it would cost his life.

It is not by accident that the liver is mentioned here. Sexual sin does physical damage to vital organs. There are more than twenty-five sexually transmitted diseases. Some are incurable.

7:24. The father was so moved by his own vivid portrayal of the fall of a young man that he burst out into another fervent plea. This time it is directed to his children, not just his son.

7:25. They should be wise to the wiles of the evil woman and stay severely away from her neighborhood.

7:26. She has caused the downfall of many wounded, yes, hordes of men who were physically strong but morally weak were slain by her. Many young men involved in illicit sex may die from venereal disease or be killed by an angry husband.

7:27. Her house is a sure route to hell, descending as it does to the realm of the dead. If it sounds scary, it's because it is, and is meant to make a lasting impression upon us so that we avoid immorality at all costs (cf. Prov. 5:5; 9:18).

Once again we must remind ourselves that the sin can be forgiven (1 Jn. 1:9) and fellowship with the Lord can be restored. But there is often a bitter after-taste. In some cases there are restrictions on public ministry or positions in the church.

Young people should realize that sexual sin is a "killer." Dr. Howard Hendricks made a list of 246 men in full-time ministry who flamed out in moral failure within two years. The fact that they were full-time workers didn't save them from falling.

Another prominent Christian suggested that only one out of ten men who started strong will still be continuing strong at sixty-five.[8]

Here are some safeguards designed to prevent this from happening to you:

- If you are a believer, remember that your body is the temple of the Holy Spirit (1 Cor. 6:19ff).
- Keep close to the Word (Ps. 119:11).
- Pray that the Lord will take you home to heaven rather than let you fall into sin.

---

8 Steve Farrar, *Finishing Strong*, Sisters, Multnomah Books, 1995, pp.6-7.

- Pray that the temptation to sin and the opportunity to sin will never coincide.
- Remember that lustful sins are among the sins that nailed the son of God to the cross. Continuing in those sins is like re-crucifying Him.
- Have the strength to say no, to swim against the tide. Don't be ashamed to be different.
- In the moment of fierce temptation, call upon the Lord to deliver you (Prov. 18:10). He always will.
- Sometimes it is necessary to flee, as Joseph did. One preacher said, "It's good to fight the good fight, but there are times when it is better to flee the good flight."
- Never counsel alone with a woman who is not your wife, even if you yourself are single.
- Don't give reason to the enemies of the Lord to blaspheme (2 Sam. 12:14).
- Don't disappoint those Christians who have trusted you, prayed for you, and perhaps invested in you financially.

Proverbs 8

1 *Does not wisdom cry out,*
And understanding lift up her voice?

2 *She takes her stand on the top of the high hill,*
Beside the way, where the paths meet.

3 *She cries out by the gates, at the entry of the city,*
At the entrance of the doors:

4 *" To you, O men, I call,*
And my voice is to the sons of men.

5 *O you simple ones, understand prudence,*
And you fools, be of an understanding heart.

6 *Listen, for I will speak of excellent things,*
And from the opening of my lips will come right things;

7 *For my mouth will speak truth;*
Wickedness is an abomination to my lips.

8 *All the words of my mouth are with righteousness;*
Nothing crooked or perverse is in them.

9 *They are all plain to him who understands,*
And right to those who find knowledge.

10 *Receive my instruction, and not silver,*
And knowledge rather than choice gold;

11 *For wisdom is better than rubies,*
And all the things one may desire cannot be compared
with her.

12 *" I, wisdom, dwell with prudence,*
And find out knowledge and discretion.

13 *The fear of the LORD is to hate evil;*
Pride and arrogance and the evil way
And the perverse mouth I hate.

14 Counsel is mine, and sound wisdom;
I am understanding, I have strength.

15 By me kings reign,
And rulers decree justice.

16 By me princes rule, and nobles,
All the judges of the earth.

17 I love those who love me,
And those who seek me diligently will find me.

18 Riches and honor are with me,
Enduring riches and righteousness.

19 My fruit is better than gold, yes, than fine gold,
And my revenue than choice silver.

20 I traverse the way of righteousness,
In the midst of the paths of justice,

21 That I may cause those who love me to inherit wealth,
That I may fill their treasuries.

22 "The LORD possessed me at the beginning of His way,
Before His works of old.

23 I have been established from everlasting,
From the beginning, before there was ever an earth.

24 When there were no depths I was brought forth,
When there were no fountains abounding with water.

25 Before the mountains were settled,
Before the hills, I was brought forth;

26 While as yet He had not made the earth or the fields,
Or the primal dust of the world.

27 When He prepared the heavens, I was there,
When He drew a circle on the face of the deep,

28 When He established the clouds above,
When He strengthened the fountains of the deep,

29 When He assigned to the sea its limit,
So that the waters would not transgress His command,
When He marked out the foundations of the earth,

30 Then I was beside Him as a master craftsman;
And I was daily His delight,
Rejoicing always before Him,

31 Rejoicing in His inhabited world,
And my delight was with the sons of men.

32 " Now therefore, listen to me, my children,
For blessed are those who keep my ways.

33 Hear instruction and be wise,
And do not disdain it.

34 Blessed is the man who listens to me,
Watching daily at my gates,
Waiting at the posts of my doors.

35 For whoever finds me finds life,
And obtains favor from the LORD;

36 But he who sins against me wrongs his own soul;
All those who hate me love death."

Chapter 8

The lady called Wisdom (8:1-21)

8:1. This chapter is a classic tribute to wisdom. To get the maximum benefit from it, apply the words to the Lord Jesus whenever possible because He is wisdom personified.

8:2. As a woman of excellence, wisdom positions herself so as to be easily heard by all. See the Introduction for an explanation of how feminine gender is used in connection with wisdom and can still be applied to Christ.

8:3. She is as ubiquitous as Coca-Cola. Wherever there are people, she is there, whether on a hilltop or at a highway intersection. You can find her at the gates to the city, the official meeting place, or at other entrances. There is really no excuse for not finding her.

Notice the resemblance between wisdom and the Lord Jesus. He is not far from any of us.

8:4. She calls out to the race of mankind as they hurry by. The Lord said, *"Come to Me, all you who labor and are heavy laden..."* (Matt. 11:28). See also Isa. 55:1-3; Rev. 22:17.

8:5. To the stupid and naïve she offers prudence and to fools an understanding heart. Jesus said, *"...learn from Me, for I am gentle and lowly in heart"* (Matt. 11:29).

8:6. Everything she says is excellent. When her lips move, the words are right. *"So all bore witness to Him, and marveled at the gracious words which proceeded out of His mouth"* (Luke 4:22).

8:7. Wisdom tells only the truth and wickedness is abomination to her lips. The Lord Jesus said, *"I am the way, the truth, and the life..."* (John 14:6).

8:8. Her talk is uniformly free from what is unclean or suggestive. Speaking of Jesus Christ, the Apostle John said, *"In Him is no sin"* (1 Jn. 3:5).

8:9. She is understandable to those who are receptive and appropriate to those who are teachable. *"If anyone wills to do His will, he shall know concerning the doctrine, whether it is from God or* *whether I speak on My own authority"* (John 7:17).

8:10. The words of wisdom are more precious than the finest silver and gold. So are the words of the Lord Jesus.

8:11. A person who is wise has something that exceeds in value the choicest rubies. So the Savior is more precious than anything we could ever imagine.

8:12. Wisdom continues to tell of her benefits. To possess her is to have good judgment, knowledge, and discretion as guides through life. It is all true of the Lord Jesus Christ.

8:13. Since the beginning of wisdom is the fear of the Lord, those who are wisdom's children hate evil, pride, arrogance, and a dirty mouth. Their lives are not dominated by the works of the flesh: fornication, uncleanness, covetousness, idolatry (Gal. 5:5). Hating sin and the destruction it causes is a good thing (see Ps. 45:7).

8:14. Wisdom is the source of sound advice and good judgment. She gives understanding, insight, and strength of character. This is also true of Christ.

8:15. It is by wisdom that kings reign well and guarantee justice to the people. This is partially true today and will be perfectly fulfilled when the Lord Jesus reigns in the Millennium.

8:16. It is true also of princes, nobles and judges. As servants of God, they are enabled to make right decisions. If a person really wants to know, he will be told (John 7:17).

8:17. A love relationship exists between wisdom and her disciples. How true!

8:18. When the disciples get wisdom, they will get riches that last, together with honor and a righteous life. It is a priceless heritage.

8:19. Money can't buy the blessings that come from wisdom. Believers are blessed with every spiritual blessing in heavenly places in Christ (Eph. 1:3).

8:20. Wisdom travels with those who love her, who do the right thing and those who render just decisions. Our Lord never leaves or forsakes us.

8:21. Again we see the importance of loving wisdom. She fills the lives of those who love her with wealth and their treasuries with riches. Paul said to Christians, *"All things are yours"* (1 Cor. 3:21).

Wisdom the active agent in Creation (8:22-31)

8:22. The next ten verses describe wisdom's role in creation. Wisdom may be taken literally, that is, God's superb intelligence in creation. Or it may be a type of the Lord Jesus as a partner with God when He made the universe. We will employ the second interpretation, although the first is equally true. (See notes in Introduction.)

The expression that God possessed His Son may include the fact that the Lord Jesus was with the Father, a distinct personality.

God the Father possessed the Lord Jesus at the beginning of His way. The beginning here could be the beginningless beginning mentioned in John 1:1, *"In the beginning was the Word, and the Word was with God, and the Word was God."* But in the immediate context, it could mean the beginning of God's creation work: *"In the beginning God created the heavens and the earth"* (Gen. 1:1).[9]

8:23. Wisdom incarnate was established or appointed in eternity, long before the earth ever existed.

This verse and the following one teach that the Lord Jesus, as wisdom, predated creation and was not a part of it.

He was established from the beginning, before there was an earth. The word "established" has the meaning of "appointed." Before Genesis 1 the Lord Jesus Christ was appointed to be a partner with God in the work of creation.

8:24. Before there were Atlantic and Pacific oceans or great fountains of the deep, the Lord Jesus was ever-present. Here we have day two of creation (Gen. 1:6-8).

8:25. Before Everest or the Mount of Olives, Jesus was appointed to the wonderful work of creating the world. *"Lands"* (vv. 25-26) points to the third day of creation (Gen. 1:9-13).

8:26. All this was before He had made the earth, the fields,

---

9 Some versions of the Bible translate "brought forth" (vs. 24) as "created" and thus support the Arian heresy that Jesus was a created being. But whether you think of wisdom as an attribute of God or as personified in Christ, it was never created. It is better to understand the verse as saying, "The Lord appointed me in the beginning of His ways." In other words, God appointed Jesus as the Maker of all things. It was the birth of a role, not of a Person.

and the primeval dust of the earth. The writer clearly emphasizes Christ's eternity. He existed before there was any created thing.

8:27. Now we learn that He was there not only before matter existed but He was also present at the time of creation. When God designed the atmospheric and stellar heavens, the Son was there. That was when God drew a circle on the face of the deep, making the earth a sphere or globe. This is best seen when you observe a distant ship slipping down over the horizon. Here again you find the Bible stating a scientific fact long before science discovered it. The Bible never taught that the earth was flat.

8:28. God established the clouds and turned on the fountains of the deep in His program for making the earth habitable for man. This was the second day of creation.

8:29. This is when He said to the oceans, *"This far you may come but no farther, and here your proud waves must stop"* (Job 38:11). It is when He laid the foundations of the earth. The dry land appeared on the third day.

8:30. The Lord Jesus was with God the Father as a skilled workman. He was the active agent in creation and was a continual delight to His Father as He rejoiced in the works of creation. We share that rejoicing when we learn of the wonders of the human body, of plant life, of the stellar universe, and of all God's marvels.

8:31. The earth brought great joy to Him but His special delight was with the sons of men. They were the crown of creation.

We pause here to remind ourselves that God's works of creation express His wisdom and power, but it is Calvary that tells His love.

> All worlds His glorious pow'r confess.
> His wisdom all His works express;
> But, O His love, what tongue can tell?
> Christ Jesus has done all things well.
> —Samuel Medley

William Cowper captured something of the grandeur of Christ's role in creation in this majestic hymn, based on our passage in Proverbs:

Ere God had built the mountains
 or raised the fruitful hills,
Before He filled the fountains
 that feed the running rills,
In Thee from everlasting,
 the wonderful I AM,
Found pleasures never wasting,
 and Wisdom is Thy name.

When like a tent to dwell in
 He spread the skies abroad,
And swathed about the swelling
 of ocean's mighty flood,
He wrought by weight and measure,
 and Thou wast with Him then,
Thyself the Father's pleasure
 and Thine, the sons of men.

And could'st Thou be delighted
 with creatures such as we,
Who when we saw Thee slighted,
 and nailed Thee to the tree?
Unfathomable wonder and mystery divine!
The voice that speaks in thunder
 says, "Sinner, I am thine."

And art Thou, Lord,
 delighted to call us now Thine own—
The love no longer slighted
 which Thou to us hast shown?
Oh, way of purposed blessing
 in death told out to man!
The fruit we're now possessing
 of Wisdom's wondrous plan.

In all your getting, get wisdom (8:32-36)

8:32. Wisdom now pronounces a blessing on all those who live in obedience to her instruction.

8:33. Her children should be careful not to scorn her teachings but to adhere to them religiously.

8:34. The happy person is the one who daily awaits some word from wisdom, watching at her gates and waiting for her to appear at the door. The Lord Jesus opened His ear every morning to get instruction from His Father for that day (Isa. 50:4). So we should begin every day by reading the Word of God and spending time in prayer.

8:35. The one who finds wisdom finds the abundant life and experiences the Lord's favor. How true this is when we equate Wisdom with the Lord Jesus.

8:36. Whoever sins against wisdom and rejects it does himself a great disfavor. Whoever hates wisdom loves death (cf. 5:12). Once again, we should apply these verses about wisdom to the Savior. Whoever rejects Him spells his own doom. He chooses eternal death rather than everlasting life.

Proverbs 9

1 Wisdom has built her house,
She has hewn out her seven pillars;

2 She has slaughtered her meat,
She has mixed her wine,
She has also furnished her table.

3 She has sent out her maidens,
She cries out from the highest places of the city,

4 " Whoever is simple, let him turn in here!"
As for him who lacks understanding, she says to him,

5 " Come, eat of my bread
And drink of the wine I have mixed.

6 Forsake foolishness and live,
And go in the way of understanding.

7 " He who corrects a scoffer gets shame for himself,
And he who rebukes a wicked man only harms himself.

8 Do not correct a scoffer, lest he hate you;
Rebuke a wise man, and he will love you.

9 Give instruction to a wise man, and he will be still wiser;
Teach a just man, and he will increase in learning.

10 " The fear of the LORD is the beginning of wisdom,
And the knowledge of the Holy One is understanding.

11 For by me your days will be multiplied,
And years of life will be added to you.

12 If you are wise, you are wise for yourself,
And if you scoff, you will bear it alone."

13 A foolish woman is clamorous;
She is simple, and knows nothing.

14 For she sits at the door of her house,
On a seat by the highest places of the city,

15 *To call to those who pass by,*
Who go straight on their way:

16 *" Whoever is simple, let him turn in here";*
And as for him who lacks understanding, she says to him,

17 *" Stolen water is sweet,*
And bread eaten in secret is pleasant."

18 *But he does not know that the dead are there,*
That her guests are in the depths of hell.

Chapter 9

Wisdom's universal invitation (9:1-12)

9:1. There are two prominent women in this chapter, wisdom in verses 1-12 and the foolish woman in verse 13-18. In this first section wisdom appears as a wealthy matron with a magnificent mansion and a door always open to those who would like to partake of her gourmet delicacies. The seven pillars suggest a huge house with room to accommodate plenty of guests.

9:2. Everything is ready—the roasted meat and the vintage wines. The table is set with exquisite splendor.

9:3. Now it is time for her maids to go out with the invitation. It is within everyone's earshot. The words of the invitation are given in verses 4 through 12.

9:4. It is for those who realize their need—the simple, the naïve, the gullible, and those who do not have practical knowledge. It is for those who are not savvy and are willing to admit it (cf. Jas. 1:5). It is for those who do not have all the intuition or street smarts that they need to get through life, which basically means all of us, although some are not willing to admit it about themselves. Remember this: only God is truly wise.

9:5. Wisdom's door is open and her feast is spread. Bread and wine might sound rather commonplace but here they stand for priceless benefits and favors.

9:6. Guests should quit acting like fools and choose the way of real living. They should get on the highway of holiness.

These verses have a direct application to the gospel invitation. They say, in effect:

> If you only knew the blessings
>   that salvation brings,
> You would never stay away.
> If you only saw the table spread
>   with lovely things,

You would come to the feast today.
The door is open wide, the Savior bids you come,
There's nothing you will have to pay.
So be wise and step inside
　and do not be like some
Who have thrown their only chance away.
　　　　　　　　　　—Author unknown

The next three verses deal with the reception that teachers can expect.

Scorners will mock wisdom's invitation. They are not good at taking advice. They are unteachable. Anyone who dares to correct a scoffer gets shame, just as the one who rebukes a sinner gets bruises. There is a price to pay but it is necessary. Modern scoffers sneer at conservative, right wing Christians. These scoffers are pro abortion, pro same-sex marriage, pro live-in partners, against family values, pro any religion but Christianity, and of course, against absolute truth. These are the kind that foolishly declare, "there are no absolutes," which is itself an absolute!

9:8. Another reward for rebuking a scoffer is to be hated by him (12:1b; 13:1b). Not so with a wise person; he will really appreciate you.

9:9. He knows this is the way to get wiser, and to increase in knowledge.

9:10. Again we come to the key verse of the book. We had it before in 1:7 in a slightly different wording. When Solomon says here, *"The fear of the Lord is the beginning of wisdom, and the knowledge of the Holy One is understanding,"* he is saying in effect, "The wisest thing a person can do is to put his trust in the Lord, henceforth to acknowledge Him as Lord of his life." A person hasn't started to be wise until he has received the gift of salvation by faith. It is the most sane, sensible, reasonable thing he can do. There is everything to gain and nothing to lose. Salvation is without money and without price.

9:11. The believer's life tends to steer clear of the perils of sin that bring premature death. Holiness generally fosters longevity.

9:12. We all have a choice to make. If we choose wisdom, we are the ones who will benefit most. If we mock the clean life, we suffer the consequences.

The prowling seductress (9:13-18)

9:13. Again we meet one of the greatest temptations in the life of a believer—sexual immorality as pictured by a foolish woman. In other passages she is called an evil woman, a harlot, an adulteress, and a seductress. She is loud in her insistence and not knowledgeable.

What will be the results in the life of one who commits adultery?

- He violates the seventh and tenth commandments (Ex. 20:14, 17). In God's sight, he is doubly worthy of death.
- It is sin against God. When Potiphar's wife tried to seduce Joseph, he resisted the temptation, saying, *"How …can I do this great wickedness, and sin against God"* (Gen. 39:9).
- It is a sin against Christ. It caused His death.
- It is a sin against the Holy Spirit. The believer's body is the temple of the Spirit (1 Cor. 6:19).
- It is a sin against the body like no other sin (1 Cor. 6:18).
- It is an extravagant waste of a person's procreative powers (Prov. 5:15-16).
- It exposes a person to sexual diseases, some of which are incurable (Prov. 7:23).
- It leaves a trail of regret, remorse, shame, and guilt (Ps. 32:3-4).
- It exposes the guilty one to blackmail and extortion.
- It destroys marriages and families. The wreckage on children is incalculable.
- It makes the guilty one the target of the murderous rage of the offended spouse (Prov. 6:34-35).
- It causes the enemies of the Lord to blaspheme (2 Sam. 12:14).
- Although the sin may be forgiven (2 Sam. 12:13), it is impossible to escape the consequences (2 Sam. 12:9-12; 14).

All this for a moment of carnal passion. Is it worth it?

9:14. The evil woman makes herself as conspicuous as possible, whether at her front door or at the city's heights.

9:15. She calls the passersby, those who are going about their business.

9:16. Her special appeal is to those who are like herself, dimwitted.

9:17. She takes advantage of a tendency of fallen human nature; there is a special pleasure in doing what the law forbids. Apples stolen from a neighbor's tree seem to taste much better than those that are bought at the supermarket. Any boy knows that.

9:18. But what they don't realize is that illicit sex has deadly consequences. For a moment of lustful indulgence and passion, a man sells his birthright. If he does not repent and forsake the sin, it spells hell in the life to come.

Proverbs 10

1 *The proverbs of Solomon:*
A wise son makes a glad father,
But a foolish son is the grief of his mother.

2 *Treasures of wickedness profit nothing,*
But righteousness delivers from death.

3 *The LORD will not allow the righteous soul to famish,*
But He casts away the desire of the wicked.

4 *He who has a slack hand becomes poor,*
But the hand of the diligent makes rich.

5 *He who gathers in summer is a wise son;*
He who sleeps in harvest is a son who causes shame.

6 *Blessings are on the head of the righteous,*
But violence covers the mouth of the wicked.

7 *The memory of the righteous is blessed,*
But the name of the wicked will rot.

8 *The wise in heart will receive commands,*
But a prating fool will fall.

9 *He who walks with integrity walks securely,*
But he who perverts his ways will become known.

10 *He who winks with the eye causes trouble,*
But a prating fool will fall.

11 *The mouth of the righteous is a well of life,*
But violence covers the mouth of the wicked.

12 *Hatred stirs up strife,*
But love covers all sins.

13 *Wisdom is found on the lips of him who has understanding,*
But a rod is for the back of him who is devoid
of understanding.

14 *Wise people store up knowledge,*
But the mouth of the foolish is near destruction.

15 *The rich man's wealth is his strong city;*
The destruction of the poor is their poverty.

16 *The labor of the righteous leads to life,*
The wages of the wicked to sin.

17 *He who keeps instruction is in the way of life,*
But he who refuses correction goes astray.

18 *Whoever hides hatred has lying lips,*
And whoever spreads slander is a fool.

19 *In the multitude of words sin is not lacking,*
But he who restrains his lips is wise.

20 *The tongue of the righteous is choice silver;*
The heart of the wicked is worth little.

21 *The lips of the righteous feed many,*
But fools die for lack of wisdom.

22 *The blessing of the LORD makes one rich,*
And He adds no sorrow with it.

23 *To do evil is like sport to a fool,*
But a man of understanding has wisdom.

24 *The fear of the wicked will come upon him,*
And the desire of the righteous will be granted.

25 *When the whirlwind passes by, the wicked is no more,*
But the righteous has an everlasting foundation.

26 *As vinegar to the teeth and smoke to the eyes,*
So is the lazy man to those who send him.

27 *The fear of the LORD prolongs days,*
But the years of the wicked will be shortened.

28 *The hope of the righteous will be gladness,*
But the expectation of the wicked will perish.

*29 The way of the LORD is strength for the upright,
But destruction will come to the workers of iniquity.*

*30 The righteous will never be removed,
But the wicked will not inhabit the earth.*

*31 The mouth of the righteous brings forth wisdom,
But the perverse tongue will be cut out.*

*32 The lips of the righteous know what is acceptable,
But the mouth of the wicked what is perverse.*

Chapter 10

Solomon's gems of wisdom (10:1-29:27)

10:1. What a joy it is for a father to see his son leading an exemplary life. On the other hand a foolish son breaks his mother's heart. He doesn't want anyone to insult his mother, but he is oblivious to the fact that he himself is hurting her. Rudyard Kipling captured something of the emotions of a joyful father as he counseled his son in his poem "If."

> If you can keep your head when all about you
> Are losing theirs and blaming it on you;
> If you can trust yourself when all men doubt you,
> And make allowance for their doubting too;
> If you can wait and not be tired by waiting,
> Or being lied about don't deal in lies;
> Or being hated don't give way to hating,
> And yet don't look too good, nor talk too wise;
>
> If you can dream—and not make dreams your master;
> If you can think and not make thoughts your aim;
> If you can meet with Triumph and Disaster
> And treat those two imposters just the same;
> If you can bear to hear the truth you've spoken
> Twisted by knaves to make a trap for fools,
> Or watch the things you gave your life to, broken,
> And stoop and build 'em up with worn-out tools,
>
> If you can talk with crowds and hold your virtue,
> Or walk with kings—nor lose the common touch;
> If neither foes nor loving friends can hurt you,
> If all men count with you, but not too much;
> If you can fill the unforgiving minute
> With every second's worth of distance run—

Yours is the Earth and everything that's in it,
And—which is more—you'll be a Man, my son!

It is a special joy for Christian parents to see their children living for Christ as adults and serving Him acceptably.

Ed McCully was one of five young missionaries who were killed by Ecuadorian Indians. After the martyrdom, his father told me that Ed was a son who never caused his parents an anxious moment. With tears zig-zagging down his checks, he added, "I'm so glad I didn't discourage him from going to the mission field."

10:2. No amount of money gained dishonestly can stop a person's appointment with death, but a life of honesty and integrity delivers from the fatal consequences of sin.

10:3. The Lord guarantees the righteous that they will not hunger (Ps. 37:25), but He *"thwarts the craving of the wicked"* (NIV). They don't succeed in having their desires fulfilled. Godly people have the best of the bargain. Only those who have God have security.

10:4. A person who is negligent in his work is assured of poverty and the curse of God (Jer. 48:10 KJV). His work is shoddy. The diligent man earns rich rewards. This is true spiritually as well as materially. We should strive for excellence in all that we do.

10:5. It isn't enough just to plant a crop. You have to take it in to the barn when harvest time comes. Harvest is not the time for sleeping during daylight hours. As Longfellow wrote:

> "The heights by great men gained and kept
> Were not attained by sudden flight,
> But they, while their companions slept,
> Were toiling upward in the night."

For the Christian, now is the time for harvest. Jesus said, *"Lift up your eyes and look on the fields, For they are already white for harvest"* (John 4: 35b).

Perishing, perishing! Harvest is passing,
Reapers are few and the night draweth near:

Jesus is calling thee, haste to the reaping.
Thou shalt have souls, precious souls for thy hire.
—Lucy R. Meyer

10:6. The head and the mouth are contrasted. The head of
the righteous is crowned with blessings from the Lord. The
mouth of the ungodly is a hiding place for violent schemes.

There are many benefits to a righteous life. The speech of
the wicked conceals violence. There is a contrast here between
a head showered with blessings and a mouth hiding sin.

The expression *"covers the mouth"* here and in verse 10 is an
idiom of uncertain meaning. It is rendered "shuts the mouth,"
"conceals," and "overwhelms the mouth."

10:7. We speak with hushed praise when we think of saints
who have gone to be with the Lord, but mention of an evil monster evokes words of disgust. Twenty million people passed from
life to death under Hitler's savagery and an even greater number
under Stalin, though the exact figure is unknown. But think of
the people who passed from death to life through the preaching
of Spurgeon and Moody. *"The memory of the just is blessed."*

10:8. It is a mark of wisdom when a person welcomes Biblical instruction and obeys it. A talkative fool disregards it and
crashes to the dust. The contrast is between a teachable and
obedient person, and a foolish, senseless one. Here are some
other ways by which you can recognize a fool.

- He knows it all, and converses freely on any topic.
- You can't tell him anything.
- He thinks that wisdom will die with him.
- He doesn't listen to advice.
- He questions authority.
- He staggers from one failure or crash to another.
- He is allergic to work.
- When trouble strikes him, he blames God.
- His motto is, "I do it my way."

A wise person realizes that the Lord's commands are for his
own good, not for God's. What does it mean to the Great God

whether we obey His Word? But it means a lot to us.

Here are some examples:

- Why did He forbid us to worship idols? Idolatry is linked with immorality. Immorality keeps a person out of heaven (1 Cor. 6:9).
- Why did He command Israel to keep the Sabbath? Because man's constitution ideally requires one day of rest for every six days of work.
- Why did He forbid adultery? Because it has built-in punishment in the bodies and souls of those who commit it.

10:9. There is security in a life of integrity, but a person who follows crooked paths eventually exposes himself for what he is and is punished. No one can sin and get away it. Sin is sure to find out the guilty.

10:10. Not all winks are evil. They can be instruments of joviality and fun. On the other hand they can be malicious. That is the kind in verse 10. *"Winks with the eye"* seems redundant, since all winking is done with the eye. It is probably for emphasis.

Here the man who winks is a liar. He says one thing to the crowd but his wink tells someone in the crowd not to believe it. This deceiver is looking for trouble. A prating fool is one who talks endlessly without saying anything. He never comes up for air. Neither winking nor prating are recommended.

All conversation should be filtered through these ten questions: Is it…

- Worthwhile?
- Kind?
- Gracious?
- Honest?
- Edifying?
- Appropriate?
- Free from oaths?
- Free from gossip?
- Free from flattery?
- Necessary?

A friend and I were talking about a mutual acquaintance. He started to say something that would have been negative. Then he stopped in the middle of the sentence and said, "No, that wouldn't be edifying." (I've been dying of curiosity ever since.)

10:11. The speech of the godly is like a life-giving fountain. Behind the covered mouth of the wicked hides life-taking violence. How am I affecting others? How do I influence them?

> My life shall touch a dozen lives
> before this day is done—
> Leave countless marks for good
> or ill ere sets the evening sun.
> Shall fair or foul its imprint prove
> on those my life shall hail?
> Shall benison my imprint be,
> or shall a blight prevail?
> —Strickland Gilliland

10:12. Hatred is the soil from which conflict grows. This agrees with what Jesus said in the Sermon on the Mount. *"You have heard that it was said to those of old, 'You shall not murder, and whoever murders will be in danger of the judgment.' But I say to you that whoever is angry with his brother without cause shall be in danger of the judgment"* (Matt. 5:21-22a). It also agrees with the apostle John who said, *"Whoever hates his brother is a murderer"* (1 Jn. 3:15). It doesn't mean that he has already committed murder, but that hatred is the pit from which murder flows. It is murder in embryo.

"Love covers all sins." This is not an Old Testament way of atoning for sins. It is simply saying that if I really love a person, I will show it by not gossiping about some sin he has committed. The sin has probably been confessed and forgiven long ago, so why should I resurrect it, unless my objective is to do him harm?

10:13. God has bound together wisdom and understanding. Also inseparable are a lack of understanding and the rod of correction. No one can part them. Also inseparable are dust on the Bible and ice in the heart. The proverb contrasts where wisdom is found and what happens when it is missing.

10:14. One of the marks of a wise man is that he is always growing in understanding. The fool's talk leads to his own undoing.

Excessive talking increases the danger of saying something sinful. That, in turn, requires an apology for the wrong. The path of wisdom is to speak guardedly and thoughtfully, weighing one's words in advance. Then you won't have it said of you, "He can talk the stink out of an onion!"

10:15. A rich man thinks that his money makes him impregnable. The poor have no such cushion against trouble and loss. Their poverty leaves them relatively helpless. But if they have the Lord as their Shepherd, they will not want.

It is a common rule of life that people work in order to provide for their own personal needs. But the Christian *"works with his hands what is good, that he may have something to give to him who has need"* (Eph. 4:28).

10:16. What righteous people earn is used for life-giving or life-sustaining purposes. Too often the wages of the wicked are squandered to finance evil.

10:17. The person who shapes his life on biblical principles is on the right path. Show me a man who rejects such principles and I'll show you one who is on the wrong route.

10:18. Whoever hates a person, yet professes to love him, is a lying hypocrite. Call a gossip by his real name—fool.

10:19. The more you talk, the more apt you are to sin. The tongue is in a wet place where it is apt to slip. The best policy is to think before you speak. The more careful we are in talking, the less we have to repent.

I have seen this proverb lived out when people are telling jokes. Each one tries to outdo the other until finally someone tells a joke that is off-color. The offender has the shameful duty of saying, "I am sorry. A man of God would not have told that joke."

Robert Frost said wryly, "Half the world is composed of people who have something to say and can't, and the other half who have nothing to say and keep on saying it."

Peter's tendency to speak impulsively led to embarrassment.

10:20. The conversation of the righteous is precious because it is edifying. The thoughts of the wicked are worthless.

There are 915 verses in the book of Proverbs. A high percentage of these have to do with speech. This is a startling indication of the potential of our talk for good and for evil.

"The tongue of the righteous" refers to what they say. It is as priceless as high quality silver. In contrast, the heart (or mind) of evil people brings forth conversation of trifling value. Our prayer should be, *"Let the words of my mouth and meditation of my heart be acceptable in Your sight, O LORD, my strength and my Redeemer"* (Ps. 19:14).

10:21. Righteous people can edify many by their worthwhile conversation. Fools don't have enough good judgment to keep themselves alive.

10:22. We are fabulously enriched by the blessings of the Lord. They are spiritual blessings (Eph. 1:3) such as salvation, justification, sanctification, forgiveness of sins, and eternal life.

"He adds no sorrow with it." This doesn't mean that believers are exempt from sorrows. It means that sorrows are not a necessary part of His blessings. Material blessings such as monetary riches have sorrows that are implicitly connected with them but it is not so with God's blessings.

10:23. For fools it's like a game, a form of amusement, to do evil. A man of understanding has too much sense for that kind of behavior. For him it's like a game to exercise wisdom.

10:24. That which the wicked fear eventually comes on them, if not in life, certainly in death and afterwards, in hell. What the godly desire will come to them—heaven, eternal joy and the Lord's *"Well done."* Every one will be recompensed, either with judgment or with blessing.

10:25. When the tornado strikes, the wicked are blown away. Not so the godly. Rain descends, floods follow, and the wind blows but the house stands, for it was founded on the Rock (cf. Matt. 7:25). That Rock is Christ, an everlasting foundation. Security and salvation are found only in the Lord Jesus.

10:26. Vinegar is sour to the taste and smoke is an irritant to the eyes. So a lazy messenger is a bitter and irritating nuisance to the boss. He is independent and useless.

10:27. Trusting the Lord is good for your health. It contributes to a long life. Living in sin reduces your life expectancy.

10:28. The hope of the believer for happiness will never be disappointed because it is based on the Word of God. It will have a joyful fulfillment because it is based on the Word of God. It is as sure as if it had already happened.

> The wicked can only look forward to destruction. Citing four of the world's most powerful rulers, G. S. Bowes wrote: "Alexander the Great was not satisfied, even when he had completely subdued the nations. He wept because there were no more worlds to conquer and he died at an early age in a state of debauchery. Hannibal, who filled three bushels with the gold rings taken from the knights he had slaughtered, committed suicide by swallowing poison. Few noted his passing, and he left the earth completely unmourned. Julius Caesar, 'dyeing his garments in the blood of one million of his foes,' conquered 800 cities, only to be stabbed by his best friends at the scene of his greatest triumph. Napoleon, the feared conqueror, after being the scourge of Europe, spent his last years in banishment." [10]

10:29. When we walk with the Lord in the light of His Word, we get strength for the way and grace for the day. Destruction is all the workers of iniquity can look forward to. They have no promise of better things to come.

10:30. God's people are assured of a firm, unmovable foundation. Sinners have no hope of inhabiting the earth. To inhabit the earth expresses an Old Testament idea of ultimate bliss. It would be similar to the Christian's dwelling in heaven.

10:31. Wise people speak words of wisdom, but those with the tongue of deceivers will be forcibly silenced. The mouth here speaks of a person's speech while the tongue refers to the instrument of evil speech.

10:32. Godly people know what kind of speech is appropriate. The talk of sinners is contrary to acceptable standards. Believers should be ready to resort to transitions to keep conversations from degenerating into unkind, unclean, vain or vul-

---

10 Quoted by H. G. Bosch in *Our Daily Bread*, January 18.

gar talk. This means finding something in the conversation to make the listeners think of something that is morally, spiritually, or ethically higher. By introducing this meaningful subject they transfer the conversation from the inane to the sublime.

For example, the conversation in the living room is about mutual acquaintances and usually with negative undertones. It is time for you to say, "With over 6 billion people in the world, do you think it is possible for God to take a personal interest in each one?" From then on the conversation is in the hands of the angels.

When you sense that a conversation is not going anywhere profitable, change its direction. Don't be like a thermometer that just registers the temperature. Be like the thermostat that changes it.

Proverbs 11

1 Dishonest scales are an abomination to the LORD,
But a just weight is His delight.

2 When pride comes, then comes shame;
But with the humble is wisdom.

3 The integrity of the upright will guide them,
But the perversity of the unfaithful will destroy them.

4 Riches do not profit in the day of wrath,
But righteousness delivers from death.

5 The righteousness of the blameless will direct his way aright,
But the wicked will fall by his own wickedness.

6 The righteousness of the upright will deliver them,
But the unfaithful will be caught by their lust.

7 When a wicked man dies, his expectation will perish,
And the hope of the unjust perishes.

8 The righteous is delivered from trouble,
And it comes to the wicked instead.

9 The hypocrite with his mouth destroys his neighbor,
But through knowledge the righteous will be delivered.

10 When it goes well with the righteous, the city rejoices;
And when the wicked perish, there is jubilation.

11 By the blessing of the upright the city is exalted,
But it is overthrown by the mouth of the wicked.

12 He who is devoid of wisdom despises his neighbor,
But a man of understanding holds his peace.

13 A talebearer reveals secrets,
But he who is of a faithful spirit conceals a matter.

14 *Where there is no counsel, the people fall;*
But in the multitude of counselors there is safety.

15 *He who is surety for a stranger will suffer,*
But one who hates being surety is secure.

16 *A gracious woman retains honor,*
But ruthless men retain riches.

17 *The merciful man does good for his own soul,*
But he who is cruel troubles his own flesh.

18 *The wicked man does deceptive work,*
But he who sows righteousness will have a sure reward.

19 *As righteousness leads to life,*
So he who pursues evil pursues it to his own death.

20 *Those who are of a perverse heart are an abomination*
to the LORD,
But the blameless in their ways are His delight.

21 *Though they join forces, the wicked will not go un-*
punished;
But the posterity of the righteous will be delivered.

22 *As a ring of gold in a swine's snout,*
So is a lovely woman who lacks discretion.

23 *The desire of the righteous is only good,*
But the expectation of the wicked is wrath.

24 *There is one who scatters, yet increases more;*
And there is one who withholds more than is right,
But it leads to poverty.

25 *The generous soul will be made rich,*
And he who waters will also be watered himself.

26 *The people will curse him who withholds grain,*
But blessing will be on the head of him who sells it.

27 *He who earnestly seeks good finds favor,*
But trouble will come to him who seeks evil.

28 He who trusts in his riches will fall,
But the righteous will flourish like foliage.

29 He who troubles his own house will inherit the wind,
And the fool will be servant to the wise of heart.

30 The fruit of the righteous is a tree of life,
And he who wins souls is wise.

31 If the righteous will be recompensed on the earth,
How much more the ungodly and the sinner.

Chapter 11

11:1. The terms "weights" and "measures" generally have to do with honesty in business transactions. God recognizes the standards that governments have established, and expects His people to observe them with integrity. Artist Leslie Thrasher painted an unforgettable picture of false weights. A butcher has a whole chicken on the scale but he also slyly has a finger on the scale, gently pressing it down. Not to be outdone, his old-fashioned matronly customer has a finger on the other side of the scale gently pushing it up.

A false balance may include dishonest tax returns, school exams, insurance claims, building permits, or expense accounts. God hates, loathes, despises, and abominates dishonesty. What He loves is a just weight, that is, an honest exchange of value. It means giving 60 minutes of work for every hour of pay. It means giving sixteen ounces of a product for the advertised cost per pound.

"A just weight is His delight." He is pleased with a man like a Christian builder named Crawford. In his entire career, it was never necessary for him to sign a contract. His promise was all that was needed. The community knew that his word was his bond.

There is a spiritual application here. In communicating the gospel, be sure to give full measure. Don't rush or pussyfoot over the subject of sin. Take time to point out Scriptures that emphasize the necessity of repentance. Don't leave out the blood of Christ. A gospel without the blood is no gospel at all.

In teaching the Word be sure to declare all the counsel of God (Acts 20:27). It's easy to avoid those subjects that might offend your audience.

11:2. Pride has a way of ending in disgrace and the humiliation of falling flat on one's face. The wisdom of humble folks keeps them low and therefore with no danger of their falling. Remember, lightning strikes the tallest object. So keep a low profile.

Pride is the parent sin. It took place in heaven when Satan tried to dethrone God and take His place. Everyone of us has enough pride to sink a battleship, and some are too proud to admit it!

11:3. Integrity serves as a guide to the godly, but the crookedness of unbelievers leads them astray and thus destroys them. Much of the news on the radio and TV illustrates the second part of the proverb. Dishonesty ends in scandal and sometimes in a prison sentence.

11:4. A big bank account is no savior at the time of disaster, death, and the day of judgment (cf. v. 28). It is godly people, those who have been justified, declared righteous, who can face the future unafraid. They know it is well with their soul.

11:5. Their Scriptural code of conduct shows blameless people the way to go. Blameless does not mean sinless. It means that no serious charge can be sustained against them.

The wickedness of ungodly people leads them to a fall. Sin leads to destruction as night follows day.

11:6. Righteousness is the safety net of the believer whereas lust takes the unbeliever captive.

11:7. When a wicked man dies, he passes into eternity without God, without Christ, and without hope in the world (cf. Luke 16:19-31). Any expectation of good is gone. He has passed the redemption point, and the point of no return. There is no second chance. As a tree falls, so shall it lie.

11:8. God's people are saved from much trouble. The proverb doesn't mean that the believer is entirely free from troubles, but his troubles are not the result of his own folly. Trouble comes to the wicked instead. The three faithful Israelites survived the fiery furnace whereas their executioner was killed by the flame outside the furnace (Dan. 3:22, 27).

11:9. By false accusation a hypocrite can destroy his neighbor and cause untold suffering. It's a form of character assassination and is abominable to the Lord. This kind of accuser loves back channels and "confidential" whispering, that help him to avoid discovery. He is like a sniper who fires lethal shots from a concealed location. However, upright people are vindicated when the truth is revealed, although this may not happen in some cases until judgment day arrives.

11:10. When righteous citizens are accepted and honored, the populace has reason to rejoice. When the wicked are no longer in power, there is a sense of relief and satisfaction.

11:11. If a city enjoys the blessing of having godly citizens, it is exalted. But that same city can be overthrown by the speech of rabble-rousers.

11:12. It's wrong to disparage your neighbor. You're supposed to love him. And some day he may save your life by warning you of danger. When tempted to belittle him, it's best to say nothing.

Here two men are contrasted. The first is short-sighted and foolish because he disparages his neighbor, perhaps for some minor fault or failure. The second is intelligent. He says nothing to disturb the important role the neighbor plays in sharing tools and equipment, in sounding an alarm when there is danger, in sharing information about common concerns, and in friendship.

11:13. A gossip blabs about things that are supposed to be secret. A faithful person knows how to keep a confidence. Early in his Christian life, a believer should learn to refrain from telling all he knows.

11:14. Pity the state or church where there are no competent advisors. Safety lies in having a group of knowledgeable people who can see all sides of an issue and can give wise counsel. But safety is not in numbers alone. King Ahab had 400 false prophets to advise him, but all of them were wrong. Wise counsel comes from those who fear the Lord and know His Word.

This is why believers should consult their elders before making major decisions.

11:15. It's unwise to guarantee that a stranger will pay back his loan. If the stranger's credit rating were any good, he probably wouldn't need you to co-sign the agreement. Use common sense. Don't act as surety unless you would be content to lose the money.

11:16.A refined, genteel woman is honored for her graciousness. In contrast, ruthless men are known for their riches. When the world asks, "How much is that man worth?" they mean "How much money does he have?" That is a poor standard for judging a person's value. Grace is better than wealth. Character is better than gold. It is better to retain honor than to retain riches.

11:17. A person's kindness and compassion are good for his health, whereas a man who is cruel suffers harmful physical effects. That is what holistic medicine is all about.

11:18. The contrast here is between a man who does shoddy, deceptive work and one who is honest in all he does. The wages of the former are transient. The latter will not fail to receive lasting reward.

11:19. Eternal life in heaven is at the end of a consistently righteous life, while eternal death awaits those who practice evil. Notice how Solomon hammers away at the link between holiness and destiny. But be clear—we are not saved or lost according to the life we've lived. A holy life is the evidence of a saved soul. Those who practice evil show that they have never been born again.

Timothy McVey illustrates the second line of the proverb. *"He who pursues evil pursues it to his own death."* Timothy McVey parked a truck full of explosives next to the Federal Building in Oklahoma City and blew it up with great loss of life and injury. McVey drove away probably confident that he had committed the perfect crime. However, a highway patrolman happened to notice that the car had no rear license plate. While he was writing a ticket for McVey's minor infraction of the law, his radio crackled with news of the explosion. Tim McVey fit the description of the suspected terrorist. He was arrested, convicted, and executed.

11:20. People whose hearts are corrupt and crooked are detestable to the Lord. It's the blameless ones who please Him.

11:21. Even though evil men mobilize an army, they will not escape punishment. Godly people will be delivered without benefit of military might.

11:22. Here are two inappropriate mergers. Just as a gold ring is not appropriate in a pig's snout, so a beautiful woman who lacks discretion is not a fitting combination.

11:23. Upright people can look forward to blessing (cf. 10:23). On the other hand, only punishment awaits the corrupt.

11:24. This is one of the delightful enigmas or seeming contradictions that Solomon mentioned in 1:6. The liberal person gains more by giving, but the one who holds on to what he should give loses what he has. If you shovel it out, God will shovel it in, and God's shovel is bigger than yours. No one can outgive the Lord.

A. T. Pierson said it well:

> "Increase comes by imparting, and decrease by withholding. If you want to get, give, and if you want to lose, keep. Even mental riches come by constant spending of intellectual capital. A thought or fact is a seed to be sown if you want a crop. No man learns as fast as he who teaches. Acquisition comes from imparting. There is gain in grain only as it is sown in the soil. 'Sowing in the field is better than sewing in a napkin.' All gifts are for trading. Coin is for circulation."

11:25. A generous person is enriched. In sharing with others, he himself is blessed. John Bunyan said it in a little ditty:

> "There was a man, and some did count him mad;
> The more he gave away, the more he had."

11:26. A farmer may withhold grain in a time of famine, hoping that the price will rise and he will profit more. But the one who sells what he has is the one who earns the favor and gratitude of the people.

11:27. What you seek determines what you get. Seek good and you will find favor. Seek evil and you're in for trouble.

11:28. Don't trust in wealth. It will fail you. Trust in the Lord. He never fails. You will prosper like verdant foliage.

11:29. The one who troubles his own family can expect nothing of lasting value. He can trouble his house, through drunkenness, drugs, massive debts, gambling, abusive behavior, and immorality.

Fools wind up serving wise folk.

11:30. The first part of this proverb cites the benefits of a righteous life. It is like nutritious fruit. Then Solomon adds, *"and he who wins souls is wise."* In other words, he who wins people to the paths of righteousness is wise.

Today when we think of winning souls, we think of zealous evangelism designed to lead souls to faith in Christ. That is certainly a valid use of the words, but it is probably asking too much to think of that as the interpretation in an Old Testament setting.

> Lead me to some soul today,
> O teach me, Lord, just what to say.
> Friends of mine are lost in sin,
> And cannot find their way.
> Few there are who seem to care,
> And few there are who pray.
> Melt my heart and fill my life.
> Give me one soul today.
> —Will H. Houghton

11:31. This is an argument from the lesser to the greater. If believers receive parental discipline in this life for their misdeeds, how much more will the wicked receive judicial punishment for theirs in the life to come.

This proverb is echoed is 1 Peter 4:18. Christians get all their suffering in this life. For the wicked, the worst is still to come.

Proverbs 12

1 *Whoever loves instruction loves knowledge,*
But he who hates correction is stupid.

2 *A good man obtains favor from the LORD,*
But a man of wicked intentions He will condemn.

3 *A man is not established by wickedness,*
But the root of the righteous cannot be moved.

4 *An excellent wife is the crown of her husband,*
But she who causes shame is like rottenness in
his bones.

5 *The thoughts of the righteous are right,*
But the counsels of the wicked are deceitful.

6 *The words of the wicked are, "Lie in wait for blood,"*
But the mouth of the upright will deliver them.

7 *The wicked are overthrown and are no more,*
But the house of the righteous will stand.

8 *A man will be commended according to his wisdom,*
But he who is of a perverse heart will be despised.

9 *Better is the one who is slighted but has a servant,*
Than he who honors himself but lacks bread.

10 *A righteous man regards the life of his animal,*
But the tender mercies of the wicked are cruel.

11 *He who tills his land will be satisfied with bread,*
But he who follows frivolity is devoid of understanding.

12 *The wicked covet the catch of evil men,*
But the root of the righteous yields fruit.

13 *The wicked is ensnared by the transgression of his lips,*
But the righteous will come through trouble.

14 *A man will be satisfied with good by the fruit of
his mouth,
And the recompense of a man's hands will be rendered to him.*

15 *The way of a fool is right in his own eyes,
But he who heeds counsel is wise.*

16 *A fool's wrath is known at once,
But a prudent man covers shame.*

17 *He who speaks truth declares righteousness,
But a false witness, deceit.*

18 *There is one who speaks like the piercings of a sword,
But the tongue of the wise promotes health.*

19 *The truthful lip shall be established forever,
But a lying tongue is but for a moment.*

20 *Deceit is in the heart of those who devise evil,
But counselors of peace have joy.*

21 *No grave trouble will overtake the righteous,
But the wicked shall be filled with evil.*

22 *Lying lips are an abomination to the LORD,
But those who deal truthfully are His delight.*

23 *A prudent man conceals knowledge,
But the heart of fools proclaims foolishness.*

24 *The hand of the diligent will rule,
But the lazy man will be put to forced labor.*

25 *Anxiety in the heart of man causes depression,
But a good word makes it glad.*

26 *The righteous should choose his friends carefully,
For the way of the wicked leads them astray.*

27 *The lazy man does not roast what he took in hunting,
But diligence is man's precious possession.*

28 *In the way of righteousness is life,
And in its pathway there is no death.*

Chapter 12

Maintain your integrity (12:1-16)

12:1. Anyone who is anxious to learn is intelligent, but the person who is not open to correction is stupid. Knowing that the Bible is the Word of God, believers should have an insatiable desire to study it.

12:2. The Lord is on the side of the one who leads a clean life. He is against those who plot evil schemes. Think of what it means to have God against you.

12:3. Wickedness does not give anyone a solid foundation on which to build his life. A righteous person, on the other hand, has roots that enable him to stand straight and strong when the storms of life are raging. *"The righteous has an everlasting foundation"* (Prov. 10:25b).

Our Lord illustrated this verse in Luke 6:48-49. The wise man builds his house on a rock foundation. When the storms of life lash against him, he is unshakeable. The foolish man builds his house on sand. A flood comes and washes everything away.

The lesson is: Build your house on the Lord, the Rock of Ages.

12:4. A man has reason to be pleased and grateful for a virtuous wife. On the other hand, a spouse who is shameful is like rottenness or cancer in his bones. She gnaws away at his well-being.

12:5. Upright people have a clean mind. The thought-life of the wicked is polluted. The sequence of cause and effect still operates.

> Sow a thought, reap an act.
> Sow an act, reap a habit.
> Sow a habit, reap a character.
> Sow a character, reap a destiny.

12:6. The words of the wicked refer to their speech. Evil men plot evil deeds like murder. In contrast, the language of the upright is life-saving. Here Solomon contrasts the speech of the wicked and that of the righteous. The former is murderous whereas the latter is uplifting. It delivers upright people from all kinds of trouble. Often when Christians have been on trial their fearless confession of Christ has deterred their execution.

12:7. Unrighteous people tend to suffer defeat and even extinction. Godly people have houses that will stand. The word "houses" here can mean posterity.

12:8. An honorable man is praised for his wisdom. Those who practice sin are despised. Since the fear of the Lord is the beginning of wisdom, a person's relation to Christ determines his eulogy.

12:9. A man who is belittled but has a servant is better off than one who exalts himself but has to go hungry. True greatness is not determined by his social status or by his self esteem. It's *"better to be a nobody"* (NIV).

12:10. A righteous man is kind to dumb animals, but the greatest kindness a wicked man shows to his animals is actually brutal. Even when he is at his best behavior, he is cruel. God cares for His creatures. He even legislates about a bird's nest in Deuteronomy 22:6. Not even a sparrow falls to the ground without His knowledge and presence (Matt. 10:29). He expects us to treat animals kindly.

12:11. This is a portrait of opposites. The diligent farmer has a harvest of food to show for his labor. The playboy type wastes his time, talents, money, and life itself. A life is a terrible thing to waste.

12:12. Wicked men are jealous when others bring in a lot of stolen goods. A righteous person can depend on fruit, not loot. A godly man is assured of fruit, not loot. The "catch" in this verse mean plunder or spoils.

12:13. The careless lying speech of the ungodly eventually traps them. They need a good memory; otherwise they will be forever contradicting themselves. Upright people don't have that problem. In Spanish there is a proverb that says, "You can catch a liar quicker than you can catch a lame man." Liars beware.

12:14. Profitable conversation and hard work both bring

their own reward. It is encouraging to know that something you have said has been a help to someone else. Also satisfying is a job well done.

> If any little word of mine
> Can make one life the brighter,
> If any little song of mine
> Can make one heart the lighter,
> God help me speak that little word,
> And take my bit of singing
> And drop it in some lonely vale,
> To set the echoes ringing.
> —Author Unknown

12:15. A fool thinks he is always right. He never thinks it possible that he has done anything wrong. He shifts the blame. It's the wise person who listens to correction and advice.

Years ago in Spain, a passenger jet crashed into the side of a mountain, killing everyone on board. When investigators rushed to the scene and recovered the black box, they were able to hear the conversation in the cockpit just before the crash. A computerized voice from the recorder had said urgently and insistently, "Pull up. Pull up. Pull up. Pull up." Then they heard the pilot's voice saying, "Shut up, Gringo," and he snapped off the voice recorder. He would have been wise to listen to the synthesized voice. His cocksureness cost him his life and the lives of all the others on board.

12:16. The fool can't restrain his anger when he is treated offensively. An intelligent person disregards an insult, leaving it to the Lord to defend him, instead of taking the bait and getting into a fight.

Control your tongue (12:17-22)

12:17. A truthful witness says what is right. The deceiver stoops to lies. Lies often seem to triumph but the last chapter hasn't been written yet.

12:18. Some people specialize in sharp, cutting remarks. Not so the wise person. His speech is uplifting and healing.

Parents should praise and encourage their children and not tell them they're dumb and hopeless.

> A little word of kindness spoken
>   —a motion or a tear—
> Has often healed the heart
>   that's broken and made a friend so dear.
> Then deem it not an idle thing
>   a pleasant word to speak;
> The face you wear, the thought you bring,
>   a heart may heal or break.
> > —John Greenleaf Whittier

12:19. A truth is forever. Lies have a short life. A Christian should not lie *"since he has put off the old man with his deeds"* (Col. 3:9).

12:20. Evildoers find their joy in deceiving, but real joy comes from making peace. Liars follow the devil's example since *"he is a liar and the father of it"* (John 8:44). *"All liars shall have their part in the lake which burns with fire and brimstone"* (Rev. 21:8).

12:21. Upright people escape the serious troubles of the wicked. The latter get a full dose of them. Christians have troubles but they escape more than they endure.

12:22. God despises liars. They are an abomination to Him. He takes great delight in honest folks.

12:23. An intelligent man doesn't parade his knowledge. He handles it with true humility, saving his hearers from feeling inferior. Fools, on the other hand, can't conceal their stupidity.

12:24. Diligent people rise to positions of power. Lazy people are reduced to slave labor. A lazy man went to the employment office. This is what the interview was like.

"What have you been doing?"
"O, this and that."
"Where have you been doing it?"
"O, here and there."
"How long have you been doing it?"
"O, off and on."
"Well, come back here now and again."

One of the best examples of diligence is the border collie. An article in the *Smithsonian* proves it:

> "Border collies are obsessive-compulsive. They are capable of working themselves to death for their owners. Besides herding sheep, their ruling passion is to turn everything they do—even play—into work. Mine, for instance, has no sheep, but if you interrupt a backyard Frisbee session by offering a bit of a dog biscuit, she spits it out contemptuously and glares at you, demanding another throw. One way handlers discipline border collies is to refuse them the reward of working with sheep.
>
> "A youthful competitor told me, 'My husband says, "You love that dog more than me." I say, "Well, he's always trying to please me."'"[11]

12:25. Anxiety often leads to depression. A cheerful, encouraging remark lifts the spirit.

12:26. Wise people choose good company. There's always the danger of being led astray by untrustworthy people. A friend of mine shared this prayer request with me: "Lord, lead me to significant people and significant books." It works.

12:27. A lazy person hunts for amusement, kills an animal and leaves it where it fell. If he went to work and butchered it, he would have something to eat. You should roast what you take in hunting. If you are diligent, you will do just that.

It is not enough to read the Bible. We should meditate on it, appropriate its promises, and obey its precepts. That is one way of roasting what we take in hunting.

12:28. The upright life leads to life. It's the best life. A righteous person avoids the sins that lead to guilt, shame, illness, suffering, sorrow, and premature death.

---

11   Timothy Foote, "A Good Dog Knows What to Do", *Smithsonian*, October 1999, pp. 73-75.

Proverbs 13

1 *A wise son heeds his father's instruction,*
But a scoffer does not listen to rebuke.

2 *A man shall eat well by the fruit of his mouth,*
But the soul of the unfaithful feeds on violence.

3 *He who guards his mouth preserves his life,*
But he who opens wide his lips shall have destruction.

4 *The soul of a lazy man desires, and has nothing;*
But the soul of the diligent shall be made rich.

5 *A righteous man hates lying,*
But a wicked man is loathsome and comes to shame.

6 *Righteousness guards him whose way is blameless,*
But wickedness overthrows the sinner.

7 *There is one who makes himself rich, yet has nothing;*
And one who makes himself poor, yet has great riches.

8 *The ransom of a man's life is his riches,*
But the poor does not hear rebuke.

9 *The light of the righteous rejoices,*
But the lamp of the wicked will be put out.

10 *By pride comes nothing but strife,*
But with the well-advised is wisdom.

11 *Wealth gained by dishonesty will be diminished,*
But he who gathers by labor will increase.

12 *Hope deferred makes the heart sick,*
But when the desire comes, it is a tree of life.

13 *He who despises the word will be destroyed,*
But he who fears the commandment will be rewarded.

14 *The law of the wise is a fountain of life,*
To turn one away from the snares of death.

15 Good understanding gains favor,
But the way of the unfaithful is hard.

16 Every prudent man acts with knowledge,
But a fool lays open his folly.

17 A wicked messenger falls into trouble,
But a faithful ambassador brings health.

18 Poverty and shame will come to him who
disdains correction,
But he who regards a rebuke will be honored.

19 A desire accomplished is sweet to the soul,
But it is an abomination to fools to depart from evil.

20 He who walks with wise men will be wise,
But the companion of fools will be destroyed.

21 Evil pursues sinners,
But to the righteous, good shall be repaid.

22 A good man leaves an inheritance to his
children's children,
But the wealth of the sinner is stored up for the righteous.

23 Much food is in the fallow ground of the poor,
And for lack of justice there is waste.

24 He who spares his rod hates his son,
But he who loves him disciplines him promptly.

25 The righteous eats to the satisfying of his soul,
But the stomach of the wicked shall be in want.

Chapter 13

13:1. Two kinds of sons are here, the intelligent and the foolish or stupid. The first are educable. The second are immune to instruction because they don't listen; it doesn't sink in. They are full of their own ideas and will. But there is always hope for the stupid. They can be born again and become a new creation.

13:2. A good man finds joy and satisfaction by his uplifting conversation. It is helping others. Unbelievers dwell on unprofitable subjects such as violence. The empty talk of empty heads yields no good results. It is an enormous waste of time.

13:3. Guard your tongue. It's in a wet place where it's apt to slip. Constructive talk saves a person from heaps of trouble. The blabber-mouth is asking for a fall. More people have repented of talking too much than of being silent.

The one who guards his mouth by careful selection of his words saves himself from heaps of trouble. It is the one who speaks carelessly who misses the best in life. The word destruction here does not mean loss of being, but loss of well-being. It is failure to realize the high purpose for which a person was created.

Learn to be a good listener. Then after you have patiently endured a prolonged monologue, your talkative friend will tell his acquaintances what a great conversationalist you are –even if you had not been able to get a word in edgewise.

13:4. "If wishes were horses, then beggars would ride." The lazy man keeps desiring but never getting. It's the desires of the diligent that are fulfilled.

13:5. An upright man wins approval by hating deception. The wicked liar is disgusting and wins disgrace.

13:6. The blameless man is preserved from danger by his clean life. The sinner is toppled by his evil.

13:7. You can't always judge by appearance. A man may put on a big show of being rich and yet be destitute. He is a hypocrite. On the other hand, a person may look poor, yet have great possessions. He is humble and self-effacing.

The Christian who has forsaken all to follow Jesus may look poor to the world but in Christ he has wealth beyond computation.

Alexander the Great thought he was rich because he had conquered the world, but when he died, his hands were empty.

13:8. The rich tend to depend on their money to ransom them from difficult or dangerous situations. They think nearly all problems can be solved by money. This is a mistake.

The poor man doesn't hear the charges, threats, and legal squabbles that go with wealth. He is not as apt to be subject to robbery, kidnapping, extortion, and embezzlement.

13:9. The upright enjoy a good life, but the wicked die prematurely. The light of the righteous is his life of purity. He has good reason to rejoice. The lamp of the wicked is his short life of shame.

13:10. Pride leads inevitably to jealousies and quarrels. Intelligent people know how to avoid them.

13:11. Riches gained dishonestly have a tendency to leak out. Income from honest work has increased buying power.

Money won by gambling is not won by honest work, and therefore does not enjoy the blessing of God. It is won by trusting in the gods of chance and luck and is therefore a form of idolatry. This includes the lottery.

Most people who gamble are the ones who can least afford it.

Those who gamble are mathematically impaired. The chances of winning are infinitesimal. In one super lotto, the chance was 1 in 41 million. In an even bigger lottery, the chance was 1 in 120 million. The gambler might as well have thrown his money down the sewer.

We hear about the few people who win millions, but we don't hear about the trail of troubles and heartaches that follow: conflicts, the jealousies, broken lives, broken homes, and broken families.

It is not uncommon for those who lose heavily in gambling to embezzle money so they can gamble some more, hoping to recoup their losses. They then have time to consider their folly in a prison cell.

Gambling is a form of covetousness. It says, "I'd rather get rich quickly than trust God to supply my needs." Covetousness is therefore idolatry (Col. 3:5). Having food and covering, we should be content (1 Tim. 6:8).

Gambling can become addictive. Paul warns against anything that is enslaving (1 Cor. 6:12b).

If you want great gain, you'll find it in godliness, not in gambling (1 Tim 6:6).

The last part of the proverb describes the person who wins God's approval. *"But He who gathers by labor will increase."* God's favor rests in a special way on the person whose income is earned by honest toil. Longfellow speaks of the village blacksmith as a man "whose brow was wet with honest sweat." That's the kind of person who wins the Lord's smile.

13:12. It's discouraging when your hopes are repeatedly delayed. This has special meaning when connected with the Lord's return. How often we cry out with Sisera's mother, *"Why is his chariot so long in coming? Why tarries the clatter of his chariots"* (Judg. 5:28). We long like the sons of Korah who said, *"As the deer pants for the water brooks, so pants my soul for you, O God. My soul thirsts for God, for the living God. When shall I come and appear before God"* (Ps. 42:1-2). Our souls *"wait for the Lord more than those who watch for the morning—I say, more than those who watch for the morning"* (Ps. 130:6).

> Weary was our heart with waiting,
> And the night watch seemed so long;
> But His triumph day is breaking,
> And we hail it with a song.
> —Henry Burton

When the fulfillment comes, it is like a new lease on life, like unparalleled joy. The thrill of seeing Him will make the years of waiting seem like only a few days.

> It will be worth it all when we see Jesus;
> Life's trials will seem so small when we see Christ;
> One glimpse of His dear face
> All sorrow will erase,

So bravely run the race
Till we see Christ.
— Esther Kerr Rusthoi

"The walk to Emmaus (Luke 24) illustrates this verse. The heart was sick, i.e., faith was enfeebled, but when the Desire of all Nations came, the two disciples found Him to be a 'tree of life' to their sad hearts" (George Williams).

13:13. The word here is the Word of God. A person who rejects it is sure to perish. A great reward is for those who obey it.

Jehoiakim showed his contempt for the Word by cutting the scroll with a knife and throwing it into the fire (Jer. 36:23). His punishment was to be *"buried with the burial of a donkey, dragged and cast out beyond the gates of Jerusalem"* (Jer. 22:19).

Zedekiah rejected Jeremiah's wise counsel and was carried into captivity (Jer. 39:7).

Jehoiakim's father, Josiah, feared the Word and was rewarded (2 Chron. 35:27)

13:14. Wise teaching is a life-guarding fountain, teaching people to avoid the traps that lead to death. Sin looks beautiful in prospect, but hideous in retrospect.

13:15. Straight thinking wins the respect of others. People recognize it as good sense. The thought-life of an unbeliever has hard problems connected with it. It does not have the ring of truth.

13:16. A discerning man behaves wisely. He thinks before acting. A fool can't hide his foolishness. He shamelessly brags about it.

13:17. There are two kinds of messengers, dependable and destructive. You should check them thoroughly to make sure they are worthy of your confidence and will advance your agenda. An unreliable messenger creates all kinds of problems, but a dependable ambassador pleases the sender by accomplishing his mission. 'Ambassador' here means messenger. Believers are ambassadors for Christ. Our duty is not to represent ourselves, but God, and to implore unbelievers on Christ's behalf to be reconciled to God (2 Cor. 5:20).

13:18. Reject good advice and the result will be poverty and shame. Benefit by correction and you will be honored.

A woman who had lived a miserable life said to a godly elder, "I wish I had listened to your counsel." A man who had rejected biblical counsel said, "I am 70 and have done nothing with my life." A life is a terrible thing to waste.

13:19. To accomplish a good task brings satisfaction. A fool doesn't think so. He shudders at the thought of abandoning his aimlessness and sin.

It often happens that one line of a proverb clarifies the other. Here the first line speaks of a desire accomplished but it doesn't tell what that desire is. The second line speaks of departing from evil. To godly people, every victory over temptation is a desire accomplished. To fools it is abhorrent.

13:20. Fraternize with wise men and their wisdom will rub off on you. Associate with fools to your own downfall.

The book of Proverbs doesn't specifically mention mind-altering drugs, but they certainly fit this verse. On campuses everywhere druggies pressure their peers to experiment with marijuana, methamphetamine, crack, heroin, cocaine, and ecstasy, for examples. Young people who think straight have the good sense to refuse all such offers. No one needs those kinds of "friends." A Spanish proverb says, "Better to be alone than in bad company."

"The companion of fools will be destroyed." Some drugs can destroy the liver and the kidneys. Some can open a person's being to demons and result in demon possession. Others can result in changes in brain function, paranoia, depression, and suicide. In certain cases, addiction comes with the first use of a drug.

13:21. Punishment chases transgressors, whereas the upright are rewarded with blessings. It's another way that we reap what we sow.

13:22. A good man remembers his grandchildren in his will, but the sinner's money ends up with the godly. In the world-wide ebb and flow of capital, the Lord is able to divert it where it will be used righteously.

In writing his will, a wise parent is aware of the dangers

involved in leaving wealth to his children. Andrew Carnegie, American industrialist said,

> "The almighty dollar bequeathed to a child is an almighty curse. No man has the right to handicap his son with such a burden as great wealth."[12]

Dr. James Dobson of Focus on the Family agrees:

> "Giving large amounts to kids who haven't earned it can be extremely destructive. It can make them unhappy, greedy, and cynical. It detracts from their motivation to trust in God and provides opportunities to give in to new temptations. It has also been our observation that nothing divides siblings more quickly than money. Many loving families have been devastated over inheritances or even by arguments about 'Who gets Grandma's dining room table.'"[13]

W. H. Vanderbilt said, "The care of $200 million is enough to kill anyone. There is no pleasure in it."

John Jacob Astor confessed, "I am the most miserable man on earth."

John D. Rockefeller admitted, "I have made many millions, but they have brought me no happiness."

Andrew Carnegie observed that "millionaires seldom smile."

Henry Ford looked back to the time he was happier doing a mechanic's job.

The best inheritance a father can leave is a spiritual one – a godly upbringing in a Christian home where the Bible is read and the family is bathed in prayer. Children of wealthy parents seldom go on for the Lord.

---

12 Quoted by Randy Alcorn, *The Treasured Principle*, Sisters, OR: Multnomah Publishers, 2001, pp.70-71.
13 *Dr. Dobson's Bulletin*, March 2003.

"A nominal inheritance is in order as a token of the parent's love, but beyond that a father and mother should put their wealth into the work of the Lord where it will earn eternal dividends. This will prevent the Lord's money from being "a windfall coming to people who are financially independent and already have more than they need."[14]

"The wealth of the sinner is stored up for the righteous." In his book *Searching for Heaven on Earth*, David Jeremiah writes:

"God's eye is on all the wealth of this world, and He says that the wealth of the sinner is being gathered and stored up to accomplish His purposes in due time."[15]

13:23. Fallow ground has the potential for raising a good crop of grain, but injustice and oppression can sweep it away. Scottish history tells of poor farmers who were driven from their crofts by wealthy landowners. Poor people may do everything right in raising a crop, and yet be cheated out of the profit. It's not enough to be a good farmer. It also helps to have discernment and to be able to detect shysters.

13:24. When a parent withholds needed punishment, it is evident that he does not love his child as he should. A good parent administers discipline promptly.

When a national magazine wrote an article saying that it was wrong to spank a child, one reader wrote in, agreeing. She wrote: "You give wise advice to a parent to stop spanking. Not only does it model violence; it humiliates and chips away at the parent-child bond. Unbelievably, 22 states still allow school personnel to administer spankings with wooden paddles for students as a method of punishment." A wiser reader wrote, "When I told a police officer about this article, his reply was simple: 'If parents take this advice, I'll always have job security.'

---

14 Randy Alcorn, op.cit.,p. 70.

15 David Jeremiah, *Searching for Heaven on Earth*, Nashville: Integrity Publishers, 2004, p. 42.

By getting spanked in a loving home, kids learn there are serious consequences for bad behavior."

Dan wasn't his real name but it will do. You've probably met him with other names, and not all complimentary. The landscape is dotted with spoiled Dan's. To put it bluntly, Dan was a brat. He was the center and circumference of his life. Everything had to revolve around him. It was not a pleasant experience to be a guest in the house. He would interrupt adult conversations and bring the spotlight back on himself, usually with a tantrum. He was his mother's only child and she could never bring herself to discipline him. If her husband remonstrated with her about her darling's behavior, she would reply, "After all, he's only human." The father finally gave it up as hopeless.

13:25. A godly person has food to enjoy. Not so the wicked. He has an empty stomach. Many who read this proverb will say, "That doesn't seem to be the way it is in life. The wicked have plenty whereas the godly are on slim rations." If you have that problem, then think in terms of spiritual food and the difficulty will disappear. The believer has food about which the world knows nothing.

Proverbs 14

1 *The wise woman builds her house,*
But the foolish pulls it down with her hands.

2 *He who walks in his uprightness fears the LORD,*
But he who is perverse in his ways despises Him.

3 *In the mouth of a fool is a rod of pride,*
But the lips of the wise will preserve them.

4 *Where no oxen are, the trough is clean;*
But much increase comes by the strength of an ox.

5 *A faithful witness does not lie,*
But a false witness will utter lies.

6 *A scoffer seeks wisdom and does not find it,*
But knowledge is easy to him who understands.

7 *Go from the presence of a foolish man,*
When you do not perceive in him the lips of knowledge.

8 *The wisdom of the prudent is to understand his way,*
But the folly of fools is deceit.

9 *Fools mock at sin,*
But among the upright there is favor.

10 *The heart knows its own bitterness,*
And a stranger does not share its joy.

11 *The house of the wicked will be overthrown,*
But the tent of the upright will flourish.

12 *There is a way that seems right to a man,*
But its end is the way of death.

13 *Even in laughter the heart may sorrow,*
And the end of mirth may be grief.

14 *The backslider in heart will be filled with his own ways,*
But a good man will be satisfied from above.

15 The simple believes every word,
But the prudent considers well his steps.

16 A wise man fears and departs from evil,
But a fool rages and is self-confident.

17 A quick-tempered man acts foolishly,
And a man of wicked intentions is hated.

18 The simple inherit folly,
But the prudent are crowned with knowledge.

19 The evil will bow before the good,
And the wicked at the gates of the righteous.

20 The poor man is hated even by his own neighbor,
But the rich has many friends.

21 He who despises his neighbor sins;
But he who has mercy on the poor, happy is he.

22 Do they not go astray who devise evil?
But mercy and truth belong to those who devise good.

23 In all labor there is profit,
But idle chatter leads only to poverty.

24 The crown of the wise is their riches,
But the foolishness of fools is folly.

25 A true witness delivers souls,
But a deceitful witness speaks lies.

26 In the fear of the LORD there is strong confidence,
And His children will have a place of refuge.

27 The fear of the LORD is a fountain of life,
To turn one away from the snares of death.

28 In a multitude of people is a king's honor,
But in the lack of people is the downfall of a prince.

29 He who is slow to wrath has great understanding,
But he who is impulsive exalts folly.

30 A sound heart is life to the body,
But envy is rottenness to the bones.

31 He who oppresses the poor reproaches his Maker,
But he who honors Him has mercy on the needy.

32 The wicked is banished in his wickedness,
But the righteous has a refuge in his death.

33 Wisdom rests in the heart of him who
has understanding,
But what is in the heart of fools is made known.

34 Righteousness exalts a nation,
But sin is a reproach to any people.

35 The king's favor is toward a wise servant,
But his wrath is against him who causes shame.

Chapter 14

14:1. Women of wisdom tend to their household, caring for the family. Foolish ones destroy their home-life by gadding around on transient pleasures. Instead of building a model family, she tears it down.

14:2. The godly man shows that he loves the Lord by his clean life. Unrighteous people don't care for the Lord or what He commands.

14:3. The rod speaks of punishment. Pride speaks of the fools conceit. The mouth stands for his speech. The proud fool's conversation backfires on him, calling for rebuke and perhaps an apology.

The lips also refer to the wise person's talk. It saves him from shame and regret.

14:4. If you want a clean barn, don't have any livestock. But if you want a productive farm, be willing to put up with a little mess. If you can't stand a few crumbs on the floor, don't entertain visitors. Great writers often have desks piled high with books and papers. Some disorder is the price of literary achievement. It's better to have a Sunday School full of rambunctious kids dropping candy wrappers than a chapel with clean floors.

14:5. A good witness in court tells the truth, the whole truth, and nothing but the truth. A false witness lies like a trooper. Truth is self-authenticating. Liars should have a good memory; otherwise they will soon be contradicting their own testimony.

14:6. A scoffer wants the benefits of wisdom, but he doesn't give the Lord His proper place in life. Anyone who sincerely wants wisdom can find it by seeking for it diligently, expending personal effort in study and prayer, searching and digging as he would for silver and hidden treasure (Prov. 2:1-6).

What will it profit, when life here is o'er,
Though great worldly wisdom I gain,
If, seeking knowledge, I utterly fail
The wisdom of God to obtain?
—Grace E. Troy

14:7. When you hear a fool spouting his nonsense, leave him by himself. It caters to his ego to have an audience.

14:8. A prudent person charts his course with real discernment. The folly of fools is that they not only deceive others; they deceive themselves.

14:9. Fools make light of sin, as if it weren't serious. They joke about things that are sinful and offensive to God, and laugh about them. But we cannot join them, because sin is not to be joked about or laughed at. It is a serious matter to God. People of wisdom, or upright people, obtain favor by reckoning themselves dead to sin and alive to God.

14:10.There are bitter things in life that no one can share. It's also true that there are joys that are all our own. This could be the discovery of a great truth or the completion of a great task.

14:11. The words "house" and "tent" may refer to a person's life or to his household. The house in this verse refers to all that goes into the life of the wicked man – his family, business and social life. We usually think of a house as being more stable than a tent, and here it is the opposite. In real life, it is also the opposite. A well-placed tent is one of the most stable structures known to man.

The proverb contrasts the fleeting span of the wicked with the enduring prosperity of the good.

We are pilgrims here on earth, just passing through. A tent is the badge of a pilgrim, because it is a temporary dwelling. Heaven is our home. It is an eternal dwelling.

14:12. The world's religion is salvation by good works or good character. It is like fool's gold, it looks like the real thing but it is worthless and deadly (16:25). It seems so logical that God saves good people. But that is wrong. God saves ungodly people who do not work for their salvation but who repent of their sins and accept Jesus as Lord and Savior. Romans 4:5

declares, *"But to him who does not work but believes on Him who justifies the ungodly, his faith is accounted for righteousness."*

When a person goes his own way according to what seems right to him, instead of being guided by the Lord, that way ends in death. That death may be his own, or the death of a loved one, the death of a dream or the death of hope.

14:13. In this life there is no such thing as unadulterated laughter. There is a tinge of sorrow in every laugh. And mirth may be transient. It often ends in grief. That's the way life is.

14:14. As in 1:31, allowing you to have it your way can be a form of divine punishment. A backslider in heart is a professing believer who is out of fellowship with God. As the text says, the problem is in his heart. He is living with sin that is unconfessed and therefore unforgiven. He professes to be a Christian but his life does not match his profession. As someone has well said, the only proof that he really is a believer is that he repents and returns to the Lord. The bitter fallout from his folly boomerangs on him. Here are some of the results of his waywardness:

- He brings dishonor on the name of the Lord.
- He delights in sins that caused the death of his Creator-God. It is almost like a re-crucifying of the Son of God.
- It is a shameful response to God's love. It not only breaks His law; it breaks His heart.
- God's hand is heavy upon him. His vitality is turned into the drought of summer (Ps. 32:4).
- He stumbles, confuses and discourages other believers, and unbelievers as well.
- He disappoints believers who have trusted, encouraged, and supported him.
- He suffers shame, remorse, and guilt.
- He exposes himself to illness and even to death.
- He may live in constant fear of being publicly exposed for scandalous or criminal activity.
- He may live to see his sin repeated in the lives of his children.
- He loses the joy of his salvation.
- He has no meaningful prayer life.

- He cannot testify for Christ without exposing the contradiction between his words and his walk.

What a contrast is the life of a good man. He receives constant encouragement from the Lord. His life is excitingly charmed. It is a great adventure.

14:15. A naive man is gullible. He believes anything you tell him. This is not what 1 Corinthians 13:7 means when it says that love believes all things, which is to have faith in others and believe the best about them. Believers should discern between truth and lies. A man of discernment considers carefully before acting. He knows that often people tell you only what they want you to know. He knows that there are no free lunches. He knows the devil is in the fine print. He remembers *caveat emptor* from Latin class: "Let the buyer beware."

Two tour buses stopped at a vista point so people could get out and admire the view. One driver said to the other, "I have a group of Christians on my bus."

"Really. What do they believe"

"Anything I tell them."

Believers should not be gullible.

14:16.The fear of the Lord makes a believer wise and keeps him from dabbling in sin. He looks at temptation like a loaded trap ready to snap shut, and avoids it. A fool, on the other hand, acts with boldness and bluster.

14:17. Anyone with a short, uncontrolled temper acts like a fool. He yells curses, slams doors, breaks dishes, and destroys furniture.

When the prophet Hanani rebuked King Asa in the name of the Lord for depending on Syria, the king was enraged. Out of control, he threw God's prophet into jail and dealt harshly with some of his people. Because he had acted like a fool, God doomed him to have wars for the rest of his reign (2 Chron. 12:1-10).

Another unpopular character is the one who plots evil schemes. People hate him.

14:18. Simple people gain nothing but folly. The prudent are ever increasing in discernment and knowledge.

14:19.   Some day the tables will be turned. Ungodly people will bow in respect to believers, and evil men will honor the just who are then in places of prominence.

14:20.   Sometimes life seems unfair. The people next door avoid a poor man, while they curry the friendship of the rich (19:4, 6). It's a great mistake rooted in the love of money. We should measure a person by his character and spirituality, not by his bank accounts.

14:21.   The one who shuns his poor neighbor sins in doing so (Jas. 2:1-9). A blessing rests on the one who has compassion on the poor (v. 31), because this is what God does.

In his book *The Magnificent Defeat*, Frederick Buechner wrote,

> "The love for the less fortunate is a beautiful thing —a love for those who suffer, for those who are poor, the sick, the failures, the unlovely. This is compassion, and it touches the heart of the world....And then there is the love for the enemy—love for the one who does not love you, but mocks, threatens, and inflicts pain. The tortured's love for the torturer —this is God's love. It conquers the world."[16]

14:22.   Evil thoughts are sin (Isa. 55:7; 59:7; Mark 7:21). Plotters of crimes stray far from mercy and faithfulness. These virtues belong to those who plan acts of kindness.

14:23.   All honorable work is profitable, but empty chatter accomplishes nothing but poverty.

The mention of idle chatter makes us think of the compulsive talker. He or she goes on talking long after he has stopped saying anything. He never comes up for air. The listener tunes him out, hearing only sound but no substance. The earth itself cannot bear the weariness of it all.

14:24.   A crown speaks of rule, reward and honor. The wise person is rewarded with riches, both material and spiritual. All a fool can expect is more foolishness.

14:25.   A faithful witness delivers a defendant or a falsely

---

16   Frederick Buechner, *The Magnificent Defeat*, Harper One, 1985

accused person from injustice. Lies are the trademark of false witnesses (12:17). If their testimony is accepted, they make justice impossible.

14:26. Those who trust in the Lord have good reason to be confident. He is a refuge to them in times of trouble.

14:27. Faith and obedience contribute to a long life, protecting from the pitfalls along the way.

14:28. It is honorable for a king when he has many loyal subjects. When he has few citizens like that, his reign is hollow and of short duration.

14:29. Anyone who has his temper under control is commendable (16:32). The person who flies off the handle quickly doesn't understand the senselessness of it.

14:30.A sound heart means a life that is tranquil and contented. Envy registers a decline on the health chart. A satisfied spirit is good for health. Envy eats away at a person's physical well being. Doctors know that nervous problems are caused by such things as boredom, resentment, selfishness, guilt, jealousy, anxiety, an unforgiving spirit, and frustration. By a figure of speech, the word "bones" in this verse stands for the entire body.

14:31. Treating poor people unfairly insults God, their Maker (17:5). Those who are godly show mercy to the needy (19:17), and God will repay them.

This verse has two of the 37 references to the poor in Proverbs. Several of them tell of the divine displeasure at those who mistreat the poor. Unfortunately, even young people can be cruel to the poor, laughing at their non-name-brand clothing, shunning them and otherwise discriminating against them because of their poverty, where they live or what job their parents have. The fact that children do it doesn't lessen God's displeasure. On the other hand, several other Scriptures promise a blessing to those who consider the poor (cf. Ps. 41:1-3).

14:32. The last chapter for the wicked is to be destroyed (cf. Ps. 73:16-19). Only God's people have a safe refuge when they die.

14:33. A wise person doesn't have to advertise his wisdom; it's apparent to all. A fool lets others know how senseless he is.

14:34. It is an honor to any government when liberty, justice, equality, and tranquility characterize it. Any corrupt government is a disgrace, regardless of whether it was begun on so-called "Christian principles" or not. "Sin is a disgrace to any people."

14:35. A ruler favors a faithful subject, but a scandalous person angers him.

Proverbs 15

1 *A soft answer turns away wrath,*
But a harsh word stirs up anger.

2 *The tongue of the wise uses knowledge rightly,*
But the mouth of fools pours forth foolishness.

3 *The eyes of the LORD are in every place,*
Keeping watch on the evil and the good.

4 *A wholesome tongue is a tree of life,*
But perverseness in it breaks the spirit.

5 *A fool despises his father's instruction,*
But he who receives correction is prudent.

6 *In the house of the righteous there is much treasure,*
But in the revenue of the wicked is trouble.

7 *The lips of the wise disperse knowledge,*
But the heart of the fool does not do so.

8 *The sacrifice of the wicked is an abomination to the LORD,*
But the prayer of the upright is His delight.

9 *The way of the wicked is an abomination to the LORD,*
But He loves him who follows righteousness.

10 *Harsh discipline is for him who forsakes the way,*
And he who hates correction will die.

11 *Hell and Destruction are before the LORD;*
So how much more the hearts of the sons of men.

12 *A scoffer does not love one who corrects him,*
Nor will he go to the wise.

13 *A merry heart makes a cheerful countenance,*
But by sorrow of the heart the spirit is broken.

14 *The heart of him who has understanding seeks knowledge,*
But the mouth of fools feeds on foolishness.

15 *All the days of the afflicted are evil,*
But he who is of a merry heart has a continual feast.

16 *Better is a little with the fear of the LORD,*
Than great treasure with trouble.

17 *Better is a dinner of herbs where love is,*
Than a fatted calf with hatred.

18 *A wrathful man stirs up strife,*
But he who is slow to anger allays contention.

19 *The way of the lazy man is like a hedge of thorns,*
But the way of the upright is a highway.

20 *A wise son makes a father glad,*
But a foolish man despises his mother.

21 *Folly is joy to him who is destitute of discernment,*
But a man of understanding walks uprightly.

22 *Without counsel, plans go awry,*
But in the multitude of counselors they are established.

23 *A man has joy by the answer of his mouth,*
And a word spoken in due season, how good it is!

24 *The way of life winds upward for the wise,*
That he may turn away from hell below.

25 *The LORD will destroy the house of the proud,*
But He will establish the boundary of the widow.

26 *The thoughts of the wicked are an abomination to the LORD,*
But the words of the pure are pleasant.

27 *He who is greedy for gain troubles his own house,*
But he who hates bribes will live.

28 *The heart of the righteous studies how to answer,*
But the mouth of the wicked pours forth evil.

29 *The LORD is far from the wicked,*
But He hears the prayer of the righteous.

30 The light of the eyes rejoices the heart,
And a good report makes the bones healthy.

31 The ear that hears the rebukes of life
Will abide among the wise.

32 He who disdains instruction despises his own soul,
But he who heeds rebuke gets understanding.

33 The fear of the LORD is the instruction of wisdom,
And before honor is humility.

Chapter 15

15:1. A soft answer deflates the anger of someone who wants to engage in verbal battle. In Judges 8:2 we see how Gideon's wise reply to the men of Ephraim prevented a fight. A bitter, hostile reply serves only to increase the strife.

A speaker had emphasized that Christ is the only way to heaven. Then there was a question and answer period for the audience of college students. One of them asked testily, "Do you mean to tell us that Mahatma Ghandi is in hell?" The soft answer was, "No, what I mean to tell you is that if, prior to his death, Mr. Ghandi trusted Jesus Christ as his Lord and Savior, he is in heaven."

The answer defused wrath without compromising truth.

15:2. A man of discernment speaks words of knowledge and understanding. Fools speak only words of senselessness and emptiness. The Apostle Paul advises, *"Let no corrupt word proceed out of your mouth, but what is good for necessary edification, that it may impart grace to the hearers"* (Eph. 4:29).

15:3. Here is a reminder about divine optics. Our God is all-seeing. Nothing escapes His notice (Heb. 4:13). He sees everything done by sinners and saints. Years ago there was a popular song that claimed that "no one knows what goes on behind closed doors." That is patently false, because no closed door can keep God out. He sees all, and the secret sin on earth is open scandal in heaven. The omniscience of God should be a great motivation to holiness. "You-Are-the-God-Who-Sees" (Gen. 16:13).

15:4. Wholesome conversation has healing power, whereas sharp, cutting words can cause great hurt.

J.C. Penney, having built a flourishing business, became filled with despair, checked himself into a hospital, and waited to die. No doctor could do a thing for him.

One evening, the certainty of impending death flooded across Penney's troubled soul. He was writing farewell notes to his wife and his loved ones when he heard the singing of nurses in a chapel down the hall. "No matter what may be the test," they sang, "God will take care of you."

To Penney these were the voices of white-clad angels. Something was suddenly born within his soul: an absolute assurance that the old faith was true—that he was completely in the loving hands of Jesus, and need fear no more.

A perverse tongue breaks the spirit.

One socialite said to another, "How do you like my new dress?" The other replied, "It's lovely, dear. It's too bad they didn't have your size." Lady Astor said to Winston Churchill, "If I were your wife, I'd put poison in your coffee." To which Winston replied, "If I were your husband, I'd drink it."

An insensitive person said to a sick lady, "I've seen many a corpse that looked better than you." We should think before speaking, and avoid telling horror stories about malpractice, sickness, death to those who are ill or about to have an operation. Ask the Lord to give you the wisdom and sensitivity to have something encouraging to say.

15:5. It is the height of folly to reject parental instruction and advice (10:17; 12:1, 15; 13:1, 18). Whoever takes it and profits by it is the sensible person.

15:6. A godly Christian home has untold advantages. Ill-gotten gain has untold troubles.

> "What a source of moral salvation is the home! … Home life properly hallowed is a citadel of the soul, a magazine of martial resources against the spiritual war. Drinking at its pure fountain, we lose our taste for stolen waters. Its simplicity and purity are charms against a garish world. Its exquisite relationships call forth the noblest qualities of the soul. Its unity is strength for good. Its joys and sorrows impart a brightness and tenderness."[17]

15:7. The speech of the godly is worthwhile but that of fools

---

17 Watkinson, *The Duty of Imperial Thinking*, pp. 66-67.

has nothing of lasting value.

15:8. God hates it when evil people come to Him with a sacrifice (21:27). For example, members of the Mafia give some of their wicked loot to a church. God doesn't want it. He wants their lives to be clean. One of the things that He really loves is the prayer of righteous people (v. 29).

Since this is the first of only three references to prayer in the book of Proverbs, we would like to suggest a few pointers in this important subject.

- Pray both at set times and also on the spur of the moment.
- Pray according to the will of God as it is revealed in His Word.
- Pray believing that He hears and answers your prayers just as you would answer them if you had His wisdom, love, and power.
- Make every major decision a matter of prayer, and seek the prayers and counsel of your elders before deciding.
- By prayer move God's hand to do things that He would not otherwise have done.
- By prayer learn to move men through God.
- Pray big. We honor God by great petitions.
- Pray believing that the work of God is done more by prayer than in any other way.
- Never ask God to do something if you can do it yourself.

15:9. The Lord detests the conduct of the wicked. His delight is in those who live uprightly.

15:10. Those who wander from the straight and narrow way are ripe for harsh discipline. If they refuse correction, they are ripe for death.

15:11. Hell (or Sheol) means the disembodied state or the grave. Destruction (or Abaddon) meant the pit. If God knows all about such mysteries as the unseen world, how much more can He read men's thoughts and intents (Heb. 4:12-13).

Old Testament saints had dim and indistinct views concerning the afterlife. They knew there was Hell, and they knew there was Sheol. The meaning of "Sheol" was not easily defined. I suggest that it means nothing more definite than the disembodied state.

There are only a few references to heaven in the Old Testament. Here are a few of the most prominent:

- Job 19:25-27 *"For I know that my Redeemer lives, and He shall stand at the last on the earth; and after my skin is destroyed, this I know, that in my flesh I shall see God, whom I shall see for myself, and my eyes shall behold, and not another. How my heart yearns within me."*
- Psalm 16:11 *"In Your presence is fullness of joy; at your right hand are pleasures forevermore."*
- Psalm 17:15 *"As for me, I will see Your face in righteousness; I shall be satisfied when I awake in your likeness."*

The prominent hope of the Jews in the Old Testament was the earthly kingdom of the Lord. This does not mean that they did not also have a heavenly hope. Abraham *"waited for the city which has foundations, whose builder and maker is God"* (Heb. 11:10). But less space is given to that hope than in the New Testament.

The word *sheol* in the Old Testament is the same as Hades in the New. Christ's soul was not left in Sheol (the disembodied state), nor did His flesh (His physical body) see corruption (see Acts 2:31).

Christ *"has brought life and immortality to light through the gospel"* (1 Tim. 1:10). What was unclear in the Old Testament is revealed in the New.

15:12. Many people behave like the scoffer—they don't like anyone who corrects them (9:8-9), and they don't go for advice to someone whose advice would be contrary to what they want to do. They are not really looking for advice, but for a rubber stamp approving their plans.

15:13. Our emotions are usually reflected in our facial appearance. A smiling face reveals a happy spirit, and a sad face may tell of a broken heart.

15:14. An intelligent person wants to be learning all the time. All a fool wants is more foolishness.

15:15. The life of a neurotic person is one trouble after another, a litany of woes. For a cheerful person, life is a continual banquet. Junior was one of those upbeat persons. One day at school went like this. He fell from the school bus, hitting his head on the concrete. It required three stitches to close the wound. During recess he and another boy bumped into each other. This broke two of Junior's teeth and cut his lip. During the afternoon he fell and broke his arm. The teacher decided to take him home before anything else could happen. On the way, the teacher saw him clutching something in his hand. Junior showed him a quarter that he had found in the playground. Then Junior smiled and said, "Teacher, I've never found a quarter before. This is my lucky day." For him life was a continual feast.[18]

15:16. This is one of twenty one "better" verses in the book of Proverbs. A poor peasant who loves the Lord is better off than a rich person with all the problems that go with wealth.

Howard Hughes was one of the world's richest men. Yet *TIME* magazine reported that at the end of his life,

> "He lived a sunless, joyless, half-lunatic life…a virtual prisoner, walled in by his own crippling fears and weaknesses. Once a dashing, vibrant figure, he neglected his appearance and health during his last 15 years until he became a pathetic wraith. His physical appearance was horrifying. Although four doctors rotated in taking care of Hughes, his medical condition was appalling. He lived week after week on a diet that a ten-cent store clerk would have spurned."
> He left an estate estimated at $2.3 billion.[19]

In his book *Strengthening Your Grip*, Charles Swindoll points out that money can buy medicine but not health, a house but not a home, companionship but not friends, a bed but not sleep, the good life but not eternal life.

15:17. A vegetable blue-plate special served with love in a congenial, pleasant environment is better than a feast of filet mignon where there is underlying animosity.

15:18. A man of quick temper causes conflicts. It takes a self-controlled person to solve controversial matters.

---

18 *Quarterly News Letter*, Canadian Bible Society, Winter '91.
19 *TIME Magazine*, Dec. 13, 1976, pp. 20-41.

An angry man (or woman) is not a pretty picture. His flushed face and squinty eyes suggest that trouble is brewing. Then his shouting and yelling remove all doubt. You can expect his language to be laced with expletives, profanity, and multiplied curses. He is miserable and makes everyone else miserable. Pity the person who is victim of his furious ranting. And pity the wife and children who have to endure this out-of-control hothead.

In sharp contrast, admire the person who can take an attack without retaliating. Under verbal assault, he has power to remain silent, remembering that where there is no fuel, the fire goes out. He could squelch his adversary with a few well-chosen words, but he chooses to exercise restraint. His soft answer turns away wrath. He models the meekness and gentleness of the Savior.

15:19. The life of a sluggard is strewn with thorny problems, but the upright travel on a smooth highway,

15:20. A son who models wisdom and maturity gladdens the heart of his father, but the behavior of a foolish son shows that he treats his mother's advice with contempt.

15:21. Those who lack discernment enjoy their freedom and foolish lifestyle. One who has sense lives uprightly.

15:22. Without good advice a person's plans often fail. There is safety in having several wise counselors. Together they are often able to see all sides of a problem. That is why we have elders (plural) in the church.

15:23. There is something satisfying in being able to say the right word at the right time. Advice that exactly fits a situation is beautiful. It is a blessing to the one who gives it and to the one who receives it. At the end of a gospel meeting, the preacher greeted the people as they were leaving. When a visiting sailor came to him, the preacher asked, "Are you saved, young man?"

"No, I'm not," came the honest reply.

"Why aren't you saved?"

"Because I can't believe."

The preacher asked, "Whom can't you believe?"

That did it! The sailor realized that it was God he wasn't believing, and that therefore he was calling God a liar. There at the chapel door, he passed from darkness to light and from death to life.

15:24. The godly life is ever upward to heaven. Those who choose it escape hell.

> "The gracious and faithful man obtains more grace and more means of usefulness, while the unfaithful man sinks lower and lower and grows worse and worse. We must either make progress or lose what we have attained. There is no such thing as standing still in religion."
> —Charles Haddon Spurgeon

15:25. The house of the proud lacks security, but the Lord protects the property of a poor widow.

15:26. The schemes of wicked men are hateful to the Lord (16:5). It's the words of the upright that He appreciates.

15:27. He who uses bribes to get rich fast causes trouble at home. The one who doesn't use bribes enjoys the good life.

15:28. The upright think before speaking. The wicked are unrestrained in pouring forth sin.

15:29. When the wicked call for help, the Lord is far away. It's the prayers of the righteous that reach Him and bring answers (1 Jn. 5:14-15).

15:30. The light of the eyes suggests a hearty smile or a pleasant countenance. A loving smile warms the heart of a friend, and good news is beneficial for the recipient's physical welfare. A cheerful smile lifts the spirit and good news fortifies the hearer (25:25).

15:31. The person who heeds correction is one of the perennial minority of earth's wise men. The reproof of life suggests "beneficial counsel."

15:32. To refuse rebuke is a form of self-hatred. Those who obey are the ones who grow in understanding. It is remarkable how much rebuke and reproof can contribute to the making of a life. There are times in all our lives when we need to be confronted on matters of speech and behavior. The wise person drinks it down like medicine. The fool rejects it as a waste.

Most of us are paralyzed when it comes to delivering needed rebuke. We fear an unpleasant blowup. We fear the death of a friendship. We fear offending the person. Love has to overcome those fears and do what is right.

15:33. By heeding the Word of the Lord a person grows in wisdom. Just as wisdom follows obedience, so does honor follow humility.

Proverbs 16

1 *The preparations of the heart belong to man,*
But the answer of the tongue is from the LORD.

2 *All the ways of a man are pure in his own eyes,*
But the LORD weighs the spirits.

3 *Commit your works to the LORD,*
And your thoughts will be established.

4 *The LORD has made all for Himself,*
Yes, even the wicked for the day of doom.

5 *Everyone proud in heart is an abomination to the LORD;*
Though they join forces, none will go unpunished.

6 *In mercy and truth*
Atonement is provided for iniquity;
And by the fear of the LORD one departs from evil.

7 *When a man's ways please the LORD,*
He makes even his enemies to be at peace with him.

8 *Better is a little with righteousness,*
Than vast revenues without justice.

9 *A man's heart plans his way,*
But the LORD directs his steps.

10 *Divination is on the lips of the king;*
His mouth must not transgress in judgment.

11 *Honest weights and scales are the LORD's;*
All the weights in the bag are His work.

12 *It is an abomination for kings to commit wickedness,*
For a throne is established by righteousness.

13 *Righteous lips are the delight of kings,*
And they love him who speaks what is right.

14 *As messengers of death is the king's wrath,*
But a wise man will appease it.

15 *In the light of the king's face is life,*
And his favor is like a cloud of the latter rain.

16 *How much better to get wisdom than gold!*
And to get understanding is to be chosen rather than silver.

17 *The highway of the upright is to depart from evil;*
He who keeps his way preserves his soul.

18 *Pride goes before destruction,*
And a haughty spirit before a fall.

19 *Better to be of a humble spirit with the lowly,*
Than to divide the spoil with the proud.

20 *He who heeds the word wisely will find good,*
And whoever trusts in the LORD, happy is he.

21 *The wise in heart will be called prudent,*
And sweetness of the lips increases learning.

22 *Understanding is a wellspring of life to him who has it.*
But the correction of fools is folly.

23 *The heart of the wise teaches his mouth,*
And adds learning to his lips.

24 *Pleasant words are like a honeycomb,*
Sweetness to the soul and health to the bones.

25 *There is a way that seems right to a man,*
But its end is the way of death.

26 *The person who labors, labors for himself,*
For his hungry mouth drives him on.

27 *An ungodly man digs up evil,*
And it is on his lips like a burning fire.

28 *A perverse man sows strife,*
And a whisperer separates the best of friends.

29 *A violent man entices his neighbor,*
And leads him in a way that is not good.

30 He winks his eye to devise perverse things;
He purses his lips and brings about evil.

31 The silver-haired head is a crown of glory,
If it is found in the way of righteousness.

32 He who is slow to anger is better than the mighty,
And he who rules his spirit than he who takes a city.

33 The lot is cast into the lap,
But its every decision is from the LORD.

Chapter 16

16:1. We may plan in advance what we are going to say or do, but sometimes the Lord overrules and we say something completely different. The Sovereign Lord has His way.

Balaam was hired by Balaak to curse Israel. That is what he planned to do. But God overruled and Balaam paid such glowing tributes to Israel that he actually sounded like a true prophet (Num. 22-24).

16:2. Man by nature thinks of himself as good. He looks on his behavior as above reproach. He trusts his goodness for salvation. But God looks not only at what's outside. He sees the thought-life and the motives of the heart (1 Sam. 16:7). It's not what we think of ourselves that matters. It's how God sees us.

16:3. If we commit our plans to the Lord and ask for His guidance, our plans will come to pass (3:5-6; 15:22).

> "He knows. He loves. He cares.
> Nothing this truth can dim.
> He gives the very best to those
> who leave the choice with Him."

Trouble comes when we act independently of Him.

16:4. He has made everything for His glory and pleasure (Rev. 4:11). He has also decreed that sin must be punished. He has not elected anyone for the day of doom, but He has ruled that any who choose to die with sins unconfessed and unforgiven will be doomed.

16:5. God abhors proud people (15:26). Even if they marshal an army to prove that they have every reason to be proud, they will not escape His judgment.

16:6. If God is the subject, it means that in His mercy and true to His promise, He has provided a way in which our sins can be righteously dealt with. As an act of mercy and in a righteous manner, God provided atonement for sin in the Old Testament.

Atonement means covering. It produced ceremonial cleansing, but did not deal with inward purification. Atonement was made for people and for inanimate objects such as the Temple, the altar, the holy place, and the most holy place. For people it made them ceremonially clean to worship at the Temple. It made inanimate things fit to be used in the service of God. Atonement is not a New Testament word. In Romans 5:11 of the King James Version, it should have been translated "reconciliation."

Today the word has acquired the meaning of expiation. When men speak of the atoning work of Christ, they mean that by His death, burial, and resurrection, He fully satisfied all God's claims against sin. He did not merely cover our sins but put them away by the sacrifice of Himself. It is the difference between ceremonial cleansing and expiation. Atonement is a ritual covering or cleansing from pollution. Expiation is the full satisfaction for the penalty of sin through the finished work of Christ.

The writer to the Hebrews illustrates the difference. When a Jew in the Old Testament touched a dead body, he became ceremonially unclean. It was not a moral matter but a ritual one. The Jews considered one ceremony as the most potent in dealing with this ritual uncleanness. It was known as the ashes of a red heifer (Num. 19). But the writer to the Hebrews pointed out that it was only a superficial, ceremonial cleansing; it sanctified to the purifying of the flesh. In contrast, the blood of Christ purges the conscience from dead works to serve the living God (Heb. 9:13-14). His work produces inward results.

No Old Testament sacrifice could put away sins (Heb. 10:3). On the contrary, when the Jews celebrated the Day of Atonement, there was an annual remembrance of sins (Heb. 10:3).

Atonement did not give the Jewish people a clear conscience concerning their sins.

People in the Old Testament were saved by faith in whatever revelation the Lord gave them at the time (Gen. 15:6; Hab. 2:4b). They were saved on the basis of the still-future work of Christ. That is how they received eternal forgiveness.

These words have their ultimate fulfillment in the words of

Christ at Calvary.

If Solomon is referring to sins between God's people, the Lord can resolve interpersonal conflicts if the parties are willing to repent and forsake the sin.

The first two parts of this proverb tell how sins are dealt with. The last lines suggest it's better to avoid sin by fearing the Lord, that is, by obeying Him.

"By the fear of the Lord, one departs from evil." The intricate and extensive sacrificial system should have taught people that sin is serious and men should fear the Lord by refraining from it.

When a person lives in a way that is pleasing to the Lord, He can make the man's enemies to be at peace with him.

The men of Israel were supposed to attend festivals in Jerusalem three times a year. But wouldn't this expose their families and property to attack by their Canaanite enemies? No, God made a promise of protection: *"...neither will any man covet your land when you go up to appear before the Lord your God three times in the year"* (Ex. 34:24). The Lord would control the minds and wills of the enemies so that they would have no desire to attack.

16:8. It's better to have little wealth but great integrity than great wealth without justice. The question is not "How much do you have in your bank account?" but "Did you make it honestly?"

16:9. A man is free to make his plans but God can and sometimes does overrule them (Jas. 4:15). Haddon Robinson writes:

> "Life is what happens to us while we are making other plans....Make your plans. But write them on paper, not on concrete. God and life have a way of intruding and leading you on a journey that you might not have anticipated in your wildest dreams."[20]

16:10. God not only gives a ruler divine authority, but He also gives him extraordinary intelligence and skill in handling the affairs of state. However the ruler must not use his authority to make unjust decisions. The only one who has absolute power is God.

---

20 *Our Daily Bread*, November 5, 2004. Radio Bible Class.

It might seem strange to see "divination" or "oracle" (JND) mentioned approvingly when it is forbidden in Deuteronomy 18:10-12 (KJV). The problem is solved when we realize that the word has a secondary meaning of "unusual insight."

16:11. God's standards of right and wrong are absolute. He has set the official weights and measures in His Word. Our responsibility is to abide by them. We must not overcharge or give underweight. This applies to all the transactions of life.

It is a false weight when an elder's son or daughter falls into sin but is treated more leniently than others who have committed the same sin.

It is a false weight when we welcome the rich, famous and good looking with fanfare while giving the cold shoulder to the ordinary or uncultured (Jas. 2:1-10). The fact that someone is wealthy, or a popular singer, musician or athlete is no reason for special treatment.

16:12. A king is in a place of extreme responsibility. Because of this great authority, any sin is more serious. His throne is made secure when he rules with justice.

16:13. Rulers delight in those who make right decisions. They love an honest citizen. This assumes, of course, that they themselves are righteous.

16:14. A ruler's wrath can spell death for a person on trial, but a wise man will seek to avoid that wrath instead of provoking it. He aims to conciliate the ruler.

16:15. A king's smile is an expression of pleasure. His favor is refreshing and invigorating like a cloud carrying rain to the fields when it is most needed. The smile carries the promise of good things to come. Those who serve the Lord well can expect His smile of approval along with the words, "Well done, faithful servant," at the Judgment Seat of Christ.

16:16. Gold and silver are precious but not as precious as wisdom. Wisdom is not inherent in us; it must be diligently sought after and acquired. A profound knowledge of God's Word is a priceless treasure.

16:17. Upright people travel on a highway that avoids evil. Those who stay on this route are saved from damage and damnation.

True believers do not practice sin, but by resisting temptation they preserve their souls from damage. God has a special blessing for those who endure temptation (Jas. 1:12).

16:18. Pride and destruction are united as cause and effect. So are a haughty spirit and a fall. To avoid pride's fall, the Bible prescribes several pills that are effective if taken regularly.

- John 3:27 *"A man can do nothing unless it has been given to him from heaven."*
- John 15:5c *"Without Me, you can do nothing."*
- 1 Corinthians 3:7 *"So then neither he who plants is anything, nor he who waters, but God who gives the increase."*
- 1 Corinthians 4:7 *"What do you have that you did not receive?"*

Another sobering put-down is found in Acts 19:15. Seven sons of a chief priest had exaggerated ideas of their own power to exorcize demons. On one occasion the evil spirit defied them, saying, *"Jesus I know and Paul I know; but who are you."* These sons of the priest were unknown in hell. Herod Agrippa illustrates this proverb. Divine judgment struck him dead when he pridefully accepted praise as a god (Acts 12:21-23).

16:19. Better to be joined to a fellowship of lowly saints than to company with the proud upper crust. The real test of a church is its holiness and faithfulness to the Word of God, not the number or affluence of its members.

16:20. Obedience to the Word of God brings benefits, and whoever trusts in the Lord is blessed. The hymn-writer, John Sammis, put this proverb to music:

> "Trust and obey,
> For there's no other way
> To be happy in Jesus,
> But to trust and obey."

16:21. One way a person shows he is wise is by his straight thinking or good judgment. Sweetness of the lips is a figure of speech for pleasant, gracious talk. The learning process is enhanced when the subject is taught pleasantly. Gracious words make things more readily understandable.

16:22. Understanding is a source of growth and invigoration. Any attempt to instruct or correct a fool ends in folly.

16:23. Wisdom is evidenced in a man's conversation. Notice the link between the heart and the mouth (Luke 6:45). His wisdom teaches him what to say and what not to say. His lips are educated as to what is proper.

16:24. Gracious words are sweet as a honeycomb, and like a good medicine for body and soul. A. B. Simpson wrote:

> "We are not surprised that some people are sickly when we hear them talk. They have enough dislikes, prejudices, doubts, and fears to exhaust the strongest constitution. Christian, if you would retain your God-given life and physical strength, keep out those things which may destroy them."[21]

Watchman Nee told of a woman who did everything possible to please her husband but she never received a word of thanks or appreciation. She felt she had failed as a wife. Only when she was dying of tuberculosis did he find it in him to tell her she would be missed because she had done so much good. It was then that she asked him, "Why did you not say this earlier. I have worried myself to sickness and now to death because I feared I was no good." A simple "well done" could have prevented this from ever happening.

This proverb is true both for the speaker and the person addressed. Gracious words are sweet as honeycomb for the speaker. Pleasant words are good also for the person addressed. They cheer, comfort, and encourage.

Our words should always be as pleasant and considerate as possible. For example, when people are dining, we should avoid subjects that are not conducive to enjoyable eating. Avoid giving a detailed description of your major surgery or your recent seasickness crossing the English Channel. Young people should learn that gross, vulgar or suggestive vocabulary is neither cute nor appreciated. Don't confuse sarcasm with wit.

---

21 Further documentation unavailable.

16:25. Man's religion seems right to him, but his perspective is fatally distorted. Many follow a religion because they were born into it and it is what they and everyone around them have always done. Their traditions seem right to them. Man's religion is to earn or deserve his salvation. But look at the end of the road. No matter how right it seems to how many people, it only lands them in hell. Only sinners saved by the grace of God reach heaven at last.

16:26. One good reason for working is that it provides food for the laborer. His hunger rightly urges him on. It is right to work hard for the supply of your current needs.

16:27. It is a great evil to resurrect sins that someone else has committed and which may have been forgiven and forgotten long ago. But the ungodly gossip just can't keep quiet about it. It burns his lips to get out. If God doesn't remember forgiven sins, neither should we. Those who cruelly expose other people's faults should desist and spend their energy correcting their own failings.

16:28. Ungodly people start quarrels and a gossip often destroys friendships. A person with a corrupt mind likes to talk about subjects that start fights. Gossips break up friendships by spreading evil reports.

16:29. Evil men try to involve others in their crimes. As law-breakers they want partners.

16:30. Squints or winks sometimes suggest evil plans. Tightly closed lips picture determination to carry them out.

16:31. White hair on a senior citizen is an honor only if his life has been a godly one. Years of experience have taught him in the school of God.

16:32. Better is one who can restrain his anger than a powerful giant. It is a greater achievement to exercise self-control than to capture a city.

At age 10, Dwight Eisenhower became enraged with someone. He took out his rage on a nearby tree, beating it with his fist until it bled. That night when he was sobbing in bed, his mother sat by the bed. Finally she quoted this Proverb, 16:32, *"He who is slow to anger is better than the mighty, and he who rules his spirit than he who takes a city."* Dwight never forgot.[22]

16:33. The dice are thrown in order to settle a matter, but the Lord, not chance, controls the outcome. He controlled the lot to select Matthias to replace Judas (Acts 1:26). We don't need to use the lot today. We have the Bible and the indwelling Holy Spirit to guide us.

---

22 Dwight Eisenhower, *At Ease: Stories I Tell to Friends,* New York: Doubleday, 1967.

Proverbs 17

1 *Better is a dry morsel with quietness,*
Than a house full of feasting with strife.

2 A wise servant will rule over a son who causes shame,
And will share an inheritance among the brothers.

3 The refining pot is for silver and the furnace for gold,
But the LORD tests the hearts.

4 An evildoer gives heed to false lips;
A liar listens eagerly to a spiteful tongue.

5 He who mocks the poor reproaches his Maker;
He who is glad at calamity will not go unpunished.

6 Children's children are the crown of old men,
And the glory of children is their father.

7 Excellent speech is not becoming to a fool,
Much less lying lips to a prince.

8 A present is a precious stone in the eyes of its possessor;
Wherever he turns, he prospers.

9 He who covers a transgression seeks love,
But he who repeats a matter separates friends.

10 Rebuke is more effective for a wise man
Than a hundred blows on a fool.

11 An evil man seeks only rebellion;
Therefore a cruel messenger will be sent against him.

12 Let a man meet a bear robbed of her cubs,
Rather than a fool in his folly.

13 Whoever rewards evil for good,
Evil will not depart from his house.

14 The beginning of strife is like releasing water;
Therefore stop contention before a quarrel starts.

15 *He who justifies the wicked,*
and he who condemns the just,
Both of them alike are an abomination to the LORD.

16 *Why is there in the hand of a fool*
the purchase price of wisdom,
Since he has no heart for it?

17 *A friend loves at all times,*
And a brother is born for adversity.

18 *A man devoid of understanding shakes hands in a pledge,*
And becomes surety for his friend.

19 *He who loves transgression loves strife,*
And he who exalts his gate seeks destruction.

20 *He who has a deceitful heart finds no good,*
And he who has a perverse tongue falls into evil.

21 *He who begets a scoffer does so to his sorrow,*
And the father of a fool has no joy.

22 *A merry heart does good, like medicine,*
But a broken spirit dries the bones.

23 *A wicked man accepts a bribe behind the back*
To pervert the ways of justice.

24 *Wisdom is in the sight of him who has understanding,*
But the eyes of a fool are on the ends of the earth.

25 *A foolish son is a grief to his father,*
And bitterness to her who bore him.

26 *Also, to punish the righteous is not good,*
Nor to strike princes for their uprightness.

27 *He who has knowledge spares his words,*
And a man of understanding is of a calm spirit.

28 *Even a fool is counted wise when he holds his peace;*
When he shuts his lips, he is considered perceptive.

Chapter 17

17:1. A crust of dry bread with congenial company is better than a feast in an atmosphere of strife (15:16; 16:8). Meals are not an appropriate time for bringing up controversial or disagreeable subjects, nor for arguing.

17:2. A servant who lives wisely will rule over a disgraceful son, and may even share the inheritance with the brothers. The son is still a son, but he can forfeit some of the privileges of sonship. That is true in the spiritual realm. Once a person is saved, he is a son of God forever. You can't change a birth. But he may walk unworthily of his high calling.

17:3. Just as a refiner melts gold and silver in a furnace to remove dross, so the Lord refines His people to remove impurities (1 Pet. 1:7).

17:4. Wicked people listen to false reports, and liars feed on spiteful accusations. These are sins of fallen human nature. It loves to feed on falsehoods and malicious innuendos.

17:5. God has a special love for the poor and He doesn't like anyone, young or old, to mock them. Someone else He doesn't like is the one who rejoices at another person's misfortune (24:17-18). The Christian way is to have compassion, to reach out and help.

17:6. Grandfathers are honored by having honorable grandchildren. Children honor their father when they speak well of him.

17:7. You don't expect a fool to speak graciously or a prince to be a compulsive liar. You expect a ruler to be a person of honesty and integrity. You expect a fool to talk folly. The world expects Christians to walk worthy of the Name they bear.

17:8. A bribe is valuable to a man. He can use it to influence people in his favor. It's a wrong way to accomplish his plans. If he would delight himself in the Lord, He will give him the desire of his heart.

17:9. A good person shows love by keeping silent about

someone else's fault or sin. Ham failed to do this about his father's drunkenness (Gen. 9:3) and was cursed. A true friend overlooks a wrong done against himself instead of trying to settle the score by turning others against the one he has in his cross-hairs (Prov. 16:27-28). Many friendships have been shattered by a gossiping man or woman, yes, even among Christians, to our shame. Today, with the telephone and email, the malicious information travels and causes damage faster than ever. Resist any temptation to expose someone else's failings or faults.

17:10. A word of correction does more good for a wise person than a hundred lashes on a fool. How a person receives correction is a test of his character. Of course, the correction should be done lovingly and not harshly. How a person gives correction is a test of his gentleness and sensitivity.

17:11. Rebellion is an evil man's stock in trade. A cruel messenger will bring him to trial. That messenger may be an informant or the angel of death.

17:12. It's better to meet a bear robbed of her cubs than an enraged fool in his fury. A bear robbed of her cubs is a picture of extreme fury. But that is exceeded by a fool whose temper is out of control.

17:13. Whoever repays kindness with a wrong will have evil as a continual guest. David sent his faithful commander, Uriah, into battle to be killed. The rest of the king's life was one sorrow after another.

The Lord Jesus set a high standard for us. He did not repay evil with evil. *"When he was reviled, [He] did not revile in return; when he suffered he did not threaten but committed himself to Him who judges righteously"* (1 Pet. 2:23).

17:14. Strife is not static. It's like releasing water. Once it starts, it's hard to stop it. It's best to nip it in the bud (19:11; 20:3).

This reminds us of the Dutch boy who discovered a small leak in the dike. He put his finger in the hole until help came, knowing that otherwise the leak would become a torrent. The lesson, of course, is to nip problems in the bud. Stop an argument before it becomes a war. Lawsuits mushroom unless settled early (Matt. 5:25).

17:15. God despises it when the wicked are exonerated and the innocent are condemned (24:23-24). Barabbas was set free, while Christ was executed.

17:16. It is foolish to pay tuition for an education when the person doesn't really want it. Motivation is important in education. Only those who are anxious to learn should spend the money for it.

17:17. A true friend loves through thick and thin, through sunshine and rain. He is like a brother, who is by nature obligated to help his brother when times are rough. Someone said that when you have troubles, that's when you find out who your real friends are.

An enduring story of friendship comes from the battlefield where a platoon had come under heavy fire and one of the men was missing. A surviving soldier wanted to go and rescue his close friend, but the senior officer told him that his buddy would probably die, and it wasn't worth the risk to get him.

After insistent pleading, the officer-in-charge finally yielded. Immediately the soldier crawled on his stomach behind enemy lines to where his friend lay and held him in his arms. The mortally wounded soldier words were scarcely audible as he said, "I knew you'd come." Those were his last words—"I knew you'd come." That's friendship.

Anyone who pledges to guarantee his friend's debt in case the friend can't pay isn't using good sense. He might as well say good-bye to his money. Friendship doesn't require us to act unwisely.

17:19. To love strife is to love sin. The two go together. Strife is a work of the flesh (Gal. 5:20). Pride and destruction are also linked. Anyone who struts around as if he were someone important is looking for a downfall. The expression *"exalts his gate"* means "boasts his greatness by the grandeur of his property." It's like boasting about a big, expensive home or land holdings, and feeling smug and superior—pride of property.

17:20. A deceitful heart and a contrary tongue can expect no good—only trouble. The tongue reveals what's in the heart, and when a wagging tongue stirs up trouble, only evil will come of it.

17:21. A father suffers real sorrow if his son turns out to be a doubter. If the son is an unbelieving fool, the father gets no joy out of him. There is no parental sorrow like trying to raise children for God only to have them reject Christ and spend eternity in outer darkness.

17:22. The literal translation here is, *"A joyful heart causes a good healing."* (cf. 15:13). Recent research confirms this. A *New York Times* article reported, "Optimism can mean life for heart patients and pessimism can mean death. A healthy outlook helps heal the heart." It is also true that heartache and depression affect the health of one's bones or body. Franz Joseph Haydn said: "God gave me a cheerful heart, so He will surely forgive me if I serve Him cheerfully."

17:23. It is evil for one who must judge a matter to accept a gift or bribe passed secretly in order to influence his decision. Almost invariably it results in a perversion of justice.

17:24. A wise person concerns himself with matters at hand. He knows where he should be and what he should be doing. The fool fantasizes about world travel. He has failed at every job he has held, so now he thinks he should be a travel guide.

17:25. A foolish son is a bitter grief to his parents. Perhaps the first sign of waywardness in this son was that his grades in school were slipping. Soon the parents noticed that he was hanging around with a different crowd. Then he came home one day with a rebel's haircut. This was followed by a switch to the typical oversized gang clothes, droopy pants, T-shirts with vulgar, violent or demonic looking designs, etc. When the parents questioned him about his lifestyle, he reacted angrily, then withdrew into sullen silence. His father refused to believe that in addition to his general rebellion and bad attitude, he also might be using drugs.

The telephone rang at 2 a.m. It was the son calling from the police station. "Come and bail me out." He had been arrested in a drug bust. The minimum sentence would be a year.

17:26. It is utterly wrong to punish the innocent or righteous (18:6), and to attack rulers who are serving righteously.

17:27. An intelligent person is slow to speak. He thinks and chooses his words carefully before saying anything. A calm attitude is a sign of good sense.

17:28. A stupid person can hide his true character by not talking. As long as his lips are sealed, no one can tell. People think he is a model of wisdom and insight. "At times it is better to keep your mouth shut and let people wonder if you're a fool than to open it and remove all doubt" (J. G. Sinclair). There is a German saying, "When the cupboard is closed, you can't see that it's empty."

Proverbs 18

1 *A man who isolates himself seeks his own desire;*
He rages against all wise judgment.

2 *A fool has no delight in understanding,*
But in expressing his own heart.

3 *When the wicked comes, contempt comes also;*
And with dishonor comes reproach.

4 *The words of a man's mouth are deep waters;*
The wellspring of wisdom is a flowing brook.

5 *It is not good to show partiality to the wicked,*
Or to overthrow the righteous in judgment.

6 *A fool's lips enter into contention,*
And his mouth calls for blows.

7 *A fool's mouth is his destruction,*
And his lips are the snare of his soul.

8 *The words of a talebearer are like tasty trifles,*
And they go down into the inmost body.

9 *He who is slothful in his work*
Is a brother to him who is a great destroyer.

10 *The name of the LORD is a strong tower;*
The righteous run to it and are safe.

11 *The rich man's wealth is his strong city,*
And like a high wall in his own esteem.

12 *Before destruction the heart of a man is haughty,*
And before honor is humility.

13 *He who answers a matter before he hears it,*
It is folly and shame to him.

14 *The spirit of a man will sustain him in sickness,*
But who can bear a broken spirit?

15 *The heart of the prudent acquires knowledge,*
And the ear of the wise seeks knowledge.

16 *A man's gift makes room for him,*
And brings him before great men.

17 *The first one to plead his cause seems right,*
Until his neighbor comes and examines him.

18 *Casting lots causes contentions to cease,*
And keeps the mighty apart.

19 *A brother offended is harder to win than a strong city,*
And contentions are like the bars of a castle.

20 *A man's stomach shall be satisfied from the fruit of*
his mouth;
From the produce of his lips he shall be filled.

21 *Death and life are in the power of the tongue,*
And those who love it will eat its fruit.

22 *He who finds a wife finds a good thing,*
And obtains favor from the LORD.

23 *The poor man uses entreaties,*
But the rich answers roughly.

24 *A man who has friends must himself be friendly,*
But there is a friend who sticks closer than a brother.

Chapter 18

18:1. Cutting himself off from human society, the recluse gets the solitude he wants but flies in the face of all good sense. One of the first things God said after creating man was, *"It is not good that man should be alone"* (Gen. 2:18). That is why He sets the solitary in families (Ps. 68:6). Unfortunately, in many western countries, when young people reach legal age they want to get away from parents and family life and be on their own.

18:2. A fool has no desire to learn. All he wants is to parade his own nonsense. The one who hastens with his feet acts impulsively. He doesn't give due consideration to the results of his hasty action.

18:3. Just as wickedness earns the contempt of others, so disgraceful behavior brings reproach. Sin brings shame and disgrace. Confession brings forgiveness and joy. I am persuaded that many people who consult psychologists and psychiatrists need cleansing from sin, but no psychologist or psychiatrist is able to say: "Your sins are forgiven." He can, however, tell you how much you owe him for his time, and can certainly make you another appointment.

18:4. This proverb is capable of two meanings. First of all, the common language of man is like stagnant water in a cistern. Words of wisdom, on the other hand, are an inexhaustible rippling brook. "Words of wisdom are a stream that flows from a deep fountain" (Geneva Version GEV).

Or the proverb may mean that the words of a wise person are full of deep meaning. When he speaks, it is like a well of wisdom producing a gushing stream, clear and refreshing. Through knowledge of the Bible and through years of a close walk with the Lord Jesus, this man has a deep well from which to draw. His conversation is like a flowing book bringing wisdom.

18:5. This is an understatement. Not only is it not good, it is positively wrong to be partial to the wicked. And just as wrong to deny justice to the upright. Partiality is not the only miscarriage of justice that should be avoided. Consider the following: bribery, false witnesses, deliberate exclusion of witnesses so as to tilt a case, admission of secret testimony against the accused, pre-arranged verdicts (called "kangaroo court"), injustice through legal loopholes, and unjust back-room plea bargaining, deal cutting and favors between lawyers. The trial of the Lord Jesus hit a new low in the history of jurisprudence.

This is one of three times in Proverbs when we are warned against partiality or showing respect of persons. The other times are 24:23b-25 and 28:21.

None of us can claim to be completely impartial. We are all prejudiced in favor of appearances, status, and talent. It is more comfortable to favor the rich, famous and talented, and to shun the poor and disinherited.

Teachers are prone to give better grades to good-looking students. Someone has called beauty the golden coin of human worth.

Judges often pervert justice by accepting bribes. This verse refers particularly to that practice. It is specially shameful when churches err or show partiality in judgment.

Lord, deliver us from the sin of partiality!

18:6. A fool wants to start a fight and his wish is granted with some blows for good measure.

18:7. It's the fool's talk that leads to his undoing. His chatter trips him up eventually and exposes him for what he is – a fool. The words "mouth" and "lip" are figures of speech that refer to his talk. A fool's talk is his own undoing. He opens his mouth and the trap snaps shut. All doubt is removed. The man is a fool.

18:8. A gossip's slanderous rumors or reports appeal to man's fallen nature (26:20-28), especially if they are about someone who is already disliked for some reason; the hearers take them in like welcome delicacies.

18:9. The lazy person and the wrecker have this in common—they ruin instead of repair. The slothful man is probably both lazy and careless. He is not diligent (Rom. 12:11). He does not follow instructions. Instead of fixing a problem, he wrecks things beyond repair.

18:10. *"The name of the Lord"* stands for the Lord Himself. He is a fortress for His people. They run into the tower, which means they do not delay, but call on Him and He protects them.

In Proverbs, there is no clear statement of the gospel of salvation by grace through faith and apart from works. However, a good evangelist could piece together a message on the way of salvation through the following verses:

- There is a life to come. *"For surely there is a hereafter"* (Prov. 23:18).
- Man thinks he is pure. *"All the ways of a man are pure in his own eyes"* (16:2a).
- *"Most men will proclaim each his own goodness, but who can find a faithful man?"* (20:6).
- *"Who can say, 'I have made my heart clean. I am pure from my sin?'"* (20:9).
- God looks on the heart. *"...but the Lord weighs the spirits"* (16:2b; 21:2).
- Man thinks he knows the right way to heaven. *"There is a way that seems right to a man, but its end is the way of death"* (14:12; 16:25).
- God has provided an atonement. *"In mercy and truth atonement is provided for iniquity"* (16:6).
- What is God's Son's name? *"What is His name, and what is His Son's name, if you know?"* (30:4).
- How can a person be saved? *"The name of the Lord is a strong tower; the righteous run to it and are safe"* (18:10).
- What is the Lord like? *"...there is a friend who sticks closer than a brother"* (18:24).
- What happens if a person refuses Him? *"But the one who misses me has injured himself irreparably"* (8:36 Today's English Version).
- What is the future for believers? *"The righteous will never be removed"* (10:30a). And for unbelievers? *"The wicked will not inherit the earth"* (10:30b).
- What is a wise thing for believers to do? *"...he who wins souls is wise"* (11:30).

18:11. The rich mogul thinks that his money is a fortified city with high walls that protect him from assault. The truth is that this world cannot provide security. It can only be found in the Lord.

When it comes time to die, all the money in the world will not save a man. That can be done only by the precious blood of Christ. Jesus said, *"What will it profit a man if gains he whole world, and loses his own soul? Or what will a man give in exchange for his soul?"* (Mark 8:36-37).

18:12. Just as pride precedes destruction, so humility comes before honorable mention. Goliath fits the first part of this verse (1 Sam. 17:44). Mephibosheth illustrates the second (2 Sam. 9:7-8). The first king of Israel is also a good illustration. He began his reign with proper humility (1 Sam. 15:17). But through one act of disobedience, he lost the throne (1 Sam. 15:23).

18:13. Don't make a decision in a case until you've heard both sides. There are usually two sides to every dispute. You can't make an intelligent decision until you know all the facts. You'll be sorry if you decide hastily.

18:14. It is amazing how many trials and tribulations a human being can bear, but a broken heart is often beyond endurance. There was a man who endured the savagery and cruelty of one of Hitler's concentration camps. He faced it all with courage. When he was released, he was still erect and unbroken. But when he learned that it was his own son who had informed the Nazis against him, he died. "He could endure the attack by an enemy, but the attack by one whom he loved killed him."

18:15. If we want to be prudent and wise, we must have an insatiable hunger to be always learning. By naming the ear, we are told to listen carefully and pay close attention if we want to learn.

18:16. The gift in this verse is a bribe. Money can be used to get a person into palaces and before great men. That, however, is a wrong use of a gift.

The proverb could also mean that if a man has a real spiritual gift, such as in preaching, he will not lack opportunities to exercise that gift, even before influential audiences.

18:17. We always tell a story to put ourselves in a favorable light. So if you only hear my version, you'll think I'm right and the other fellow is wrong. But when someone comes along with the other side of the story, then the truth comes out. In serious matters, never make a decision on the basis of one witness.

If someone comes to you with an evil report about someone else, don't accept it or pass it on until you have obeyed the tests found in Deuteronomy 13:14. You should be careful about what you believe until you inquire, search out both sides with fairness, and ask diligently. Make every effort to know if it is not slanted, but totally true, certain and completely accurate.

18:18. One way to settle a dispute is by casting lots. It keeps contenders from coming to blows. But there is a better way. That is by love and brokenness.

18:19. Family troubles are among the hardest to heal. A close relative can be very unforgiving. Domestic strife is like the bars of a castle—cold, hard, and immovable.

18:20.Tremendous satisfaction can come to a person when he speaks wisely and helpfully. It's the same as if he had just had a feast. Here a man's mouth and lips are likened to a garden. Just as a person takes satisfaction from his garden produce, so this man can be pleased to remember his edifying conversations.

18:21. Our speech has tremendous power for good or evil, for life or death. Those who are habitual and careless talkers will suffer for it.

18:22. At first it sounds as if Solomon is calling a wife a thing. That would be disrespectful. He is not referring to a woman but to a good thing, a blessing—a divinely ordained marriage and the blessings that come from it (12:4; 19:14).

In Luke 1:35 the baby Jesus is called a holy thing, or holy one.

18:23. When a poor man needs something, he asks courteously and humbly. A man of wealth is apt to reply coldly, "Why don't you get a job?"

18:24. There are two quite different translations of the first part of this verse. First, it may mean that friendship is a two way street. If you want to have friends, then you have to be a friend. But it could also be translated *"A man of many companions may* *come to ruin"* (NIV). This is a case where a man has friends of questionable character. He is interested in quantity rather than in quality.

The second part of the verse invariably makes us think of the Lord Jesus. He is the Friend of all friends (John 15:13), the One who sticks closer than a brother.

> "Earthly friends may fail or leave us,
> One day soothe, the next day grieve us,
> But this Friend will ne'er deceive us;
> O how He loves."
> – Marianne Nunn

Proverbs 19

1 *Better is the poor who walks in his integrity*
Than one who is perverse in his lips, and is a fool.

2 *Also it is not good for a soul to be without knowledge,*
And he sins who hastens with his feet.

3 *The foolishness of a man twists his way,*
And his heart frets against the LORD.

4 *Wealth makes many friends,*
But the poor is separated from his friend.

5 *A false witness will not go unpunished,*
And he who speaks lies will not escape.

6 *Many entreat the favor of the nobility,*
And every man is a friend to one who gives gifts.

7 *All the brothers of the poor hate him;*
How much more do his friends go far from him!
He may pursue them with words, yet they abandon him.

8 *He who gets wisdom loves his own soul;*
He who keeps understanding will find good.

9 *A false witness will not go unpunished,*
And he who speaks lies shall perish.

10 *Luxury is not fitting for a fool,*
Much less for a servant to rule over princes.

11 *The discretion of a man makes him slow to anger,*
And his glory is to overlook a transgression.

12 *The king's wrath is like the roaring of a lion,*
But his favor is like dew on the grass.

13 *A foolish son is the ruin of his father,*
And the contentions of a wife are a continual dripping.

14 *Houses and riches are an inheritance from fathers,*
But a prudent wife is from the LORD.

15 *Laziness casts one into a deep sleep,*
And an idle person will suffer hunger.

16 *He who keeps the commandment keeps his soul,*
But he who is careless of his ways will die.

17 *He who has pity on the poor lends to the LORD,*
And He will pay back what he has given.

18 *Chasten your son while there is hope,*
And do not set your heart on his destruction.

19 *A man of great wrath will suffer punishment;*
For if you rescue him, you will have to do it again.

20 *Listen to counsel and receive instruction,*
That you may be wise in your latter days.

21 *There are many plans in a man's heart,*
Nevertheless the LORD's counsel—that will stand.

22 *What is desired in a man is kindness,*
And a poor man is better than a liar.

23 *The fear of the LORD leads to life,*
And he who has it will abide in satisfaction;
He will not be visited with evil.

24 *A lazy man buries his hand in the bowl,*
And will not so much as bring it to his mouth again.

25 *Strike a scoffer, and the simple will become wary;*
Rebuke one who has understanding, and he will
discern knowledge.

26 *He who mistreats his father and chases away his mother*
Is a son who causes shame and brings reproach.

27 *Cease listening to instruction, my son,*
And you will stray from the words of knowledge.

28 *A disreputable witness scorns justice,*
And the mouth of the wicked devours iniquity.

29 *Judgments are prepared for scoffers,*
And beatings for the backs of fools.

Chapter 19

19:1. It is better to be poor and yet honest than to be a rich thief. Some choices in life are easy to make. It is better to be honest and poor than to be a liar and a dishonest fool. The contrast is vivid and the choice is easy.

19:2. The picture here is of a person who is zealously propagating some falsehood. The expression *"hastens with his feet"* describes his goal in doing it. Paul uses Israel as an example of zeal without knowledge in Romans 10:2, *"they have a zeal for God, but not according to knowledge."* Zeal is good only if it is based on truth, and we need more of it. However, zeal without knowledge can be destructive. The misdirected zeal of the person in this verse makes him enthusiastic and energetic in his evil speaking. All the worse for his victims.

19:3. *"When a man's folly brings his way to ruin, his heart rages against the Lord"* (RSV). A man's own foolishness in disobeying the Lord leads him into problems. Then he turns and blames the Lord. The Lord had told him not to do it. He does it, then puts the blame on the Lord for what happened. It doesn't seem fair, does it?

19:4. Rich people may never know who their true friends are, because they have many self-seeking *"friends"* (14:20). But not so the poor. Parasitic friends avoid them because there's no hope of profiting from their friendship. This is unfortunately as true in Christian work as in the world. A Christian from abroad who has and dispenses money as offerings is anxiously awaited in a country, while a poor ministering brother is not received with the same effusion.

19:5. We are back in a court. False witnesses will get their reward, and liars will not get away with their lying. The Supreme Court will convene at the Judgment Seat of Christ, and again at the Great White Throne. The truth will come out.

19:6. People like to hobnob with royalty in hope of getting something. Anyone can gain nominal friends by generous handouts. The term "rice Christians" refers to those who profess Christianity because of the material benefits of being near the missionary who provides food, money, transportation, jobs, etc. Christian missionaries have often gained adherents by offering money, food or clothing. The balance between the gospel and social service is delicate and sometimes difficult, and calls for great discernment.

19:7. On the other hand, the brethren of the poor person treat him with scorn, and his so-called friends are even more disdainful. No matter how hard he tries to ingratiate himself, they don't want to associate with him. Why not? Because he doesn't have any money that could benefit them.

19:8. It's for a person's own good to act wisely. He who obeys good teaching gains the life that is better, richer and fuller.

19:9. This repeats the condemnation of those who bear false witness in a court of law. Destruction awaits those who lie under oath.

19:10. A fool is out of place in luxurious surroundings, just as a servant doesn't fit as a ruler over princes. Neither the fool nor the servant knows how to act appropriately.

19:11. A man who is intelligent doesn't lose his composure readily. It's to his credit if he can disregard some wrong done against him (20:3) instead of getting bent out of shape about it.

19:12. A king's anger can be as threatening as a lion's roar. His favor, on the other hand, is like dew on the grass—pleasant to see and refreshing to the soil.

19:13. A foolish, self-willed, errant son is a heartbreak to his father (v. 26), and a quarrelsome wife is a continual irritation to her husband, like the dripping of water. Wives should not quarrel or contend with their husbands, but treat them with respect (Eph. 5:33; 1 Pet. 3:5-6).

19:14. Children may inherit houses and land from their father, but a godly wife is an inheritance from the Lord. Godliness is the key characteristic that men should seek in a woman. Cosmetics and other tricks can make women appear more outwardly attractive, but only the Lord can produce godliness. Such a woman should be sought from the Lord in prayer, and when He supplies her, kneel often to give thanks.

19:15. A lazy person sleeps away his life. After all, he needs his rest, although no one knows what he needs it for. Work, toil and self-sacrifice are not in his vocabulary nor in his plans. If he refuses to work, he should go hungry (2 Thess. 3:10).

19:16. Think of the commandment here as the Word of God. Obedience to its teachings ensures a charmed life. A reckless life of disobedience leads to destruction. All God's commandments are for our benefit, not for His. That is why He commands us to have no other gods before Him. He knows that we become like what we worship, and He wants us to become like Him. To worship an idol is hurtful. Idolatry and immorality are linked.

Thomas Watson, a Puritan writer said, "God commands nothing but what is beneficial. '*O Israel, what doth the Lord require of thee, but to fear the Lord thy God, and to keep His statutes, which I command thee this day for thy good.*'" To obey God is not only our duty; it is our privilege.

19:17. God reckons kindness to the poor as a loan to Himself. He promises to repay in good measure. Think of it—a loan to Jehovah! What an exalted view of a commonplace gift! If we really believe this verse it ought to affect our giving.

> We lose what on ourselves we spend,
> We have as treasures without end,
> Whatever, Lord, to Thee we lend,
> Who givest all!
>
> Whatever, Lord, we lend to Thee,
> Repaid a thousandfold will be;
> Then gladly will we give to Thee,
> Who givest all!
> – Christopher Wordsworth

19:18. Parents should discipline their children when they are young—when they are still capable of being changed. As the twig is bent, so grows the tree. Discipline is work, and failure to discipline may mean that you love yourself more than your children. If you love them, you don't want them to be destroyed by a wild life.

The last part of the verse could also be a warning against discipline that is unfair, inconsistent or too severe.

19:19. Even if you try to change someone who has a terrible temper, he will revert to it. Only the power of God can change him through the second birth.

19:20. If you want to be wise in your old age, listen to wise instruction when you are young. It is sad to see an old man who talks endlessly about trivia and the past, or who continually tells foolish jokes.

19:21. A man may have all kinds of extravagant plans, but it's the Lord who makes the right decisions. We should fear making plans without clear guidance from Him.

19:22. Kindness is what makes a person really likeable. *"The charm of a man is his kindness"* (JND). Any poor man is better than a liar if he displays the fruit of the Spirit.

Here is a classic paraphrase of the fruit of the Spirit (Gal. 5:22-23):

> "The fruit of the Spirit is an affectionate, lovable disposition, a radiant spirit and a cheerful temper, a tranquil mind and a quiet manner, a forbearing patience with trying people, tactfulness and big souled charity, loyalty and reliability under all circumstances, humility that forgets self, in all things self-mastered and self-controlled."[23]

19:23. The fear of the Lord sometimes may mean the Word of God, as here. It leads us to salvation, sanctification, and ultimately to heaven. The Bible-centered believer finds satisfaction because the Bible is sufficient in all matters of faith and morals. It delivers us from the snares of evil (2 Tim. 3:15-16).

19:24. This man is so lazy that he can't exert himself to dip his hand into the bag to pick up a potato chip and raise it to his mouth. He goes to sleep with the bag in his hand. "He buries a hand in the dish, and will not even bring it back to his mouth. He can do the burial part of eating, but that's it. The sluggard

---

23 Quoted by Brian Powlesland in *Choice Gleanings Calendar*, March 13, 2006

will not attempt the return trip because it involves an uphill battle against the massed forces of gravity. He cannot think of a good enough reason to test those forces. In fact, he cannot think of a good reason to think" (Cornelius Plantinga).

19:25. If a thinking person sees a scoffer being rebuked, that's all he needs in order to learn. A New Testament version of this is, *"Those who are sinning rebuke in the presence of all, that the rest also may fear"* (1 Tim. 5:20 NKJV). A simple rebuke is all an intelligent person needs in order to understand.

19:26. A son who squanders his father's money and abandons his mother is a disgrace to his parents and himself. He is not worthy to be called their son. When I asked my doctor if he would accept my 96 year old stepmother who had just come to live in a retirement home in the area, the attendant replied, "Dr. Rosenthal likes to care for old folks whose relatives show an interest in them."

19:27. There are two possible thoughts here. First, as in the NKJV, it may mean that if you stop listening to advice, you will stray from the right route, the route of righteous living. In the King James Version, the thought is: *"Cease my son to hear instruction that causes to err from the words of knowledge."* A group of young people were on their way home for the semester break. One fellow began to air some doubts and denials that he had absorbed in one of his classes. Another student who had absorbed lots of Scripture verses at home spoke up: *"Cease my son to hear instruction that causes* [you] *to err from the words of knowledge."* It was the best verse for that moment and it had the effect of a bomb shell.

19:28. A disreputable witness cares nothing for laws that call for just decisions. He feeds on wickedness as if it were going out of style. He drinks it as if it were water.

19:29. Scoffers and fools laugh at the threat of punishment. They will laugh on the other side of the face when the justice they scorned catches up with them.

Proverbs 20

1 Wine is a mocker,
Strong drink is a brawler,
And whoever is led astray by it is not wise.

2 The wrath of a king is like the roaring of a lion;
Whoever provokes him to anger sins against his own life.

3 It is honorable for a man to stop striving,
Since any fool can start a quarrel.

4 The lazy man will not plow because of winter;
He will beg during harvest and have nothing.

5 Counsel in the heart of man is like deep water,
But a man of understanding will draw it out.

6 Most men will proclaim each his own goodness,
But who can find a faithful man?

7 The righteous man walks in his integrity;
His children are blessed after him.

8 A king who sits on the throne of judgment
Scatters all evil with his eyes.

9 Who can say, "I have made my heart clean,
I am pure from my sin"?

10 Diverse weights and diverse measures,
They are both alike, an abomination to the LORD.

11 Even a child is known by his deeds,
Whether what he does is pure and right.

12 The hearing ear and the seeing eye,
The LORD has made them both.

13 Do not love sleep, lest you come to poverty;
Open your eyes, and you will be satisfied with bread.

14 " It is good for nothing," cries the buyer;
But when he has gone his way, then he boasts.

15 There is gold and a multitude of rubies,
But the lips of knowledge are a precious jewel.

16 *Take the garment of one who is surety for a stranger,*
And hold it as a pledge when it is for a seductress.

17 *Bread gained by deceit is sweet to a man,*
But afterward his mouth will be filled with gravel.

18 *Plans are established by counsel;*
By wise counsel wage war.

19 *He who goes about as a talebearer reveals secrets;*
Therefore do not associate with one who flatters with
his lips.

20 *Whoever curses his father or his mother,*
His lamp will be put out in deep darkness.

21 *An inheritance gained hastily at the beginning*
Will not be blessed at the end.

22 *Do not say, "I will recompense evil";*
Wait for the LORD, and He will save you.

23 *Diverse weights are an abomination to the LORD,*
And dishonest scales are not good.

24 *A man's steps are of the LORD;*
How then can a man understand his own way?

25 *It is a snare for a man to devote rashly something as holy,*
And afterward to reconsider his vows.

26 *A wise king sifts out the wicked,*
And brings the threshing wheel over them.

27 *The spirit of a man is the lamp of the LORD,*
Searching all the inner depths of his heart.

28 *Mercy and truth preserve the king,*
And by lovingkindness he upholds his throne.

29 *The glory of young men is their strength,*
And the splendor of old men is their gray head.

30 *Blows that hurt cleanse away evil,*
As do stripes the inner depths of the heart.

Chapter 20

20:1. A light table wine was a common item on nearly every Middle Eastern table, and still is in some parts of the world. Here, however, Solomon is thinking of using wine to excess (21:17). It promises joy, relaxation, and a sense of well-being. Actually it is a depressant, reducing the body's functional activity and leading to intoxication. That is why a person who has had one too many should have a designated driver for the trip home.

A man who has a magnetic personality when sober may be a disgusting brawler when intoxicated. It changes his personality. And then, of course, there is the hangover– the disagreeable after effects. No one with good sense would pay that price.

The world can't have a good time without alcohol. It's called "social drinking." A believer doesn't need an alcoholic drink to unwind or to socialize. He finds his joy in a Book, not in a bottle.

20:2. The wrath of a ruler who has undisputed power is like a lion's roar. Whoever provokes him is playing with trouble, even endangering his own life.

20:3. A man of honor stifles the urge to quarrel (17:14; 19:11). Leave it to a fool to pick a fight. This is a good proverb to remember in the event of road rage. A driver is furious with you for his own stupidity. He may even threaten violence. "The better part of valour is discretion" (Shakespeare). Handle the situation quietly and with honor.

20:4. A lazy farmer says it's too cold to plow, then pulls the quilt over his head and goes back to sleep. It is no surprise that when harvest comes, there is no crop to bring into the barn (19:15).

The Lord Jesus warned against excusing our failure to evangelize. He said that the fields are already white for harvest (John 4:35). It's already harvest time.

20:5. Here is a man of knowledge, experience, and good judgment. He knows his Bible and walks with God in a life of obedience and devotion. His mind is full of good advice based on the Word. But he doesn't parade it. A young Christian would be wise to cultivate his company, looking to him to serve as a mentor. Those young people who do not cultivate wise older friends, but who only "hang out" with those of their own age group, are poorer for it.

The disciple could draw out valuable information by asking significant questions, including the meaning of difficult Bible verses. He could ask his mentor to share helpful lessons he has learned and seek his advice on problem areas. He could seek help on drawing up a list of significant books and another list of prayer requests.

20:6. The Fall left man blinded to his own faults. He talks glibly about his obedience to the Ten Commandments, his gifts to charity, and the number of children he has raised. He goes to ridiculous limits to show his innocence when he reports his accident to the insurance company. He sees himself as a paragon of virtue. He can see faults in others when he has those same faults to an exaggerated degree. David condemned the rich man in Nathan's parable for his lack of pity, but he had acted similarly and couldn't see it (2 Sam. 12:1-14). The Lord Jesus later told of the man who wanted to remove a speck of dust from his neighbor's eye when he had a plank in his own (Luke 6:41). The Lord warned against this in Matthew 7:1-5.

It requires the convicting work of the Holy Spirit to open a person's eyes to what God thinks of him. Then he stops proclaiming his own goodness and says, *"Father, I have sinned against heaven and in your sight, and am no longer worthy to be called your son"* (Luke 16:21). He confesses, *"I know that in me (that is, in my flesh) nothing good dwells"* (Rom. 7:18).

The Bible calls this penitent man a faithful man. For other examples of true confession, read Psalms 32 and 51.

20:7. This proverb came with power to a young father walking on the wet sand of a California beach. His little boy was lagging behind. When the dad looked back to see what was hindering, he saw his son carefully plant one little foot after the other in the father's footprints.

A careful man I've got to be,
A little fellow follows me.
I do not dare to go astray
For fear he'll go the self same way.

I must not madly turn aside
Where pleasure's paths are smooth and wide.
And join in wine's revelry,
A little fellow follows me.

I cannot once escape his eyes;
Whatever he sees me do he tries,
Like me he says he's going to be,
That little chap that follows me.

He thinks that I am good and fine,
Believes in every word of mine;
The base in me he must not see,
That little chap that follows me.

I must remember as I go
Through summer sun and winter snow,
I'm building for the years to be,
A little fellow follows me.
                    – Author Unknown

We shape our children in our own image and likeness. They benefit by the example of godly parents who model integrity and righteousness.

20:8. It is amazing how expressive the eyes can be. When a ruler sits as judge, you can tell whether he is pleased or unhappy. A glare that speaks of punishment scatters evil men. They don't want to be victims of his wrath.

20:9. No one born of human parents can claim to be perfect. Nothing he can do by himself will cleanse a man's heart or wash away his impurity. We have all sinned and fall short of the perfection of God (Rom. 3: 23). Solomon said, *"For there is not a just man on earth who does good and does not sin"* (Eccl. 7:20). The

Lord Jesus said, *"That which is born of the flesh is flesh,"* that is, it is fallen (John 3:6).

But that is not the end of the story. God has provided a way by which ungodly sinners can be cleansed. Scarlet sins can be washed as white as snow. Crimson sins can be white as wool. When a person repents of his sins and receives Christ as his Lord and Savior, the sins of a lifetime are washed away in the blood of the Lamb, and that person stands before God in all the perfection of the Savior.

The converted person is still not perfect in himself. But now he begins the process of becoming more and more like the Lord Jesus. The process continues until Christ takes him home to heaven. Then we will be perfect. *"We know that when he is revealed, we shall be like him, for we shall see him as he is"* (1 Jn. 3:2b).

20:10. False weights and measures must really aggravate the Lord. They are condemned three times in this book as abominations. The lesson for us is that we should avoid any deals that are not 100% honest. Our ethical standards should be of the highest order. We must have "a conscience live and keen to sense the first approach of sin."

20:11. Every child has characteristic behavior that defines him. It may be in part affected by heredity or environment, but more importantly, by his own will. Trees are known by their fruit (Luke 6:44), and children and adults are known by their behavior. A child's behavior may go with him through life. His behavior in youth may mark him in adulthood. An incorrigible child may turn out to be the despair of his parents.

But there is something else that we must factor into the equation, that is, the grace of God. That seemingly hopeless youngster may become a new creation in Christ Jesus and be a godly Christian. Parents should never stop praying for their children.

In Christian work remember that people are known by their doings, more than by their sayings. Their deeds are their fruit. If a person professes to know God but by his behavior he denies Him (Tit. 1:16; 1 Jn. 2:4), believe the behavior, for even a child is known by his doings.

20:12. It is God who designed the ear and the eye (Ps. 94:9). They didn't happen by random chance any more than did a watch or a computer chip. They are the result of intelligent design. We should praise the Lord for them and use them to glorify Him. We are responsible for what we do with our ears and eyes. Are we couch potatoes, spending hours before the T.V.? Do we know more about Hollywood stars or sports figures than we do about the red heifer or the book of Ezekiel?

We should be careful what we see, turning away our eyes from seeing sinful or worthless things (Job 31:1; Ps. 119:37). We should be careful what we hear, ready always to hear His will and shutting our ears to what is defiling. Proper use of the remote control, especially the "off" switch, can cut out anything on TV that is not glorifying to the Lord or spiritually edifying. Incidentally, that takes care of practically everything.

20:13. One mother warned her children, "Don't let the rising sun catch you in bed." Morning is the best part of the day for accomplishing work. Undue love of sleep spells poverty. Rising early ensures the basic needs of life. It is hard to make progress on a pillow.

> The heights by great men reached and kept
> Were not attained by sudden flight,
> But they, while their companions slept,
> Were toiling upward in the night.
> — Longfellow

Also, the morning of life – the youth – is the best time to give to the Lord.

20:14. This is such an accurate picture of business as it is. A man wants to purchase a used car. When the salesman extols its virtues, the buyer kicks a tire, then gives a litany of all its imperfections. The salesman comes down in the price and the buyer leaves with his classic Chevrolet, boasting about the bargain he got.

But not so fast! The salesman is an expert at this game. He knows all about the car, including the fact that it is not worth the reduced price. Buyer, beware!

20:15. Gold and jewelry have value but there is a greater value in wise instruction. The Bible gives that instruction, especially the gospel of salvation.

> If I gained the world, but lost the Savior,
> Were my life worth living for a day?
> Could my yearning heart find rest and comfort
> In the things that soon must pass away?
> If I gained the world but had no Savior,
> Would my gain be worth the life-long strife?
> Are all earthly pleasures worth comparing
> For a moment with a Christ-filled life?
> – Anna Olander

20:16. It appears that this proverb deals with different degrees of suretyship. A man may guarantee someone's debt, either orally or in writing. If it was a loan with small risk, as to a stranger, the surety guaranteeing the borrower might be required to give nothing more than his garment as pledge. The garment would have to be returned before nightfall because it was worn as apparel during the day but used as a blanket at night (Ex. 22:26; Deut. 24:13). If the loan was exceptionally risky because made for a questionable character such as a seductress, the surety would have to give himself as pledge. (Darby translates 20:16b: "...and hold him in pledge.") In case of default he would serve the lender for a certain period of time. In other words, the greater the risk, the more the surety would have to supply as pledge. (The passage is admittedly obscure).

In general a person is warned against guaranteeing the payment of someone else's loan in the event he cannot repay. But there may be exceptions. If so, you should consider the degree of the risk and the amount of pledge that would be appropriate.

The Lord Jesus gave His blood, that is, His life as pledge when He became surety for us. Think of that!

> Worthy of death, O Lord, we were;
> That vengeance was our due;
> In grace Thy spotless Lamb did bear

Himself our sins and guilt and shame;
Justice our Surety slew,
With Him our Surety we have died,
With Him we there were crucified.
                    —James G. Deck

20:17. If we gain something good by dishonest means, it may seem to be a bonanza, but it will turn out to be as revolting as chewing on a mouthful of pebbles. The thought of chewing with a mouth full of gravel is enough to create a severe case of shivers or goose bumps.

20:18. It is important to make careful plans before going to war. There must be intense training. Good military strategy is crucial, including the proper use of weapons.

This also applies to anyone who contemplates a life of Christian discipleship. He should ask:

- Have I counted the cost? Do I have the spiritual
  resources to endure and succeed? (Luke 14:31-33).
- Have I confessed and forsaken all known sin? (Prov. 28:13)
- Am I equipped with the whole armor of God? (Eph. 6:11-18).
- Am I consistently obedient to the Word of God? (Josh. 1:8).
- Am I dependent on the Lord Jesus, drawing my strength
  from Him? (John 15:5).
- Do I have an effective prayer life? (Col. 4:12; Jas. 5:16).
- Am I disentangled from the affairs of this life? (2 Tim. 2:4).

20:19. At first there seems to be a disconnect between a gossip and a flatterer. But the fact is that if a person can't exercise control over one area of speech, he is unlikely to be dependable in others. Gossips not only spread negative information about others, they also reveal confidences. Stay away from them. A gossip cannot be trusted to keep a secret that is damaging to someone else's reputation. He may try to justify it by saying, "I'm just telling you this for your prayer fellowship." Don't believe it. He may tell you that you are the greatest but he doesn't mean a word of it. A gossip divulges secrets. He breaks confidences. So we should be careful about the people with whom we associate. If someone flatters you to your face, you can be sure that he will condemn you behind your back. Avoid him.

20:20. Anyone who curses or speaks evil of his parents is destined for deep, dark oblivion or premature death (Lev. 20:9). God's estimate of the importance of mothers and fathers is seen in the fact that one of the Ten Commandments requires that they be honored (Ex. 20:15). It is the first commandment with promise—the promise being length of life.

20:21. There is nothing wrong in gaining an inheritance if it is done legally. The red flag in this verse is the word "hastily." That suggests that greed is involved and that questionable means are employed.

Estates are not generally settled speedily. Legal processes can be slow and frustrating, and wills can be broken. Don't spend an inheritance until you actually have it.

Families that have lived peaceably for generations may cease to be on speaking terms when an estate is divided. The strife may be over chipped dishes or early Salvation Army furniture.

Rather than involve themselves in these squabbles, many Christians have chosen to take the high road by letting the relatives have everything.

Our verse warns that no good can come from an inheritance sought by covetousness and gained by carnal means.

20:22. Taking revenge is forbidden. *"Do not say I will recompense evil."* The New Testament version is, *"Beloved, do not avenge yourselves, but rather give way* [place] *to wrath"* (Rom. 12:19a). A.T. Robertson in *Word Pictures in the New Testament* comments on Romans 12:19, *"give room for the wrath of God instead of taking vengeance into your own hands."*

Taking revenge is unnecessary.

"It is God that avengeth me" (Ps. 18:;47; 79:10; 94:1).

"Wait for the Lord, and He will save you" (Prov. 20:22; cf. 24:29).

"Stand still, and see the salvation of the Lord, which He will accomplish for you today" (Ex. 14:13).

"The battle is not yours, but God's" (2 Chron. 20:15).

Showing kindness is better than taking revenge. *"Therefore if your enemy hungers, feed him; if he thirsts, give him a drink; for in so doing you will heap coals of fire on his head. Do not be overcome by evil, but overcome evil with good"* (Rom. 12:20-21).

20:23.　Here are some of the diverse weights and false balances that the Lord hates: lying to escape punishment, using bogus immigration papers, violating traffic laws, carrying on personal business on the employer's time.

Paul Van Gorder commented,

> "There is a God of absolutes whose scales never lose their adjustment. With Him, a pound is a pound, right is right, and wrong is wrong, He says, *'I am the Lord, I do not change'* (Mal. 3:6)."[24]

20:24.　If a good man's steps are guided by the Lord, how then can anyone dare to act independently of Him? God's way is the best way, and we must seek to be conformed to His will.

> He does not lead me year by year
> Nor even day by day,
> But step by step my path unfolds;
> My Lord directs my way.
>
> Tomorrow's plan I do not know,
> I only know this minute;
> But He will say, 'This is the way;
> By faith now walk ye in it.'
>
> And I am glad that it is so.
> Today's enough to bear;
> And when tomorrow comes, His grace
> Shall far exceed its care.
>
> What need to worry then, or fret?
> The God who gave His Son
> Holds all my moments in His hand
> And gives them, one by one.
> 　　　　– Barbara C. Ryberg

24　*Our Daily Bread*, April 20, 2005.

20:25. A person should avoid promising to give something to the Lord, then changing his mind about it. If you vow, pay the vow. This applies to soldiers who make a vow in distress on the battle field, to patients in a hospital who promise God something if He will get them through an operation or sickness, and of course, to brides and grooms at the marriage altar. Vows to commit sin are not binding and should be broken. This could include vows that were made when joining certain fraternal organizations and societies. There is no honor in such vows.

20:26. A wise ruler is able to separate the guilty from the innocent and sentence the guilty accordingly. A threshing wheel separates the chaff from the grain.

20:27. Many believe that the human conscience is in view here. It is called the spirit of a man and the lamp of the Lord. It searches all the depths of the heart, revealing what is right and what is wrong.

In speaking of pagans who did not have the law, the Apostle Paul says, "[these] *by nature do the things contained in the law... [they] are a law unto themselves, who show the work of the law written in their hearts, their conscience also bearing witness, and between themselves their thoughts accusing or else excusing them*" (Rom. 2:14-15). They don't need a law to tell them that stealing is wrong. Their conscience tells them.

The conscience is not infallible. It needs to be educated by the Word of God and by the example of Christ. Paul did not know that lustful coveting was sin until he learned it from the law (Rom. 7:7). A good rule of behavior is, *"How does it appear in the eyes of Christ?"* In cases of doubt, the rule is "don't." *"Whatever is not from faith is sin"* (Rom. 14:23).

Believers have no more conscience of sins that have been confessed and forgiven. They know that Christ paid the penalty on the cross and they will never have to pay it. They can sing:

> Conscience now no more condemns us,
> For His own most precious blood
> Once for all has washed and cleansed us,
> Cleansed us in the eyes of God.
> —Tr. Mrs. Florence Bevan

They should always have *"a conscience void of offense toward God and men"* (Acts 24:16). This is known as a tender conscience.

Some unbelievers have a conscience seared with a hot iron that results in their departure from the faith (1 Tim. 4:2).

20:28. By exhibiting mercy and truth, a king maintains his position. By a reign of kindness and not tyranny, he avoids being overthrown. A righteous reign gives stability to his throne.

20:29. Young men can rejoice in their strength and physical agility. The beauty of those who are old is their white hair. This speaks of the honor that goes with wisdom, knowledge, and experience. Young men see visions of great exploits. Old men dream dreams of past glories (Acts 2:17).

20:30. Corporal punishment may not be in vogue in today's world, but in the wisdom of God it is effective in discouraging bad behavior. It affects not only the body but the thoughts and intents of the heart. The rise of psychoanalysis and psychotherapy have produced a corresponding rise in delinquent youth and crime.

Proverbs 21

1 The king's heart is in the hand of the LORD,
Like the rivers of water;
He turns it wherever He wishes.

2 Every way of a man is right in his own eyes,
But the LORD weighs the hearts.

3 To do righteousness and justice
Is more acceptable to the LORD than sacrifice.

4 A haughty look, a proud heart,
And the plowing of the wicked are sin.

5 The plans of the diligent lead surely to plenty,
But those of everyone who is hasty, surely to poverty.

6 Getting treasures by a lying tongue
Is the fleeting fantasy of those who seek death.

7 The violence of the wicked will destroy them,
Because they refuse to do justice.

8 The way of a guilty man is perverse;
But as for the pure, his work is right.

9 Better to dwell in a corner of a housetop,
Than in a house shared with a contentious woman.

10 The soul of the wicked desires evil;
His neighbor finds no favor in his eyes.

11 When the scoffer is punished, the simple is made wise;
But when the wise is instructed, he receives knowledge.

12 The righteous God wisely considers the house of the wicked,
Overthrowing the wicked for their wickedness.

13 Whoever shuts his ears to the cry of the poor
Will also cry himself and not be heard.

14 *A gift in secret pacifies anger,*
And a bribe behind the back, strong wrath.

15 *It is a joy for the just to do justice,*
But destruction will come to the workers of iniquity.

16 *A man who wanders from the way of understanding*
Will rest in the assembly of the dead.

17 *He who loves pleasure will be a poor man;*
He who loves wine and oil will not be rich.

18 *The wicked shall be a ransom for the righteous,*
And the unfaithful for the upright.

19 *Better to dwell in the wilderness,*
Than with a contentious and angry woman.

20 *There is desirable treasure,*
And oil in the dwelling of the wise,
But a foolish man squanders it.

21 *He who follows righteousness and mercy*
Finds life, righteousness, and honor.

22 *A wise man scales the city of the mighty,*
And brings down the trusted stronghold.

23 *Whoever guards his mouth and tongue*
Keeps his soul from troubles.

24 *A proud and haughty man — "Scoffer" is his name;*
He acts with arrogant pride.

25 *The desire of the lazy man kills him,*
For his hands refuse to labor.

26 *He covets greedily all day long,*
But the righteous gives and does not spare.

27 *The sacrifice of the wicked is an abomination;*
How much more when he brings it with wicked intent!

28 A false witness shall perish,
But the man who hears him will speak endlessly.

29 A wicked man hardens his face,
But as for the upright, he establishes his way.

30 There is no wisdom or understanding
Or counsel against the LORD.

31 The horse is prepared for the day of battle,
But deliverance is of the LORD.

Chapter 21

21:1. Our God is able to control the mind, emotions, and will of a king or president. He can do it just as He can turn a river this way or that. Ezra and Nehemiah both believed this and prayed for the Lord to move the heart of the king (Ezra 6:22; Neh. 1:11). Over 200 years before Cyrus was born, God called him by name and arranged that this Persian monarch would decree the restoration of Jerusalem and the rebuilding of the temple (Isa. 44:28).

Preacher DeWitt Talmage gave us this gem on the providence of God:

> "Despots may plan and armies may march, and the congresses of the nations may seem to think that they are adjusting all the affairs of the world, but the mighty men of the world are only the dust of the chariot wheels of God's providence."[25]

21:2. It's man's nature to think of himself as good. But God is able to see the inward life, that is, the thought life and the intentions. It's not how we think of ourselves that counts; it's how the Lord sees us. Check the following examples of the first part of this proverb. Insurance companies have received the following explanations (and many more!) of how accidents happened.

- The other car collided with mine without giving warning of its intention.
- A pedestrian hit me and went under my car.
- An invisible car came out of nowhere, struck my vehicle, and vanished.

---

25 John Rush, *The Authentic Life of T.DeWitt Talmage*, L. G. Stahl, 1902, p.371.

- The telephone pole was approaching fast. I attempted to swerve out of its path when it struck my front end.
- I had been shopping for plants all day and was on my way home. As I reached an intersection, a hedge sprang up, obscuring my vision and I did not see the other car.
- I collided with a stationary truck coming the other way.
- My car was legally parked as it backed into the other vehicle.
- The indirect cause of the accident was a little guy in a small car with a big mouth.

21:3. It was God who instituted the sacrifices and offerings in the Old Testament but He wanted them to come from people whose lives please Him (Isa. 1:12-15). Rituals are supposed to be outward signs of inward devotion.

That is true today of church ceremonies like baptism. It isn't the ritual that is important but the baptized life that it represents.

21:4. We know that arrogance and pride are sins, but to God even the plowing ["lamp" JND] of the wicked is sin. The Spanish Bible translates this word "thoughts." Until they repent and put their faith in Him, anything they do is sin. Sin is anything short of God's perfection.

21:5. The well-thought out plans of the diligent bring good results, but those who act hastily, without due consideration, may come to poverty. Those who believe don't have to be in a hurry (Isa. 28:16). The only time that haste is associated with God is in the story of the prodigal son. The father ran and fell on the prodigal's neck and kissed him. God is in a hurry to restore the backslider.

The Old Testament gives us two examples of ill-considered haste. When Abraham couldn't wait for the son that God promised by Sarah, he married Hagar and Ishmael was the result. This was the beginning of strife that continues to this day. Moses is the second example. One day he saw an Egyptian beating an Israelite, so he killed the Egyptian. It was a mistake. God's time to deliver Israel from Egypt hadn't come yet.

21:6. Wealth gained dishonestly is like a fleeting dream of those who are hurrying to death. In managing the affairs of mankind, the Lord has set certain laws in action. He rewards righteousness wherever He finds it. But just as surely, He acts in judgment against every form of evil. These laws are always operating.

21:7. Violence by evil and unjust men backfires on them. It destroys them. We might not always see it, but the headlines in the paper corroborate God's Word.

21:8. A guilty man does not act normally. He has to be guarded in his speech for fear of incriminating himself. He is inhibited in his contact with others. Those who live clean lives can be relaxed in their dealings with others. They have nothing to fear. They habitually do the right thing.

21:9. It is better to dwell alone in the corner of a rooftop than to live downstairs with a nagging wife. Solomon has quite a few negative things to say about certain wives, but he gives the other side of the coin with his description of the ideal wife in the final chapter.

21:10. A wicked man is consumed with evil desires. Even his neighbor can't please him. But there is Someone who can help him. His name is the Lord Jesus Christ. He can make the foulest clean and transform the incorrigible criminal into a man of God.

21:11. If you punish a scoffer, the simple realize that sin does not pay. Wise people don't need such dramatic instruction. They learn simply by being told.

21:12. Our righteous God knows what goes on in the life of the wicked and will punish him accordingly. He has not forgotten the concentration camps, the gulags, the ethnic cleansing of recent years. His judgment, though delayed, is sure.

21:13. Help the poor person when you learn of his need. Don't think that someone else should do it. Otherwise you will call for help someday and no one will answer. Anyone who has the desire to help will never lack the resources (2 Cor. 9:8).

21:14. A bribe passed secretly can pacify an angry person and a gift behind the back can allay fury. But the fact that it is recorded here does not mean that God approves bribery. God gives a faithful record of what happens in life but does not sanction the practice. That is also true of polygamy practiced by the patriarchs.

21:15. Upright people love to do what is right. There is a real sense of satisfaction in dispensing justice. Destruction, not joy, is the end of the wicked. They can't look forward to anything better.

21:16. A person who wanders in the fields of sin will come to the cemetery of the dead. This man can choose to sin but he can't choose the consequences of sin. They are written in indelible ink.

21:17. Those who spend their lives in pleasure and luxury will have only poverty to show for it. This reminds us of Paul's words in 1 Corinthians 6:13, *"Foods for the belly and the belly for foods, but God will destroy both it and them."* What a tragedy — to spend our life for self and for passing things, while above us burns the vision of the Christ upon the cross.

Wine and oil were common items in almost every Middle Eastern and Mediterranean home. But here the writer uses them as symbols of luxury and excessive consumption. Even things that are not wrong in themselves can be used to excess and thus they become wrong.

It is folly to live for the body which, in a few short years, will be eaten by worms.

21:18. A ransom is the price paid to deliver a person from captivity or punishment. Sometimes when the wicked are punished, they serve as a ransom, figuratively speaking, to liberate the righteous. This verse is similar to 11:8: *"The righteous is delivered from trouble, and it comes to the wicked instead."*

God doomed Israel to defeat because of their sin at Ai (Josh. 7:12). But when the Israelites destroyed Achan, his relatives and possessions (Josh. 7:24-25), the Lord turned from the fierceness of His anger and spared the people (Josh. 7:26). In a sense, the death of the wicked Achan served as a ransom to deliver the rest of the nation.

21:19. It is better to live alone in a waste, howling desert than with a cantankerous woman (25:24; 27:15-16). She is the opposite of the virtuous woman of chapter 31, and woe to the man who marries her. But there is hope! In *From Grace to Glory,* Murdoch Campbell tells of a Highland minister who was married to an angry woman. One day as he was sitting by the fireside, reading his Bible, she stormed in, seized the Bible, and threw it in the fire. He looked sadly into her face and said quietly, "I never sat at a warmer fire." Campbell remarks, "It was an answer that turned away her wrath and marked the beginning of a new and gracious life. His Jezebel became a Lydia. The thorn became a lily."[26]

Solomon had 700 wives and 300 concubines. There must have been some pretty unhappy times in the palace.

When the godly Robert Chapman was out for a walk one day, he met a cantankerous woman who leveled a fusillade of verbal abuse at him. Chapman called a friend who was nearby and said, "Come and hear a woman tell me all that is in her heart."

21:20. The wise person keeps supplies on hand to meet current needs. A foolish man is like the virgins in Matthew 25. They didn't have oil for their lamps when the bridegroom arrived. They had squandered their money.

The verse does not sanction laying up treasures on earth for the rainy day (Matt. 6:19). It deals with recurring daily needs, not with saving for the indistinct future.

21:21. Those who follow righteousness and mercy as guides will find honor and the good life. They lead without fail to that goal.

21:22. A wise man is able to do great exploits such as scaling the walls of a fortified city and tearing down a fortress. Paul gives a spiritual application in 2 Corinthians 10:4-5, *"For the weapons of our warfare are not carnal but mighty in God for pulling down strongholds, casting down arguments and every high thing that exalts itself against the knowledge if God, and bringing every thought into captivity to the obedience of Christ."* In other words, believers can destroy the godless reasonings and arguments of unbelievers, not with carnal weapons, but with the Word of God.

21:23. You can avoid a lot of trouble if you are careful with your speech. The tongue is untamable, but the Holy Spirit will give the power to those who sincerely seek it. We should all pray, *"Set a guard, O Lord, over my mouth; Keep watch over the door of my lips"* (Ps. 141:3).

21:24. Meet Mr. Snob – an arrogant and haughty man. You

26 Murdoch Campbell, *From Grace to Glory*, London: Banner of Truth Trust, 1907, p.149.

can't tell him anything he doesn't already know. He knows it all. He considers himself the final authority on all matters, great and small. He cannot be corrected. Everyone else is a dimwit. He is too proud to do what common folks are asked or expected to do. That would be below his dignity. The world has a word for one who is proud and conceited. They call him a snob.

21:25. The desire of the lazy man is to get what he wants without working for it. He is defeated by his own sloth. His hands refuse to move, when they should be working to supply his needs (Eph. 4:28). His feet are like lead. His laziness is self destructive.

21:26. The sluggard spends all day wishing for a catalog of things but that's as far as he goes. Sleep takes precedence over everything else. He always waits to be on the receiving end. If he were a good man, he would be giving endlessly.

> For we must share if we would keep
>   that good thing from above;
> Ceasing to give, we cease to have
>   —such is the law of love.
>   —R. C. Trench

21:27. It's bad enough for a wicked man to give to the Lord, but it is even worse when he does it with the hope of getting something in return or of getting away with sin. The evil of sacrificing to the Lord when the person is living in sin is vividly described in Isaiah 66:3. He might just as well commit murder.

21:28. False testimony has a short life. The testimony of a true witness endures. The verse does not mean that a true witness never stops talking. The thought is that he is spared to tell what he has heard. Notice that the word "him" is in italics. It is not found in the original.

21:29. The evil of a man's heart is reflected in the hardness of his face. The upright don't have that problem.

21:30. No plot against the Lord will ever succeed. He is invulnerable. Man has his wickedness but God has His way.

21:31.   Victory in battle ultimately comes from the Lord and not from the amount of weapons you have. It is human responsibility to prepare for battle, but faith must be in the Lord, not in technology, weapons or superior numbers.

Proverbs 22

1 *A good name is to be chosen rather than great riches,*
Loving favor rather than silver and gold.

2 *The rich and the poor have this in common,*
The LORD is the maker of them all.

3 *A prudent man foresees evil and hides himself,*
But the simple pass on and are punished.

4 *By humility and the fear of the LORD*
Are riches and honor and life.

5 *Thorns and snares are in the way of the perverse;*
He who guards his soul will be far from them.

6 *Train up a child in the way he should go,*
And when he is old he will not depart from it.

7 *The rich rules over the poor,*
And the borrower is servant to the lender.

8 *He who sows iniquity will reap sorrow,*
And the rod of his anger will fail.

9 *He who has a generous eye will be blessed,*
For he gives of his bread to the poor.

10 *Cast out the scoffer, and contention will leave;*
Yes, strife and reproach will cease.

11 *He who loves purity of heart*
And has grace on his lips,
The king will be his friend.

12 *The eyes of the LORD preserve knowledge,*
But He overthrows the words of the faithless.

13 *The lazy man says, "There is a lion outside!*
I shall be slain in the streets!"

14 *The mouth of an immoral woman is a deep pit;*
He who is abhorred by the LORD will fall there.

15 *Foolishness is bound up in the heart of a child;*
The rod of correction will drive it far from him.

16 *He who oppresses the poor to increase his riches,*
And he who gives to the rich, will surely come to poverty.

17 *Incline your ear and hear the words of the wise,*
And apply your heart to my knowledge;

18 *For it is a pleasant thing if you keep them within you;*
Let them all be fixed upon your lips,

19 *So that your trust may be in the LORD;*
I have instructed you today, even you.

20 *Have I not written to you excellent things*
Of counsels and knowledge,

21 *That I may make you know the certainty of the*
words of truth,
That you may answer words of truth
To those who send to you?

22 *Do not rob the poor because he is poor,*
Nor oppress the afflicted at the gate;

23 *For the LORD will plead their cause,*
And plunder the soul of those who plunder them.

24 *Make no friendship with an angry man,*
And with a furious man do not go,

25 *Lest you learn his ways*
And set a snare for your soul.

26 *Do not be one of those who shakes hands in a pledge,*
One of those who is surety for debts;

27 *If you have nothing with which to pay,*
Why should he take away your bed from under you?

28 Do not remove the ancient landmark
Which your fathers have set.

29 Do you see a man who excels in his work?
He will stand before kings;
He will not stand before unknown men.

Chapter 22

22:1. A good reputation is better than great wealth. The apostles witness by their lives that this is true. Loving favor is preferable to gold and silver.

22:2. In the game of life the playing field is level in this respect; rich and poor all have the same Creator. Robert Burns, the Scottish poet, captured this truth in his poem, "For a' that and a' that." He says that we pass by the coward-slave but dare be poor for all that. What does it matter if we eat common food and dress in common clothes? Let fools have their silks and knaves their wine; a man's a man for all that. Let them have their tinsel show; an honest man, though ever so poor, is king of men for all that. We see a smart assertive person and call him lord and all that. Though he parades ribbons and stars, and hundreds worship at his word, he's only a dolt for all that.

As you can tell, Burns was a friend of the common man.

22:3. A careful thinker foresees troubles and seeks shelter (27:12). Unthinking persons carry on heedlessly and perish. This has a special application to the gospel. A sensible person foresees the coming judgment and hides himself in the Rock of Ages, Christ Jesus the Lord. Reckless sinners neglect their soul's salvation and perish in their sins.

Noah illustrates this proverb. Forewarned by God that a flood was coming, he built an ark and saved his family.

22:4. Humility and godliness bring three things: true riches, honor, and the good life. The believer who is humble and godly earns spiritual riches, the approval of the Lord and of His people, and a life worth living.

22:5. Difficulties and problems beset the path of the wicked. The way of transgressors is hard (Prov. 13:15). There are inescapable trials and sufferings connected with a life of sin. He who walks uprightly escapes them.

22:6. Proper training in youth determines much of what a child will be in old age. For years North American parents raised their children according to *Child Care* by Dr. Spock. Toward the close of his life, he confessed that it was all a mistake. His permissive teachings had resulted in a generation of "brats." But it was too late.

Those parents would have been wiser to bring up their children according to the book of Proverbs. Susanna Wesley, mother of John and Charles Wesley, raised her 19 children according to the principles of the Word, which she condensed as follows:

> "Subdue self-will in the child and thus work together with God to save his soul. Teach him to pray as soon as he can speak. Give him nothing he cries for, and only what is good for him if he asks for it politely. To prevent lying, punish no fault that is freely confessed, but never allow a rebellious, sinful act to go unnoticed. Commend and reward good behavior. Strictly observe all promises you have made to your child."
>
> "I cannot yet dismiss this subject. As self-will is the root of all sin and misery, so whatever cherishes this in children insures their after-wretchedness and irreligion; whatever checks and mortifies it promotes their future happiness and piety. This is still more evident if we further consider that religion is nothing else than the doing the will of God and not our own: that the one grand impediment to our temporal and eternal happiness being this self-will, no indulgences of it can be trivial, no denial unprofitable. Heaven or hell depends on this alone. So that the parent who studies to subdue it in his child works together with God in the renewing and saving a soul. The parent who indulges it does the devil's work, makes religion impracticable, salvation unattainable; and does all that in him lies to damn his child, soul and body forever."[27]

---

27 *The Journal of John Wesley*, Chicago: Moody

There is another way of understanding this proverb. Training up a child in the way he should go could mean that parents should observe a child's natural aptitudes and encourage him accordingly. It is a mistake to think that every adolescent should go to college. Often it would be wiser and just as honorable for him to go to a technical or trade school. Exposing a young person to various occupations soon reveals the ones which best suit his abilities and interest. Therefore young people should learn to work, and not waste their youth hanging out, chilling out and playing games.

A third interpretation of verse 6 is this: Train up a child in his own way, and when he is old he will not depart from it. This is a warning. If you train a child in the way he wants to go, he will follow that selfish way all through life.

More than we would like to admit, parents are responsible for how their children turn out. Almost anyone can have a child, but raising and training a child obviously requires more wisdom and devotion than some parents are willing to give. But there are two other factors that must be added to the equation. First, after the parents have done their best, the child still has a will of his own. He can choose which way to go. The second is that parents should never give up hope or stop praying. The grace of God sometimes triumphs over all our parental failure.

Dr. S. D. Gordon in his *Quiet Talks on Home Ideals* says, "A father and mother living together with their children, tender in their love, pure in their lives, strong in their convictions, simple and orderly in their habits, do infinitely more than presidents and governors, legislators and clergymen can do in making a strong nation."

22:7. Rich people are able to dictate to the poor. Money is their power. They use it to get their own way. A borrower is slave to anyone to whom he owes money. The lender dictates the deadline for payment, the principal to be returned, and the amount of interest that is due. There may be a penalty for failure to meet the terms. The borrower is not a free man until he has repaid in full on time.

22:8. Sow iniquity and reap sorrow (Job 4:8; Gal. 6:7-8). David sowed adultery and murder. The rest of his life brought funeral after funeral to his family. The baby died (1 Sam. 12:18) and three sons, Amnon (Ch. 13); Absalom (Ch. 18) and Adonijah (1 Kgs. 2) were slain. His sins were forgiven but sorrows never ceased.

A man's ability to hurt others by his anger will soon vanish. The wicked Haman applies here. His anti-Semitism and attempt to exterminate the Jews had a short life. So did he. His anger did not produce the righteousness of God (see Jas. 1:20).

22:9. The generous giver will be blessed, especially if he has been kind to the poor.

> For the heart grows rich in giving,
> All its wealth is living gain;
> Seeds which mildew in the garner,
> Scattered, fill with gold the plain.
> – Author unknown

The poor in this verse may have a double meaning. The surface reference, of course, is to people who lack food and possessions. But it can also refer to those who are spiritually poor. A generous Christian will give liberally in order to share the gospel with them. No poverty is worse than that of the soul. •

22:10. Cast out the troublemaker and strife will end. This man is trouble with a capital T. He is a loud mouth, spreading vitriolic reports about others. He is a hot-head, unwilling to listen to gracious men who try to conciliate him. He has never done anything wrong. It's others who are wrong. Quarreling is his forte.

Such a person can wreck an assembly if allowed to continue. It is necessary to take strong disciplinary action before he does. Removal from fellowship until he repents is often the only way to solve the problem.

22:11. The king favors those with pure hearts and gracious speech. He can trust them. Daniel and his three friends fit that job description. Both inwardly and outwardly they made an impact on Nebuchadnezzar.

22:12. God protects those who have knowledge, that is, the faithful. They have little concept of how many times He saves them on the highway, at work, and at home. He rescues them from germs, allergies, viruses, and broken bones. He delivers them from fires, floods, and hurricanes.

He renders the speech of unbelievers ineffective. Christians are often the object of lies, threats, curses, and other forms of verbal abuse. The Lord knows all about it. All the foul language falls powerless to the ground.

22:13. The lazy man invents excuses for not working (26:13-16). To go to work might imperil his life. But there is not a lion in the street. The lion is only in his mind. Or perhaps he actually did see an animal; it was a pussy cat. The point is that the one who is allergic to work will resort to ridiculous excuses.

22:14. An immoral woman's talk is as dangerous as a deep pit, commonly used for capturing animals. It was camouflaged with leafy branches and other vegetation. The evil woman uses flattery, promises, and blatant lies as her camouflage. She appeals to man's sensuous nature, stirring up his fleshly appetite. If he hesitates, she rushes in with a plausible encouragement. Her trap is set. Her persistence pays off. His resistance breaks down.

Those who sin with her appear to be hated by the Lord because of the results of falling into her pit. They knew it was wrong, yet they yielded to temptation. The backlash of this sin is so severe on mind and body that it appears that God is far more angry with it than He is with other sins.

- It is a sin against God. All sin is against Him
- It is a sin against Christ. It amounts to re-crucifying Him.
- It is a sin against the Holy Spirit. It defiles a body in which He dwells.
- It is a sin against the body; bringing disease and other ills.
- It is an unspeakable waste of a person's procreative powers.
- It leaves a trail of regret, remorse, shame, and guilt.
- It exposes a person to blackmail, guilt, and public scandal.
- It destroys marriages and families.
- It makes enemies of the Lord to blaspheme.
- It disappoints friends who have trusted the guilty one.

All this for a moment of pleasure. Is it worth it?

22:15.A child is foolish (self-willed) by nature, but the paddle will drive the naughtiness from him (13:24). Today the psychologists tell us that this is all wrong. They say that children are basically good, and we must not spank them. They say, "Just reason with them." This is bad advice, but it appeals to many parents who want to believe their children are good, and don't want to go through the pain of a struggle of wills in disciplining them. They want the easy road of just reasoning with them.

But children are not basically good. They are all sinners by nature (Rom. 3:10). It doesn't take long for them to prove this, as anyone knows who has raised children.

The Creator's advice is that the rod of correction will drive naughtiness far from them. This does not mean cruel, abusive treatment that leaves scars. But it does mean a sting that is strong enough to tell the child that what he did is not acceptable and to remind him that it should not be repeated.

God has wisely designed the rod of correction and the backside to which it should be applied. Millions will testify as they look back on their childhood that it worked for them.

22:16. Oppressing the poor, perhaps in this case by paying starvation wages, is a bad way to get rich; it leads to poverty. And giving to the rich to curry their favor is a bad way to be generous; the rich don't need it. Poverty is the punishment.

22:17. From this verse to 24:34, we have what are called "Sayings of the Wise." They begin with an appeal to listen to these words and to abide by them.

22:18. It is a pleasure to be guided by them and to let them shape our conversation.

22:19. The goal of this instruction is to trust in the Lord. This is the most sensible thing that anyone can do, because He is completely trustworthy. There is no risk in trusting Him; He always keeps His promise. Believing Him is the pathway to blessing; it's His great delight to bless us. It is the sure way to eternal life.

22:20-21. These excellent words of advice are written so that the reader will not only grow in knowledge of the truth but will pass it on to others. God does not intend us to be terminals of His blessings but channels.

22:22-23. Here are examples of the counsel of the wise. Don't rob the poor because he is defenseless or take advantage of the crippled at the court of justice. The Lord will defend them and plunder the plunderers.

22:24-25. Keep your distance from a person who flies into a rage, or burns with slow resentment, or gets what he wants by intimidating others with his anger. Don't associate with him. *"Evil company corrupts good habits"* (1 Cor. 15:33).

22:26-27. Once again we are warned to avoid suretyship. Why should you lose the furniture in your house in order to pay someone else's debt?

However, if Christ had not become Surety for our debts, we would all have perished eternally.

> My God I have found—the thrice blessed ground,
> Where life and where joy and true comfort abound.
> 'Tis found in the blood of Him who once stood
> My refuge, my safety, my surety with God.
> He bore on the tree the sentence for me,
> And now both the Surety and sinner are free.
> – J. Denham Smith

22:28.   Don't move the stones that mark the boundaries of property (23:10; Hos. 5:10). The fathers knew what they were doing when they set them.

A spiritual application is this: don't tamper with the boundaries of sound doctrine. A curse rests on those who do. Also, don't try to find novel ways of expressing Bible truth—*"hold fast the pattern of sound words"* (2 Tim. 1:13).

Another application in this: don't be in a hurry to discard traditions. First, stop to ask why those traditions started in the first place. Maybe the reasons are still valid. Not all change is good.

There are two kinds of tradition in the New Testament. The Lord Jesus denounced the traditions of the Jewish elders because they made void the commandments of God (Matt. 15:2). These were traditions of men that had no Scriptural authority. But Paul told the Thessalonians to hold the traditions that they were taught, whether orally or by letter (2 Thess. 2:15). He referred to the inspired teachings that were handed down to us by the apostles.

22:29. A man who does excellent work is sure to be promoted to stand before men of distinction. He will not stand before common people. The best way to go forward in your work is to try to be the best and do the best at your job. Honest, diligent, hard workers will be rewarded whereas employees who goof off, waste time and do sloppy work will not. A Christian's work is part of his testimony.

Proverbs 23

1 *When you sit down to eat with a ruler,*
Consider carefully what is before you;

2 *And put a knife to your throat*
If you are a man given to appetite.

3 *Do not desire his delicacies,*
For they are deceptive food.

4 *Do not overwork to be rich;*
Because of your own understanding, cease!

5 *Will you set your eyes on that which is not?*
For riches certainly make themselves wings;
They fly away like an eagle toward heaven.

6 *Do not eat the bread of a miser,*
Nor desire his delicacies;

7 *For as he thinks in his heart, so is he.*
" Eat and drink!" he says to you,
But his heart is not with you.

8 *The morsel you have eaten, you will vomit up,*
And waste your pleasant words.

9 *Do not speak in the hearing of a fool,*
For he will despise the wisdom of your words.

10 *Do not remove the ancient landmark,*
Nor enter the fields of the fatherless;

11 *For their Redeemer is mighty;*
He will plead their cause against you.

12 *Apply your heart to instruction,*
And your ears to words of knowledge.

13 *Do not withhold correction from a child,*
For if you beat him with a rod, he will not die.

14 You shall beat him with a rod,
And deliver his soul from hell.

15 My son, if your heart is wise,
My heart will rejoice—indeed, I myself;

16 Yes, my inmost being will rejoice
When your lips speak right things.
Do not let your heart envy sinners,
But be zealous for the fear of the LORD all the day;

18 For surely there is a hereafter,
And your hope will not be cut off.

19 Hear, my son, and be wise;
And guide your heart in the way.

20 Do not mix with winebibbers,
Or with gluttonous eaters of meat;

21 For the drunkard and the glutton will come to poverty,
And drowsiness will clothe a man with rags.

22 Listen to your father who begot you,
And do not despise your mother when she is old.

23 Buy the truth, and do not sell it,
Also wisdom and instruction and understanding.

24 The father of the righteous will greatly rejoice,
And he who begets a wise child will delight in him.

25 Let your father and your mother be glad,
And let her who bore you rejoice.

26 My son, give me your heart,
And let your eyes observe my ways.

27 For a harlot is a deep pit,
And a seductress is a narrow well.

28 She also lies in wait as for a victim,
And increases the unfaithful among men.

29 Who has woe?
Who has sorrow?
Who has contentions?
Who has complaints?
Who has wounds without cause?
Who has redness of eyes?

30 Those who linger long at the wine,
Those who go in search of mixed wine.

31 Do not look on the wine when it is red,
When it sparkles in the cup,
When it swirls around smoothly;

32 At the last it bites like a serpent,
And stings like a viper.

33 Your eyes will see strange things,
And your heart will utter perverse things.

34 Yes, you will be like one who lies down in the midst of the sea,
Or like one who lies at the top of the mast, saying:

35 "They have struck me, but I was not hurt; They have beaten me, but I did not feel it. When shall I awake, that I may seek another drink?"

Chapter 23

23:1-3. This is a section of do's and don'ts regarding table manners. When you sit at a ruler's table, think ahead as to how to be moderate. If you usually eat large meals, this is a time to cut back on your helpings. Your host may have an ulterior motive in inviting you. He may be testing you. He may be a stingy host who grudges what you eat. Don't let him trap you with his gourmet food.

23:4-5. Don't work excessively overtime to get rich. Be sensible about this. Money is not real wealth. The extra money you make may fly away like an eagle. For example, you may have to pay it to a doctor or a garage mechanic.

Riches can be good if used for the Lord. They can be the source of much heartache if used exclusively for self. The children of wealthy Christians seldom go on well for the Lord.

23:6-8. Don't even desire to eat with a stingy miser or covetous person (1 Cor. 5:11). He may encourage you to help yourself, but it's what he is thinking that matters. He doesn't mean it when he tells you to eat and drink. The food will come back on you like acid reflux and spoil your pleasure in eating. Your thanks are wasted.

23:9. It's useless to reason with a fool. He will reject anything you say. This reminds us of Matthew 7:6 where the Lord said, *"Do not give what is holy to the dogs, nor cast your pearls before swine, lest they trample them under their feet and tear you in pieces."*

23:10-11. Don't steal land by meddling with the ancient landmarks or by taking possession of an orphan's property. You will have to give account to his mighty Redeemer, who will plead the cause of the dispossessed. The word Redeemer here has the meaning of Advocate.

23:12. Be diligent in gaining instruction and in applying knowledge to your life. The best place to get the instruction is in the Bible. We test all other instruction by the Word.

23:13-14. Don't be an unloving parent by failing to discipline your child when he has done wrong (13:24; 22:15). When you spank him, he may cry and howl as if you were killing him, but the spanking will not be fatal. Actually you'll be saving him from premature death. Spank like you mean it, don't just go through the motions. Break the child's will, but not his spirit. If he cries in anger or comes out moping or sullen, he is not broken yet. Better go back and finish the job. Deliver the corporal punishment and deliver the soul.

We need more fathers who are on speaking terms with God and mothers who are on spanking terms with their children. We need more children who are brought up at the knees of a devoted father and over the knees of a determined mother.

23:15-16. A wise son brings joy to a parent's heart. A father is happy when he hears his son speaking intelligently and correctly (vv. 24-25).

23:17-18. This *"do not"* echoes the words of David in Psalm 73. He envied the prosperity of the wicked until he went in to the sanctuary and considered their latter end. Envy is an insult against God. It is dissatisfaction with the way He has ordered our lives. It accuses Him of mistakenly denying us the prosperity, power, and pleasures of His enemies. The believer should steadfastly continue trusting the Lord, knowing that there is a hereafter when his hope will be fulfilled.

We have the hope of eternal glory in heaven and this hope is sure because it is based on the Word of God, the surest thing in the universe.

Portrait of a drunkard (23:19-35)

23:19-21. A wise son should keep his life on track, avoiding companionship with wine bibbers, gluttons, drunkards, and sluggards. These people are heading for poverty and rags. They are potential street people.

It is, of course, proper to befriend these men if your purpose is to lead them to Christ and freedom. In doing this you follow the example of the Friend of sinners (Luke 7:31-35).

23:22. There is something uncommonly heart-warming to see sons and daughters showering their parents with honor, care and loving kindness. Mother is now frail and forgetful, but it makes no difference. Her children treat her like a queen.

Not so endearing is it when the family shunts father or mother off to a substandard nursing home and rarely visits. They are old, but not too old to appreciate love. They took care of their children when they were little and helpless, and now it is time for love to return the favor.

23:23. We should spare no expense in obtaining the truth or in gaining wisdom and understanding. Think of this in terms of knowledge of the Bible. We buy the truth when we discipline ourselves to spend quality time each day in studying the Sacred Scriptures. H. A. Ironside bought the truth by reading through the Bible once for every year of his life. He lived to be 75.

Having "bought" the truth, we should not use it as a means for making money. False teachers exploit people for financial gain (*"make merchandise of you"* 2 Pet. 2:3 KJV). Those who suppose that godliness is a means of gain are corrupt and destitute of the truth (1 Tim. 6:5). The commercialization of the Christian faith, also known as the selling of Jesus, turns people of the world away from the faith. The cynics say, "All the church wants is your money." We should prove them wrong.

Fritz Kreisler, one of the world's great violinists, came close to the Christian ideal when he wrote:

> I was born with music in my system. I knew musical scores instinctively before I knew my ABC's, It was a gift of Providence. I did not acquire it by my own skill. So I do not ever desire thanks for the music.
>
> Music is too sacred to be sold. And the outrageous prices the musical celebrities charge today are truly a crime against society.[28]

So-called "Christian artists" who claim their musical ability is a gift from God should remember what the Lord said, *"Freely you have received, freely give"* (Matt. 10:8).

23:24-25. Who can measure the gratification in the hearts of

---

28   E. Stanley Jones, *The Christ of Every Road*, Nashville:Abingdon Cokesbury Press

parents when their children go on well for the Lord? It is rich repayment for all they have done attempting to raise the children in the fear of the Lord. It means more to them than a card, flowers or a box of chocolates on Mother's Day or a new tie on Father's Day.

23:26-28. Solomon asks for his son's heart (4:23), and his rapt attention to receive and believe what he is about to say. Children should be taught to look at their parents when they are being spoken to, to listen carefully and to remember. The wisest advice is useless unless it enters the heart. He warns against sexual immorality, one of the worst traps in life. A harlot is a deep pit and a narrow well, easy to enter but hard to get out (22:14). The seductress waits for her next victim and adds another name to the roster of the unfaithful, that is, unfaithful to God and unfaithful to his wife.

When the Lord asks for our heart, He is asking for our lives. The heart is our control center, our citadel. If He has our heart, He has all of us. In view of what Christ has done for us, nothing less than total surrender is an adequate response. True faith is not superficial.

23:29-35. The next warning is against drunkenness—the cause of woe, sorrow, fights, complaints, causeless wounds, and bloodshot eyes. The victim sits at the bar, drinking all night. He is fascinated by the sight of the wine. It looks so harmless at first, but eventually it bites like a poisonous snake. As drunkenness sets in, so does delirium tremens. He sees unreal things and his speech is garbled. He is as unsteady as a person tossed about in the ocean or perched on the top of a mast that swings crazily in a storm. He protests that he is quite sober and wonders when he can go back to the bar.

What does the Bible teach about drinking wine?
- The Lord Jesus made and drank wine, and it was the best wine (John 2:3-10; 4:46; 19:30).
- It is permitted in moderation or prescribed for:
    - stomach trouble (1 Tim. 5:24),
    - heavy heartedness (Prov. 31:6),
    - terminal illness (Prov. 31:6a),

○ holy celebrations (Deut. 14:24-26),
○ Lord's Supper (Luke 22:20). The Jews use wine in the Passover cup.

• Wine is prohibited:
○ When drinking it would stumble someone else (Rom. 14:21).
○ When it leads to drunkenness (here in Prov. 23, Eph. 5:18).
○ When it affects a ruler's judgment adversely (Prov. 31:30).
○ "Much wine" is prohibited for elders and deacons in the New Testament church (1 Tim. 3:3, 8).
○ Older women are not to be given to wine (Tit. 2:3).

Rather than being drunk with wine, believers should be filled with the Spirit (Eph. 5:18).

Proverbs 24

1 *Do not be envious of evil men,*
Nor desire to be with them;

2 *For their heart devises violence,*
And their lips talk of troublemaking.

3 *Through wisdom a house is built,*
And by understanding it is established;

4 *By knowledge the rooms are filled*
With all precious and pleasant riches.

5 *A wise man is strong,*
Yes, a man of knowledge increases strength;

6 *For by wise counsel you will wage your own war,*
And in a multitude of counselors there is safety.

7 *Wisdom is too lofty for a fool;*
He does not open his mouth in the gate.

8 *He who plots to do evil*
Will be called a schemer.

9 *The devising of foolishness is sin,*
And the scoffer is an abomination to men.

10 *If you faint in the day of adversity,*
Your strength is small.

11 *Deliver those who are drawn toward death,*
And hold back those stumbling to the slaughter.

12 *If you say, "Surely we did not know this,"*
Does not He who weighs the hearts consider it?
He who keeps your soul, does He not know it?
And will He not render to each man according to his deeds?

13 *My son, eat honey because it is good,*
And the honeycomb which is sweet to your taste;

14 *So shall the knowledge of wisdom be to your soul;*

If you have found it, there is a prospect,
And your hope will not be cut off.

15 *Do not lie in wait, O wicked man,*
against the dwelling of the righteous;
Do not plunder his resting place;

16 *For a righteous man may fall seven times*
And rise again,
But the wicked shall fall by calamity.

17 *Do not rejoice when your enemy falls,*
And do not let your heart be glad when he stumbles;

18 *Lest the LORD see it, and it displease Him,*
And He turn away His wrath from him.

19 *Do not fret because of evildoers,*
Nor be envious of the wicked;

20 *For there will be no prospect for the evil man;*
The lamp of the wicked will be put out.

21 *My son, fear the LORD and the king;*
Do not associate with those given to change;

22 *For their calamity will rise suddenly,*
And who knows the ruin those two can bring?

23 *These things also belong to the wise:*
It is not good to show partiality in judgment.

24 *He who says to the wicked, "You are righteous,"*
Him the people will curse;
Nations will abhor him.

25 *But those who rebuke the wicked will have delight,*
And a good blessing will come upon them.

26 *He who gives a right answer kisses the lips.*

27 *Prepare your outside work,*
Make it fit for yourself in the field;
And afterward build your house.

28 Do not be a witness against your neighbor without cause,
For would you deceive with your lips?

29 Do not say, "I will do to him just as he has done to me;
I will render to the man according to his work."

30 I went by the field of the lazy man,
And by the vineyard of the man devoid of understanding;

31 And there it was, all overgrown with thorns;
Its surface was covered with nettles;
Its stone wall was broken down.

32 When I saw it, I considered it well;
I looked on it and received instruction:

33 A little sleep, a little slumber,
A little folding of the hands to rest;

34 So shall your poverty come like a prowler,
And your need like an armed man.

Chapter 24

24:1-2. It is foolish to envy wicked men or to want to associate with them (3:31; 23:17). All they can think of is violence and crime.

Psalm 73 is a classic in this subject. This is an appropriate time to read it again.

The Apostle Paul reminds us that godliness with contentment is great gain (1 Tim. 6:6). If you are content, you have what money cannot buy.

24:3-4. Building a house involves a lot of wise planning, then considerable skill in actual construction. After that it is time to equip it with furniture and necessary fixtures.

There is a parallel in building a life, a home, a marriage, a family, and a church. It doesn't just happen. It takes discipline, patience, and prayer.

24:5-6. A wise man is morally and spiritually strong, not in himself but in Christ Jesus. With wisdom he fights the battles of life and finds safety in seeking the counsel of others.

Wisdom is better than strength. A general may have the weapons to defeat his enemy, but without wisdom, he may not take into account the weather conditions that he might meet. Napoleon had the power to invade Russia, but wisdom would have taught him to go at a time when the weather was favorable. He was defeated by something as feeble as snowflakes. Wisdom would have taught the Nazis to profit by Napoleon's mistake. They didn't count on the snow.

24:7-9. There are all kinds of people in the world. A fool is incapable of dealing with lofty matters. Wise decisions are beyond his reach. He doesn't participate when great issues are discussed in the city square. He is silent in the presence of rulers. He has nothing to contribute.

The schemer is always plotting some evil (6:18). The man who devises foolishness is sinning in his thoughts. The scoffer is an irritating nuisance to everyone.

24:10. Don't slack off when it is time to work, or give up when the going gets rough. If you do, your strength is small. *"Be strong in the grace that is in Christ Jesus"* (2 Tim. 2:1).

Elvina Hall must have had this proverb in mind when she wrote:

> I hear the Savior say,
> 'Thy strength indeed is small,
> Come to Me. I'll be thy stay,
> Find in Me thine all in all.'
> Jesus paid it all. All to Him I owe.
> Sin had left a crimson stain,
> He washed it white as snow.

We are also reminded of Jeremiah 12:5: *"If you have run with the footmen and they have wearied you, then how can you contend with horses? And if in the land of peace, in which you trusted, they wearied you, then how will you do in the flooding of the Jordan?"*

A modern version of this proverb might be, "When the going gets tough, the tough get going."

24:11-12. Think of these verses in connection with personal evangelism. Everyone will die. The time of death is unknown. There is a hereafter. In the future life, it is either heaven or hell. Without Christ people are drawn toward death, that is eternal separation from God. They are stumbling to the doom of eternal punishment. Believers have the privilege and responsibility of delivering people by sharing the good news with them and saving them from slaughter.

Christians should not excuse themselves by saying they did not know. The One who weighs the hearts in His scales and who knows the full truth will reward every believer according to his faithfulness in soul winning.

Verses 11 and 12 have also been a mandate for those who have openly protested against abortion with marches and other demonstrations. And is there not a cause? Between 1973 and 2005, there were over 50 million abortions in the United States. It is staggering to think of that number of unborn babies murdered.

A car had two stickers on the rear bumper. One said, "Save

the whales." The other said, "Abortion – A woman's right." What's wrong with this picture? Whales are more important than babies? *"Does not He who weighs the hearts consider it? He who keeps your soul does He not know it? And will He not render to each man according to his deeds?"*

24:13-14. Just as honey is good and the honeycomb especially sweet, so should wisdom be to our souls. It holds out hope for the future, a hope that will not be disappointed.

24:15-16. A criminal may lie in wait to plunder a good man's house. The righteous have a built-in resiliency. They may suffer seven calamities but they will rise again.

> Yes, I to the end shall endure
> As sure as the Earnest is given.
> More happy but not more secure
> The souls of the blessed in heaven.
> – Augustus M. Toplady (1740-1778)

The wicked will be wiped out by calamity and it will be final.

In his book *The Pursuit of Holiness*, Jerry Bridges says that he often uses this verse when he fails in the battle with sin:

> "The person who is disciplining himself toward holiness falls many times, but he doesn't quit. After each failure he gets up and continues the struggle. Not so with the unrighteous. He stumbles in his sin and gives up. He has no power to overcome because he does not have the Spirit of God at work in him."[29]

24:17-18. It is a trait of fallen human nature to be glad when an enemy suffers a mishap or loss. Gloating violates the law of love. God is so displeased when His people rejoice at the calamity of others, He may even turn His wrath away from the enemy and onto those who gloat. See Proverbs 17:5 and Obadiah 12.

24:19-20. We should not fret at the prosperity of the wicked or envy them for their success. They have no prospect of bless-

---

29 Jerry Bridges, *The Pursuit of Holiness,* Colorado Springs, CO:Navpress,1983, p.106.

ing and their life will be extinguished. We should pity them and pray for their salvation. This is the only heaven they will ever have if they die without Christ.

24:21-22. Our obligation is to recognize God's authority and the ruler's. Three words describe how we do it in the case of a ruler—obey, pray, and pay. We obey up to the point where we would disobey the Lord. Then the rule is "We ought to obey God rather than men."

We should not join with those who seek to overthrow the government. Those who are thus "given to change" are asking for punishment by both God and the ruler.

Further Sayings of the Wise

24:23-25. Wise people live in the light of the following: they are not partial in judgment but treat all alike, they do not reverse moral distinctions by judging the wicked to be innocent (28:21). This will incur the curse and hatred of the people. They punish the wicked and are blessed in doing so.

The Lord also pronounces a curse on those *"who call evil good and good evil, who put darkness for light and light for darkness, who put bitter for sweet and sweet for bitter"* (Isa. 5:20). What would He say about those who say there are no moral absolutes or that sin is only a sickness?

Those who have the courage to rebuke the wicked win the praise of the populace.

24:26.   A kiss is a universal expression of love. So the proverb tells us. Just as it is welcome, pleasing, and good, so is a correct answer. People love anyone who gives a right answer. The appropriate word at the right time is as good as a kiss, because it exactly fits the situation. Test your love quotient by answering the following questions:

- What is man's chief purpose in life?
- What should be our major goal?
- What is God's way of salvation?
- What is the greatest thought you have ever had?

24:27. Many of the proverbs assume an agricultural economy. Before building a house, the Israelite is counseled to be sure he has what he will need. He should prepare his land for a crop. He should plow the ground, remove the rocks, and plant the seed. After he has provided a means of livelihood, he is ready to build his house and raise a family. ("House" may mean either.) This is good advice for a young man contemplating marriage. It is better than sending his new bride out to work while he continues his college education. He should not be like the man who began to build but couldn't finish (Luke 14:28-30).

Charles Bridges explains it helpfully:

> "The wise builder first prepares his work without. He collects his materials, calculates upon the quantity required; then he makes his work fit by shaping and bringing them into their place; and afterwards, having all things in readiness, he builds his house."[30]

The American settlers coming West did not build houses right away. They could still live in their tents or covered wagons. The first priority was food. They had to prepare land and plant seed.

24:28-29. The neighbor relationship is something to cherish and preserve. Testimony against a neighbor in court should never be causeless, dishonest, or vengeful. We should never try to get even with anyone (20:22).

The senseless sluggard (24:30-34)

24:30-34. Here Solomon paints the portrait of a sluggard. The man is senseless. His vineyard is overgrown with thorns and nettles. The stone wall is in disrepair. It is a living parable. All the owner is interested in is just a little more sleep, a little nap, a little relaxed folding of the hands. Then poverty comes as a bandit, and the need for money as an armed robber.

---

30 Charles Bridges, *The Book of Proverbs*, Melford, Michigan: Mott Media, 1978, pp. 541-2.

Oswald Chambers draws a valuable lesson:

> "If a man lets his garden alone, it very soon ceases to be a garden; and if a saint lets his mind alone, it will soon become a rubbish heap for Satan to make use of."

Note in verse 32 how Solomon learned from the mistakes of others: *"When I saw it, I considered it well; I looked on it and received instruction."*

The slothful person's vineyard, unkept and in disorder, describes some people's room, house or life. It takes constant effort to maintain a vineyard or garden, and the same is true in other areas of life. If there is an overgrown or unkept area in your life, don't just feel ashamed. Confess your lack of diligence to the Lord, then get busy and do something about it.

Proverbs 25

1 These also are proverbs of Solomon which the men of Hezekiah king of Judah copied:

2 It is the glory of God to conceal a matter,
But the glory of kings is to search out a matter.

3 As the heavens for height and the earth for depth,
So the heart of kings is unsearchable.

4 Take away the dross from silver,
And it will go to the silversmith for jewelry.

5 Take away the wicked from before the king,
And his throne will be established in righteousness.

6 Do not exalt yourself in the presence of the king,
And do not stand in the place of the great;

7 For it is better that he say to you,
" Come up here,"
Than that you should be put lower
in the presence of the prince,
Whom your eyes have seen.

8 Do not go hastily to court;
For what will you do in the end,
When your neighbor has put you to shame?

9 Debate your case with your neighbor,
And do not disclose the secret to another;

10 Lest he who hears it expose your shame,
And your reputation be ruined.

11 A word fitly spoken is like apples of gold
In settings of silver.

12 Like an earring of gold and an ornament of fine gold
Is a wise rebuker to an obedient ear.

13 Like the cold of snow in time of harvest
Is a faithful messenger to those who send him,
For he refreshes the soul of his masters.

14 Whoever falsely boasts of giving
Is like clouds and wind without rain.

15 By long forbearance a ruler is persuaded,
And a gentle tongue breaks a bone.

16 Have you found honey?
Eat only as much as you need,
Lest you be filled with it and vomit.

17 Seldom set foot in your neighbor's house,
Lest he become weary of you and hate you.

18 A man who bears false witness against his neighbor
Is like a club, a sword, and a sharp arrow.

19 Confidence in an unfaithful man in time of trouble
Is like a bad tooth and a foot out of joint.

20 Like one who takes away a garment in cold weather,
And like vinegar on soda,
Is one who sings songs to a heavy heart.

21 If your enemy is hungry, give him bread to eat;
And if he is thirsty, give him water to drink;

22 For so you will heap coals of fire on his head,
And the LORD will reward you.

23 The north wind brings forth rain,
And a backbiting tongue an angry countenance.

24 It is better to dwell in a corner of a housetop,
Than in a house shared with a contentious woman.

25 As cold water to a weary soul,
So is good news from a far country.

26 A righteous man who falters before the wicked
Is like a murky spring and a polluted well.

27 It is not good to eat much honey;
So to seek one's own glory is not glory.

28 Whoever has no rule over his own spirit
Is like a city broken down, without walls.

Chapter 25

Further Wise Sayings of Solomon

25:1. These also are proverbs of Solomon, which the men of Hezekiah king of Judah copied. Think of the hours of painstaking work that the king's men expended to preserve this portion of the sacred Scriptures for us.

25:2. It is God's privilege and honor to hide a subject in figurative language such as parables, types, and poetry (Deut. 29:29). It is honoring for kings to search for the deeper meanings.

The Bible has many hidden gems in its depths. It is our glory as members of the royal family to dig into the Word and to find what lies beneath the surface.

25:3. Verses like this suggest that kings enjoy special intuition from God in order for them to rule well. As servants of the Lord they need unusual knowledge and insights that peasants simply do not require.

25:4. Solomon sees a similarity between refining silver in order to make jewelry and purging a government from evil to give it stability. In one case you get rid of dross, in the other of dishonest officials. In both cases a good result follows. You get fine jewelry and a stable throne.

25:5. This is an application of verse 4. If you remove wicked men from a government, the king's throne will be an upright one.

25:6-7. There is special etiquette to be observed when you appear before kings and other nobility. It is better not to push yourself forward to a prominent place (v. 27b). It's better to wait until you are invited to come forward. Otherwise you may be humiliated by demotion below the prince whose post you may be seeking. Jesus taught us to take the lowly place in Luke 14:7-10. We should not think too highly of ourselves (Rom. 12:3).

Some think that the last line of this verse should read, *"What your eyes have seen,"* and that it is part of verse 8.

25:8-10. Don't be in a hurry to go to law with your neighbor, or the law will get you. You may lose the case through his testimony. It is better to try to work it out peacefully with him. Keep it confidential between him and you lest you be shamed when the actual facts come out. Our Lord warned against a litigious spirit in Matthew 5:25-26.

25:11-12. A word that just fits the occasion is as beautiful as golden apples in a silver bowl. A Christian family was crushed by the death of the mother. Her illness had been an emotional roller coaster, up and down from hope to despair. No one could seem to help. Then a letter cane from a valued servant of the Lord. In it he quoted Psalm 30:5: *"Weeping may endure for a night, but joy comes in the morning."* That verse snapped the chains of sorrow and brought comfort and peace. It was beautiful.

A deserved rebuke that is well received gleams like a golden earring worn with other expensive jewelry. I heard that on one occasion Dr. H. A. Ironside was on a conference platform with other speakers. When one blasphemously suggested that Jesus was born of Mary and a German soldier, Dr. Ironside got up and walked off the platform. It was a deserved rebuke, and yet not a word was spoken.

25:13. A dependable messenger is as refreshing to the senders as a cold drink in harvest time. The opposite is seen in 26:6.

25:14. One who boasts that he intends to give generously but who fails to do it is like clouds that look like rain but fail to produce. He is disappointing, undependable, and frustrating. The Native Americans had a saying for a man like this: "Heap big wind. No rain."

Ananias and Sapphira gave the impression that they had given everything to the Lord, but in reality they had kept back some. By doing this, they had lied to the Holy Spirit. Ananias died immediately and Sapphira followed three hours later (Acts 5:1-11).

God does not always punish sin so promptly. Rather He does it at chosen times to make an example and to warn future generations who might be tempted to commit the sin.

25:15. A stubborn ruler can often be persuaded by repeated entreaties, and gracious, gentle words can overcome obstinacy. To put it another way, a gentle approach can break a hard bone.

25:16. Be moderate in eating. Even honey can make you sick if you eat too much. A father became exasperated with his children by their repeated refusal to eat vegetables. All they wanted was ice cream. So he announced that ice cream would now be their menu at every meal. After a day they wanted to go back to a balanced diet.

Here is a good rule: Moderation in everything except in zeal for God.

25:17. If you spend too much time in your neighbor's house, you will wear out your welcome. He probably has work to do. Limit your visits or he will groan to see you coming. Samuel Johnson said that fish and visiting friends smell after three days.

25:18. Anyone who slanders his neighbor is like a club that beats, a sword that cuts, and an arrow that pierces. These weapons can all be lethal.

25:19. Don't put your confidence in an undependable man when you are in trouble. It's like a painful tooth or a foot out of joint. You just can't trust them to bring anything but more pain.

25:20. Singing cheerful songs to a broken heart makes matters worse. It's cruel, like taking away a person's garment on a cold, rainy day. He doesn't need more discomfort. Try something that is more comforting and less frothy.

Pouring vinegar on soda robs soda of its intended use. Singing songs to a troubled heart is ill-suited and incongruous.

25:21-22. Treat your enemy with love. Feed him when he is hungry. Give him something to drink when he is thirsty. It will make him ashamed of the way he has treated you. He will feel scalded, as if you had put burning coals on his head. Your love takes away his enmity. This is confirmed in Romans 12:20. The Lord has a special reward for those who live in this supernatural way.

25:23. Slander brings an angry reaction just as the north wind brings rain. (In some countries, it may be a different wind that brings rain. Weather conditions differ.) Critics should not use this proverb to show that the Bible contains error.

25:24. It is preferable to live by yourself exposed to foul weather on a rooftop than to live with a mean-spirited woman. When choosing a mate remember that character is a major factor. A young woman who criticizes or disobeys her parents, or shows selfish, moody, headstrong or argumentative behavior will probably not have those character flaws removed by the marriage vows.

25:25. Good news from afar does what ice water does to a thirsty person. This is never more true than in the case of the gospel. It is God's good news from heaven. One day I stood by a news stand, reading the gloomy headlines, when an African-American lady came and stood beside me. As soon as she read the headlines and shook her head, I said, "The only good news is in the Bible." She smiled and said, "You got that right, Mister."

25:26. A good man who loses his confidence before an evil man and fails to confront him is as disappointing as a murky spring or a polluted well. His impact is negative. There is room for compromise when it is not a question of doctrine, but when it comes to divine truth and principles, there can be no compromise. It was Dante who said that the hottest places in hell are reserved for those who in a period of moral crisis maintain their neutrality.

Paul teaches us to have no fellowship with the unfruitful works of darkness, but rather to expose them (Eph. 5:11). We do this by rebuking them (TLB).

Here is a preacher who has spent his life proclaiming the unsearchable riches of Christ. He has never compromised the Word. For him, the truth is not negotiable. Evangelical Christians love and respect him for his defense of the faith.

Now the time has come to honor him for his ministry. Prominent men and women from various walks of life are present. Politicians, clergymen, business executives and educators have arrived. He feels tremendous pressure to ingratiate himself with the audience. When called on to speak, he realizes that many in the audience are part of the ecumenical movement.

Incredibly, he loses it. He makes an appeal for the union of all churches. Didn't Jesus pray that they should all be one? To do this, each denomination should acknowledge that Jesus is Lord. But it would be up to each church to interpret it as they wish.

"Dr. Jones" was intimidated by his illustrious audience. He

was "like a murky spring and a polluted well." He was no longer a source of dependable water.

25:27. Attempts at self-glorification are as sickening to others as ingesting too much honey.

25:28. Whoever can't exercise self-control is like a defenseless city. The enemy has found a weak spot on which he can get a beach head.

Proverbs 26

1 *As snow in summer and rain in harvest,*
So honor is not fitting for a fool.

2 *Like a flitting sparrow, like a flying swallow,*
So a curse without cause shall not alight.

3 *A whip for the horse,*
A bridle for the donkey,
And a rod for the fool's back.

4 *Do not answer a fool according to his folly,*
Lest you also be like him.

5 *Answer a fool according to his folly,*
Lest he be wise in his own eyes.

6 *He who sends a message by the hand of a fool*
Cuts off his own feet and drinks violence.

7 *Like the legs of the lame that hang limp*
Is a proverb in the mouth of fools.

8 *Like one who binds a stone in a sling*
Is he who gives honor to a fool.

9 *Like a thorn that goes into the hand of a drunkard*
Is a proverb in the mouth of fools.

10 *The great God who formed everything*
Gives the fool his hire and the transgressor his wages.

11 *As a dog returns to his own vomit,*
So a fool repeats his folly.

12 *Do you see a man wise in his own eyes?*
There is more hope for a fool than for him.

13 *The lazy man says, "There is a lion in the road!*
A fierce lion is in the streets!"

14 *As a door turns on its hinges,*
So does the lazy man on his bed.

15 The lazy man buries his hand in the bowl;
It wearies him to bring it back to his mouth.

16 The lazy man is wiser in his own eyes
Than seven men who can answer sensibly.

17 He who passes by and meddles in a quarrel not his own
Is like one who takes a dog by the ears.

18 Like a madman who throws firebrands,
arrows, and death,

19 Is the man who deceives his neighbor,
And says, "I was only joking!"

20 Where there is no wood, the fire goes out;
And where there is no talebearer, strife ceases.

21 As charcoal is to burning coals, and wood to fire,
So is a contentious man to kindle strife.

22 The words of a talebearer are like tasty trifles,
And they go down into the inmost body.

23 Fervent lips with a wicked heart
Are like earthenware covered with silver dross.

24 He who hates, disguises it with his lips,
And lays up deceit within himself;

25 When he speaks kindly, do not believe him,
For there are seven abominations in his heart;

26 Though his hatred is covered by deceit,
His wickedness will be revealed before the assembly.

27 Whoever digs a pit will fall into it,
And he who rolls a stone will have it roll back on him.

28 A lying tongue hates those who are crushed by it,
And a flattering mouth works ruin.

Chapter 26

Verses 1-18 are mainly about fools.

26:1. Snow in summer and rain in harvest are not suitable combinations. To honor a fool is another inappropriate event. Honors are for superior excellence. A fool cannot qualify.

No unbeliever will ever receive the Savior's *"well done,"* regardless of his achievements in this life. If he dies without Christ as his Lord and Savior, he is a fool.

26:2. This proverb may well have the distinction of being the most difficult one in the book. It seems to approve the pronouncing of curses. But this participation in spiritism is forbidden in Deuteronomy 18:10-12 and Galatians 5:19-21. It compares fluttering birds with causeless curses that do not land. Birds in flight do not land without reason. Curses do not land on people who don't deserve them. Apparently it is meant to deliver believers from fear of curses by a shaman. Nothing happens by chance for the child of God. He works all things together for good to those who love Him (Rom. 8:28).

26:3. Various means are necessary to get obedience. All a donkey needs is a tug on the bridle. The horse needs the sting of the whip. But a fool needs the heavy blow of a rod.

26:4. In answering a fool, we should not stoop to his level. We should maintain self-control and courtesy.

26:5. Yet it is good to answer a fool lest he think that he is wise. Just don't make a fool of yourself in doing it. Don't lose your temper, yet do not withhold needed rebuke. Quote Scripture liberally.

26:6. Send a fool on an errand and you are crippling yourself and inviting harm in other ways. He'll take the wrong address, make frequent unnecessary stops along the way, garble the message, and lose some important papers on the way back. As a result, an important sale is lost and a customer leaves in disgust. To cut off one's own foot means to make it impossible to accomplish one's purposes. To drink violence means to bring harm to oneself.

26:7. Verses 7-9 are similes that ridicule the foolishness of fools. A proverb in the mouth of fools goes limp, failing to make proper sense. It misses the whole point of what is being discussed. One man says, "A bird in the hand is worth two in the bush." The fool replies, "Yes, the early bird gets the worm." The only connection is the single word bird.

26:8. Don't tie a stone in a sling. It has to be free to leave the sling and hit its object. Praising a fool is similar to tying the stone. It only confirms him in his folly.

26:9. A drunkard is too unsteady to handle a thorn that is stuck in his hand. It's like that with a proverb in the mouth of a fool. He doesn't know how to use it appropriately, thus he has completely mishandled the proverb and made it useless. There is a disconnect between the meaning of the proverb and the subject being discussed. Let's say that the subject is pride. To illustrate, the fool says, "He who hesitates is lost." He has complete mishandled the proverb and made no sense at all.

26:10. The Great Creator-God knows how to repay men for their folly and sin. The destruction of Sodom and Gomorrah are proof. The Hebrew text here is difficult, but the proverb is true as it stands.

26:11. A dog is stupid enough to return to its own vomit. So it is with a fool repeating his own senselessness and never learning from experience. And so it is with sinners who have experienced a moral reformation short of the new birth. They are deceived by false teachers and become more polluted than before (2 Pet. 2:18-22).

26:12. After all the critical things that Solomon has said about a fool, it is surprising to learn that a conceited, arrogant person is even worse. There is more hope for the fool. Anyone who is wise in his own conceit seldom changes.

26:13. The lazy man is back with us, still excusing his shiftlessness and aversion to work by claiming there is a lion in the street. It would be too dangerous for him to go to work. (cf. Eccl. 11:4).

26:14-16. Like a door swinging on its hinges, the sluggard turns from one side to the other in bed.

Even the exertion of lifting food to his mouth is too exhausting for him. His laziness extends to even the simplest activities of life.

He considers himself wiser than seven sensible men who can give a good reason why he should get a job.

26:17. Here is a person who comes across two people who are having a fierce argument. He tries to help. Both disputants unite in condemning him for interfering. He might as well have tried to hold a vicious dog by the ears.

26:18-19. The one who hurls slanderous remarks is like one who says, "I was just kidding" after misleading the man next door. Once the words are out, they cannot be retracted. You can't put the toothpaste back in the tube. And you can't un-ring a bell. Let's be honest, "it was only a joke" or "just teasing" is sometimes said so as to get away with speaking your mind or making an insulting remark. Many a truth is said in jest.

26:20. Fire goes out when there is no fuel. Quarrels cease when there is no gossip. Gossipers have no outlet if people refuse to listen to them.

26:21. Just as charcoal and wood fuel a fire, so a troublesome man fuels contention and fights.

26:22. Juicy gossip is welcomed like sweet pastries, and becomes part of your memory. It takes courage to nip it in the bud by saying, "Please don't tell me. I'm not part of the problem or part of the solution."

26:23. Sincere-sounding words spoken by a fraud are like clay pottery coated with silver. They seem to be good but hide worthlessness.

26:24. Anyone whose speech is loving but whose heart hates builds up a supply of deceit in his heart.

26:25. This man in the previous verse may speak kindly but he is lying. He is totally abominable. His preliminary remarks may be designed to disarm any suspicion you might have about his hatred and resentment. "I love brother so-and-so, but...", or "He really is a good Bible teacher, but...." As a rule, when you hear the "but," forget everything that went before it. Now he is going to tell you what he really wanted to say. The kind words were the camouflage for his hateful criticism. He may even preface his remarks by, "Now this is not speaking against so-and-so, but...." His disclaimer doesn't change the true nature of his remarks.

The phrase "seven abominations in his heart" is an idiomatic expression meaning that his thought life is full of disgusting and hateful subjects. The seven stands for fullness. The hater may speak kindly but don't be deceived by that.

26:26. His hatred may be well enough disguised to fool some people and help him achieve his goal of bringing down his target, but it will be brought to light some day before his acquaintances, and certainly at the Judgment Seat, if not sooner.

26:27. The person who wants to trap or harm someone else is in danger of his plan recoiling. There is a boomerang effect. Jacob deceived with a kid (goat) and was deceived by one. He deceived his father with the skins of two kids and got the blessing that was Esau's (Gen. 27:9). He was deceived when his sons dipped Joseph's coat in the blood of a kid, creating the illusion that Joseph was dead (Gen. 37:31).

26:28. Lying about someone indicates hatred, and is a form of torture. Flattery is designed to ruin.

Proverbs 27

1 *Do not boast about tomorrow,*
For you do not know what a day may bring forth.

2 *Let another man praise you, and not your own mouth;*
A stranger, and not your own lips.

3 *A stone is heavy and sand is weighty,*
But a fool's wrath is heavier than both of them.

4 *Wrath is cruel and anger a torrent,*
But who is able to stand before jealousy?

5 *Open rebuke is better*
Than love carefully concealed.

6 *Faithful are the wounds of a friend,*
But the kisses of an enemy are deceitful.

7 *A satisfied soul loathes the honeycomb,*
But to a hungry soul every bitter thing is sweet.

8 *Like a bird that wanders from its nest*
Is a man who wanders from his place.

9 *Ointment and perfume delight the heart,*
And the sweetness of a man's friend gives delight by
hearty counsel.

10 *Do not forsake your own friend or your father's friend,*
Nor go to your brother's house in the day of your calamity;
Better is a neighbor nearby than a brother far away.

11 *My son, be wise, and make my heart glad,*
That I may answer him who reproaches me.

12 *A prudent man foresees evil and hides himself;*
The simple pass on and are punished.

13 *Take the garment of him who is surety for a stranger,*
And hold it in pledge when he is surety for a seductress.

14 He who blesses his friend with a loud voice,
rising early in the morning,
It will be counted a curse to him.

15 A continual dripping on a very rainy day
And a contentious woman are alike;

16 Whoever restrains her restrains the wind,
And grasps oil with his right hand.

17 As iron sharpens iron,
So a man sharpens the countenance of his friend.

18 Whoever keeps the fig tree will eat its fruit;
So he who waits on his master will be honored.

19 As in water face reflects face,
So a man's heart reveals the man.

20 Hell and Destruction are never full;
So the eyes of man are never satisfied.

21 The refining pot is for silver and the furnace for gold,
And a man is valued by what others say of him.

22 Though you grind a fool in a mortar with a pestle
along with crushed grain,
Yet his foolishness will not depart from him.

23 Be diligent to know the state of your flocks,
And attend to your herds;

24 For riches are not forever,
Nor does a crown endure to all generations.

25 When the hay is removed,
and the tender grass shows itself,
And the herbs of the mountains are gathered in,

26 The lambs will provide your clothing,
And the goats the price of a field;

27 You shall have enough goats' milk for your food,
For the food of your household,
And the nourishment of your maidservants.

Chapter 27

27:1. We should not take tomorrow for granted. Life is uncertain. While we have to make some plans for the future, we should always do so with the proviso "Lord willing." This saves us from presuming too much (cf. Jas. 4:13-14).

Real estate developer Larry Silverstein fulfilled a long time obsession by obtaining a 99 year lease on the Twin Towers of the World Trade Center in New York. He paid $3.2 billion. Six weeks later, on September 11, the towers were destroyed by terrorists.

27:2. It's better for praise to come from an outside source, not from one's self. Self-praise is the opposite of meekness and humility. One's own estimate of personal grandeur might be seriously flawed (Rom. 12:3).

Modern research confirms that people are not competent to judge themselves accurately. They consider themselves smarter, better looking, and more important than they actually are.

> "Incompetent people are doubly handicapped because they lack not only the requisite skills but the ability to recognize their own deficiencies."[31]

27:3. A fool's anger is heavier than a large stone or a barrel of sand. Heavier can mean having "greater" weight or it can mean harder to bear or more grievous. Both usages are found in this verse.

27:4. Anger is cruel and torrential but envy and jealousy are worse. Often when a man finds his wife having an affair with another man, he becomes insanely jealous and murders the culprit. Professional envy in the workplace, envy of others' friendships, and envy of others' spiritual gifts or blessings are just a few of the many forms this rottenness takes (Rom. 1:29; Tit. 3:3).

---

31 Quoted in "PsychoHeresy Awareness Letter," Vol. 15, No. 2, p. 4 www.psychoheresy-aware.org

27:5. Loving rebuke is better than a love that never cares to correct another person (28:23). We hesitate to correct for fear we will lose a friend. If the rebuke is loving, it is likely that our friendship will deepen.

27:6. If a friend criticizes you, it's because he wants to help you, but an enemy's commendation or kiss is deceitful. It's a great gift to be able to criticize graciously, constructively and lovingly. Not everyone can do it.

In the days of Absalom's rebellion, there was a power struggle between two military commanders, Joab and Amasa. Pretending to salute Amasa in a friendly manner, Joab pulled him forward by the beard. But instead of kissing him, he took his sword and stabbed him fatally in the stomach (2 Sam. 20:8).

But that was not history's most deceitful kiss. That despicable distinction goes to Judas, the betrayer. He walked up to Jesus, greeted him with "Rabbi, Rabbi," then kissed him with a great show of affection (Mark 14:45 LB).

27:7. One who has had enough to eat doesn't crave a serving of honeycomb. But when he is hungry, every bit of common food is welcome. Fussiness about foods decreases in proportion to the intensity of hunger.

God was displeased when Israel complained about the manna which was a type of Christ.

In Mark 7:14-16, the Lord Jesus pronounced all food clean. It is sanctified by the Word of God and prayer. It is sanctified by the Word in the passage just cited in Mark. It is sanctified by prayer when we bow our heads and give thanks for it.

We should not be food faddists, but should eat what is set before us, asking no questions for conscience' sake (1 Cor. 10:25). We should sing, "Where he leads me I will follow; what He feeds me I will swallow." Good missionary training!

27:8. A young person who leaves home too soon is like a chick that abandons its nest before it can fly. The teenager is apt to say, "I'm tired of being bossed around. I'm getting out of here." But he's not ready to face the responsibilities, temptations and problems that await him.

27:9. Perfume or cologne is sweet smelling and pleasant. That's what fellowship with a friend is like. It's a pleasure to talk with someone who accepts you as you are. You don't have to put on airs. Your conversation is relaxed, pleasing, and profitable.

> "Jesus is a Friend. He is the One who is always there; One who will always help; One whom we do not have to impress; One with whom we can talk whenever the need arises, or with whom we can just be quiet when we don't feel like saying anything at all."[32]

27:10. Be loyal to your friends and your family's friends. But a neighbor next door can be more comforting than a brother who lives far away. You don't have to choose between friends and neighbors. All should be cultivated. But in an emergency, the one who is close at hand is best.

27:11. A wise son gladdens his father and enables the father to answer any who might criticize his parenting or his son. When the son turns out to be a man of good character, criticism is silenced.

27:12. An intelligent person foresees trouble and prepares for it. The simpleton proceeds unthinkingly and suffers for it. Believers prepare for the future by trusting the Savior. Unbelievers know that the day of judgment is coming but they reject God's offer of free salvation.

27:13. There are degrees of suretyship. If a man guarantees the debt of a stranger, he should give his cloak as collateral. The Mosaic law required that the coat had to be returned to the owner by nightfall (Ex. 22:26-27). The owner might need it as a blanket (20:16).

But to guarantee a large loan made to a harlot is different. This loan is especially risky. Here the surety might have to offer himself as pledge. The last part of the verse might read "and hold him in pledge for a strange woman" (J. N. Darby's *New Translation*). In case of default, he might have to offer himself as a servant or even as a slave.

27:14. It is more of a curse than a kindness to loudly and

---

32 Editorial in *Decision Magazine*, February 1979.

cheerily rouse your friend early in the morning. That kind of thoughtless, insensitive behavior deserves a dumbbell rather than a Nobel.

27:15-16. A belligerent, argumentative or nagging woman is like a constant drip-drip-drip on a rainy day. To stop her is as impossible as holding back the wind or grasping a handful of oil. What dreadful crime did her husband commit that he should be so afflicted?

27:17. *"Just as iron sharpens iron,"* so wholesome discussions have a beneficial influence on the thinking of the participants. Dr. H. A. Ironside explains:

> "As by friction, one iron instrument is sharpened and polished by contact with another, so we may be a help to each other by interesting and profitable intercourse and exchange of thought."

27:18. Just as the one who tends a fig tree gets fruit from it, so a master rewards his servant. Faithful service does not go without recompense. Our Lord has promised a reward for every cup of cold water given in His name (Matt. 10:42). He promises, *"Them that honor me, I will honor"* (1 Sam. 2:30).

27:19. As in water, face answers to face, so the heart of man to man. As my face is reflected in water, so when I look into the face of another man, I see ways in which we are similar. He has strengths and weaknesses; so do I. He has joys and sorrows; so do I. He has victories and defeats; so do I. I see his humanity reflected in mine.

27:20. Hell and destruction always have room for more. So a man's heart is always looking for more. He is never satisfied. The musical group the Rolling Stones had plenty of money and fame, yet they sang, "I can't get no satisfaction." Hell (Sheol) and destruction (Abaddon) are synonyms here. They refer to nothing more precise than the disembodied state. Old Testament saints had very limited knowledge of the afterlife.

27:21. The *Living Bible* seems to have best caught the meaning of this proverb. It changes the word "valued" to "tested." *"The purity of silver and gold can be tested in a crucible, but a man is* *tested by his reaction to men's praise."* If he becomes puffed up, he fails the humility test. He has forgotten that it's how he ends the race of life that counts. If he reacts with true humility, dismissing the praise as undeserved, he passes the test.

Incidentally, the lavish praise that is usual in introducing Christian speakers is a violation of Colossians 1:18, *"that in all things He* [Christ] *may have the preeminence."* When one preacher was introduced with overflowing superlatives, he dismissed it by saying, "Of all the introductions I've ever received, that was certainly the most recent one."

27:22. No matter what you do with a fool, you can never rid him of his stupidity. Crush him as you crush grain with a mortar and pestle, but his folly remains. It is inseparable from him.

But we must always remember that there is hope. We must always allow for the grace of God to reach him with the gospel and make a new man out of him. Only God can say never.

27:23-27. The one who herds livestock has to give them constant care and attention. Cows have to be milked on schedule. Vigilance is also true of a ruler and his subjects. Conditions always change and disaster may come when he's not on guard.

There is an application in verse 23 for elders, as pastors of the flock of God. Elders should do pastoral work with diligence, observing, listening, visiting and interacting with the saints so as to know their spiritual condition. It would be difficult to do this by a simple greeting before or after a meeting. Shepherding is much more involved than being a shop-keeper. A shop-keeper arrives at his shop a little before opening time, turns on the lights, arranges things, and then opens the door and waits for customers. He greets them as they come in, makes his sales, and then turns off the lights and closes the shop at the end of the day. But the church is not a shop; it is the flock of God. Shepherds watch over and care for the flock. In 1 Peter 5:1-4 we learn that shepherds have a Chief Shepherd, the Lord Jesus, to whom they must give account for their care of the flock of God.

Verse 25 describes harvest time on the farm. The hay is brought to the barn. What was once green grass has disappeared. The mountain herbs are stored. As a result of this careful attention by the farmer, the lambs provide wool for clothing, and the goats produce milk. Money from the sale of the milk can be used for providing food for the whole household and for enlarging the farm.

Proverbs 28

1 *The wicked flee when no one pursues,*
But the righteous are bold as a lion.

2 *Because of the transgression of a land, many are its princes;*
But by a man of understanding and knowledge
Right will be prolonged.

3 *A poor man who oppresses the poor*
Is like a driving rain which leaves no food.

4 *Those who forsake the law praise the wicked,*
But such as keep the law contend with them.

5 *Evil men do not understand justice,*
But those who seek the LORD understand all.

6 *Better is the poor who walks in his integrity*
Than one perverse in his ways, though he be rich.

7 *Whoever keeps the law is a discerning son,*
But a companion of gluttons shames his father.

8 *One who increases his possessions by usury and extortion*
Gathers it for him who will pity the poor.

9 *One who turns away his ear from hearing the law,*
Even his prayer is an abomination.

10 *Whoever causes the upright to go astray in an evil way,*
He himself will fall into his own pit;
But the blameless will inherit good.

11 *The rich man is wise in his own eyes,*
But the poor who has understanding searches him out.

12 *When the righteous rejoice, there is great glory;*
But when the wicked arise, men hide themselves.

13 *He who covers his sins will not prosper,*
But whoever confesses and forsakes them will have mercy.

14 Happy is the man who is always reverent,
But he who hardens his heart will fall into calamity.

15 Like a roaring lion and a charging bear
Is a wicked ruler over poor people.

16 A ruler who lacks understanding is a great oppressor,
But he who hates covetousness will prolong his days.

17 A man burdened with bloodshed will flee into a pit;
Let no one help him.

18 Whoever walks blamelessly will be saved,
But he who is perverse in his ways will suddenly fall.

19 He who tills his land will have plenty of bread,
But he who follows frivolity will have poverty enough!

20 A faithful man will abound with blessings,
But he who hastens to be rich will not go unpunished.

21 To show partiality is not good,
Because for a piece of bread a man will transgress.

22 A man with an evil eye hastens after riches,
And does not consider that poverty will come upon him.

23 He who rebukes a man will find more favor afterward
Than he who flatters with the tongue.

24 Whoever robs his father or his mother,
And says, "It is no transgression,"
The same is companion to a destroyer.

25 He who is of a proud heart stirs up strife,
But he who trusts in the LORD will be prospered.

26 He who trusts in his own heart is a fool,
But whoever walks wisely will be delivered.

27 He who gives to the poor will not lack,
But he who hides his eyes will have many curses.

28 When the wicked arise, men hide themselves;
But when they perish, the righteous increase.

Chapter 28

28:1. A driver may fear even when he hasn't done anything wrong. He looks in his rear view mirror and sees a car with a ski rack on the roof. Thinking it is a police car with a light bar on the roof, he slows down, even if there are no flashing lights. Anyone who consistently obeys the law doesn't have to worry about the police.

Wasn't it Shakespeare who said, "Conscience doth make cowards of us all"?

28:2. When a country is characterized by law-breaking, you can expect a weak government with many rulers, one after another. The Northern Kingdom of Israel had 19 kings and 9 dynasties in a little over 200 years. One king reigned only one month, another only 6 months. All the kings were evil. You can read all about it in 1 Kings 12:25–2 Kings 17:41.

One godly king can use his knowledge and understanding to bring prolonged righteousness to a kingdom.

28:3. A poor man who oppresses others like him is like a driving rain that flattens the crop. Rain should help the crop, not destroy it. The poor man should help other poor people who do not have enough to eat. But some even rob their own parents (v. 24).

In the concentration camp at Auschwitz, some of the prisoners became turncoats, serving the Nazis by becoming capos, that is guards over their own countrymen. Often these capos were more cruel than the Nazi guards. And often they suffered the same fate as their prisoners.

28:4. People who flout the law exalt the wicked. Isaiah 5:20 pronounces a woe upon those who call evil good and good evil. Those who honor the law rebuke evil-doers. In other words, you judge a person's character by his attitude to the law.

28:5. Evil men don't understand the necessity of justice whereas the righteous appreciate it. The expression *"do not understand"* means they haven't a clue as to the importance of justice in any stable society.

28:6. A poor saint is better than a rich sinner, just as integrity is better than perversity. An honest car dealer is greatly to be desired over a crooked one.

28:7. A son who is law abiding has good insight. The son who spends his life eating, drinking, carousing, and sowing his wild oats is a disgrace to his father. Luke 15:13 attributes such activities to the prodigal son.

28:8. If you get rich by usury and extortion, you might see your money go to someone who would use it honestly, such as by helping the poor. Here is a possible example. A man becomes wealthy by illegal means. The law catches up with him and he is required to pay a heavy fine. The fine goes to the government and some of it is distributed to citizens who are in need of financial help.

Money is circulating all the time. The Lord is able to control its ebb and flow and to channel it to accomplish His purposes.

It was forbidden for a Jew to charge interest when lending to a fellow Jew (Lev. 25:35-38). Since that was true for a Jew living under law, how much more should it be true for a Christian living under grace!

28:9. A person who refuses to hear and obey the law prays in vain. His prayers don't reach heaven (Ps. 66:18; Isa. 1:15). Think of the law here as referring to the Word of God. 2 Timothy 4:4 warns of the time when men will no longer listen to sound doctrine, but will still be religious.

When you read the book of Proverbs, it may surprise you to find little emphasis on prayer.

When believing parents like Solomon advise their children, you would think that prayer would occupy a prominent place. But in this book it is largely missing. (15:8b; 29; 28:9; 30:7-9).

Actually the Old Testament saints did not enjoy a sense of personal intimacy with the Lord. No Jew living under the law called God by the name of Father.

There were a few notable exceptions to this lack of direct and free communion with God – men such as Abraham, Moses, David and Daniel. But prayer seems to have been the prerogative of the priests.

This all changed with the coming of Christ. Now when a person is saved, the indwelling Holy Spirit teaches him to speak to God as *"Abba Father."* *"Abba"* is the word Jewish children use to say "Daddy." It is a shockingly familiar way of addressing Him (Gal. 4:6), but it is the privilege of those who are in His family.

So if Solomon were writing the Proverbs today, he would doubtlessly train his sons and daughters to be people of prayer.

28:10. Whoever tempts a good person to sin will be trapped by his own wickedness (26:27). The Lord Jesus said, *"Whoever causes one of these little ones who believe in Me to sin, it would be better for him if a millstone were hung around his neck, and he were drowned in the depth of the sea"* (Matt. 18:6).

The other side of the proverb says that people with good character can expect blessings.

28:11. A rich man who lacks wisdom actually thinks he is a fountainhead of wisdom. He attributes his riches to his own cleverness. He doesn't realize that God is testing him.

A poor man who is wise can see through the lofty pretensions of the conceited man of wealth.

Hans Christian Anderson illustrates this proverb in "The Emperor's New Clothes." This particular emperor ordered his tailor to make him a suit of surpassing beauty. The tailor, a shady character from the get go, decided to make a suit that would be pure fiction. It would exist only in the minds of the emperor and his people. He took measurements, and then went through all the actions involved in pretending to weave, cut and sew. He often worked late into the night. A parade was scheduled for the emperor's birthday. The people were limp with anticipation and curiosity. The bubble of excitement burst when a little boy in the crowd bravely announced, "The emperor is naked."[33]

With knowledge and understanding a poor man can challenge a conceited rich man. He can see how poor the rich man really is. The Lord often uses the most unlikely agents to deflate the pride of the pompous.

Belshazzar was wise in his own eyes, but it took a humble

33 Anderson, *The Emperor's New Clothes*, New York: Harcourt Brace & Company, 1998.

nobody like Daniel to decode the handwriting on the wall (Dan. 5:29). Incidentally, Daniel wasn't at the party socializing. He was separated from them. They had to send for him. Good example.

In his book *Rich Christians in an Age of Hunger*, Ronald Sider gave this withering description of the rich fool:

> The rich fool is the epitome of the covetous person. He has a greedy compulsion to acquire more and more possessions even though he does not need them. And his phenomenal success at piling up more and more property leads to the blasphemous conclusion that material possessions can satisfy all his needs. From the divine perspective, however, this attitude is sheer madness. He is a raving fool.[34]

28:12. When godly men are in authority, a country enjoys great honor. When wicked men come to power, the populace hides in fear. A righteous ruler creates a sense of peace and safety. A tyrant sends the populace scurrying for a hiding place.

28:13. One who refuses to confess his sins does not progress spiritually (Ps. 32:3-4). Achan fits this description; he covered his transgression (Josh. 7:21). It is the one who confesses and forsakes his sins who finds forgiveness. David fits here (Ps. 32:5). When he confessed, *"I have sinned,"* the prophet Nathan said, *"The Lord also has put away your sin"* (2 Sam. 12:11).

Why is it so hard to confess when we have done wrong? It's because of pride. Yet it is the pathway to blessing.

Note in this verse that confession is not all. We must confess and forsake the sin. True confession includes the intention of refraining from doing it again.

Here we pause to consider what the Scriptures teach about confession. First of all, we deal with confession to God. A sinner receives judicial forgiveness from the penalty of his sins when he repents and believes on the Lord Jesus Christ. A believer receives parental forgiveness of his daily sins when he confesses

---

34 Ronald J. Sider, *Rich Christians in an Age of Hunger*, 1997, Nashville: Thomas Nelson

them to God (1 Jn. 1:9).

Confession should be prompt. I shouldn't go to God with a gift until I have been forgiven by the one I have wronged (Matt. 5:23-24). My access to God is interrupted until I have made things right.

- Confession should not be conditional or vague ("If I have done anything wrong").
- It should be personal (I, not we or they).
- It should be absolute ("I was wrong.")
- It should call the sin by its name rather than trivializing it ("Gossip," not "indiscretion").
- It should not criticize or implicate anyone else.

Clever phrases like "I'm sorry you were offended" are neither apologies nor confessions.

28:14. The Lord has a special blessing for those who fear His chastening. The person who hardens his heart, refusing to confess, is asking for trouble.

28:15. A tyrannical ruler over poor people is like a ferocious lion and bear. Both of these animals terrorize and destroy.

28:16. A ruler who oppresses the poor in order to get rich shortens his days in office. One who is not greedy for wealth can look forward to a long reign.

28:17. A person guilty of murder will eventually get caught and punished. No one should provide him refuge or try to have him exonerated. Let the law take its course.

Years ago a man named Daniel Mann was found guilty of murder and sentenced to die. While awaiting execution, he was converted to Christ, and in the days following, he became a phenomenally bright student of the Word.

There were considerable efforts to have his sentence reduced to life in prison. However, his spiritual guides felt that he should die. They based it on this verse, *"Let no one help him."* Daniel Mann agreed, and he was executed.

28:18. A blameless person saves himself from the results of sin. Blameless doesn't mean sinless. It means consistently righteous and good. It means that when he has done something wrong, he is quick to repent. The crooked one inevitably gets his comeuppance.

28:19. The farmer who faithfully tills his land is assured of an adequate food supply. The one who neglects his crops and lives for pleasure is assured of poverty sooner or later.

28:20. Anyone who is faithful in obeying the Word of the Lord will be richly rewarded, but the one whose goal is to get rich quick will pay for it.

28:21. Showing respect of persons is wrong (24:23), yet some of the best people can be bought with something as trivial as a crust of bread.

A TV program sent a man dressed like a homeless beggar to buy an expensive car. No one hurried to wait on him. Finally a salesman came to him reluctantly. The same man went and changed into expensive clothes, then drove up in a Ferrari. All the salesmen raced out to serve him. That's what human nature is like, but it should not be what the Christian is like.

There are those who show favoritism to someone who is wealthy, famous, or attractive (Jas. 2:1-9). But partiality isn't the only sin that some will commit for a crust of bread.

- Esau sold his birthright for a bowl of red beans (Gen. 25:30-34; Heb. 12:16).
- There are businessmen who will barter their integrity for a crooked deal.
- Or a young Christian who will swap his or her purity for a moment of passion.
- The media discovers an evangelical minister in a compromising situation and it becomes national news.
- A undercover policewoman in a sting operation arrests a preacher for soliciting sex from her.
- A young fellow brought up in a Christian home turns his back on Christ in order to be recognized as a scholar.

The precious Lord Jesus is still sold for a trifle. The South African poet William Blane expressed it well in the second half of his poem "Thirty Pieces of Silver":

It may not be for silver,
It may not be for gold,
But still by tens of thousands
Is this precious Saviour sold.
Sold for a godless friendship,
Sold for a selfish aim,
Sold for a fleeting trifle,
Sold for an empty name,
Sold in the mart of Science,
Sold in the seat of Power,
Sold at the shrine of Fortune,
Sold in Pleasure's bower
Sold where the awful bargain
None but God's eye can see!
Ponder, my soul, the question:
Shall He be sold by thee?
– William Blane, *Lays of Life and Hope*

28:22. An evil eye is the desire to become wealthy. Emerson said, "The lust of gold, unfeeling and remorseless, is the last corruption of degenerate man." Poverty is apt to be the result.

Our Lord said that those who lay up treasures on earth have an evil eye, and their whole life is full of darkness (Matt. 6:23).

28:23. A rebuke may hurt at the time it is spoken but afterwards the recipient may be grateful for it. It has been a help to him. Flattery is not a kindness, now or later.

Gordon MacDonald said that he understood this proverb.

> "I am thankful to my wife and other special friends
> who play the position of rebuker. In the end people
> appreciate frankness more than flattery."[35]

28:24. The son who robs his parents and admits no wrong destroys their livelihood and their peace of mind. This reminds us of a Jewish tradition when Jesus was on earth. If a father needed financial help, all the son had to do was say *"Corban."*

---

35 Gordon MavDonald, *Restoring Your Spiritual Passion*, Nashville :Thomas Nelson. 1986, pp.192-3.

This meant that anything that the son might have given to help his father had been dedicated to the temple. It doesn't mean that the temple ever got it. The mere utterance of the word relieved the son of any obligation to help his dad. It excused him from obeying the Fourth Commandment, *"Honor your father and your mother."* Thus the son made void the Word of God by this inexcusable tradition (Mark 7:8-13).

28:25. Show me a proud person and I will show you a troublemaker. What is the connection between pride and trouble? Perhaps it is that a proud person is play-acting, pretending to be greater than he is. He is forever keeping up appearances. Anything that interferes with his charade angers him.

Show me a contented believer and I will show you a spiritually wealthy saint. He doesn't have to put on airs. He is satisfied with what he has in Christ. Trust in the Lord and you will be blessed (Ps. 2:12; Prov. 3:5).

28:26. Anyone is foolish if he trusts in his own wisdom and power. The wise way is to trust in the Lord. That brings freedom from senseless decisions. It is a hard lesson to learn (2 Cor. 1:9).

28:27. There is great reward in giving to the poor, but great loss in closing one's eyes to their hardship. This is true not only of those who are poor economically but also of those who don't have the Savior. John is uncomfortably pointed when he asks, *"But whoever has this world's goods, and sees his brother in need, and shuts up his heart from him, how does the love of God abide in him?"* (1 Jn. 3:17).

28:28. When wicked men rise to power, the people live in fear. When those rulers die, the citizens enjoy freedom and peace.

Proverbs 29

1 *He who is often rebuked, and hardens his neck,*
Will suddenly be destroyed, and that without remedy.

2 *When the righteous are in authority, the people rejoice;*
But when a wicked man rules, the people groan.

3 *Whoever loves wisdom makes his father rejoice,*
But a companion of harlots wastes his wealth.

4 *The king establishes the land by justice,*
But he who receives bribes overthrows it.

5 *A man who flatters his neighbor*
Spreads a net for his feet.

6 *By transgression an evil man is snared,*
But the righteous sings and rejoices.

7 *The righteous considers the cause of the poor,*
But the wicked does not understand such knowledge.

8 *Scoffers set a city aflame,*
But wise men turn away wrath.

9 *If a wise man contends with a foolish man,*
Whether the fool rages or laughs, there is no peace.

10 *The bloodthirsty hate the blameless,*
But the upright seek his well-being.

11 *A fool vents all his feelings,*
But a wise man holds them back.

12 *If a ruler pays attention to lies,*
All his servants become wicked.

13 *The poor man and the oppressor have this in common:*
The LORD gives light to the eyes of both.

14 *The king who judges the poor with truth,*
His throne will be established forever.

15 *The rod and rebuke give wisdom,*
But a child left to himself brings shame to his mother.

16 *When the wicked are multiplied, transgression increases;*
But the righteous will see their fall.

17 *Correct your son, and he will give you rest;*
Yes, he will give delight to your soul.

18 *Where there is no revelation, the people cast*
off restraint;
But happy is he who keeps the law.

19 *A servant will not be corrected by mere words;*
For though he understands, he will not respond.

20 *Do you see a man hasty in his words?*
There is more hope for a fool than for him.

21 *He who pampers his servant from childhood*
Will have him as a son in the end.

22 *An angry man stirs up strife,*
And a furious man abounds in transgression.

23 *A man's pride will bring him low,*
But the humble in spirit will retain honor.

24 *Whoever is a partner with a thief hates his own life;*
He swears to tell the truth, but reveals nothing.

25 *The fear of man brings a snare,*
But whoever trusts in the LORD shall be safe.

26 *Many seek the ruler's favor,*
But justice for man comes from the LORD.

27 *An unjust man is an abomination to the righteous,*
And he who is upright in the way is an abomination to
the wicked.

Chapter 29

29:1. Anyone who repeatedly refuses to listen to good advice will end up being destroyed. The more he rejects good counsel, the more calloused he becomes. This is true with regard to the gospel. Everyone hears it for the last time. There is a place where the lights go out on the way to hell. The person has passed redemption point and there is no second chance. The more one rejects the gospel, the harder it is to accept it.

Pharaoh is a classic example of a person with a stiff neck and a hardened heart. Nine plagues failed to force him to let the Israelites go.

29:2. A righteous ruler means peace and tranquility for his people. They rejoice. When a scoundrel comes to power, they groan. Queen Victoria's 64 year reign was a blessing to Great Britain. Hitler, Stalin and Mao brought tyranny and repression to their countries.

29:3. A sensible son brings joy to his father, but one who frequents a harlot's parlor dissipates his father's money. The prodigal son fits the latter part of this proverb. After getting his share of the inheritance, he wasted it in riotous living. His brother was more specific. He said, "[Your son] *has devoured your livelihood with harlots*" (Luke 15:30).

29:4. The king who promotes justice by refusing graft has a well-established government. One who accepts bribes undermines it. Large gifts to a candidate's election campaign are a favorite way of winning his favor and support.

29:5. When you flatter someone, it is not a kindness. It is a trap that prepares him for a fall. Flattery is designed to win favor and affection, but it is dishonest and destructive. There is a huge difference between flattery and praise. Flattery is a deceitful compliment. Praise is deserved commendation. Have you praised your spouse and children lately?

29:6. Those who transgress bring sorrow and trouble on themselves, and they get caught sooner or later. Godly people have reason to rejoice and be glad. There is no condemnation for them (Rom. 8:1). They can sing:

> Death and judgment are behind me,
> Grace and glory lie before.
> All the billows rolled o'er Jesus;
> There they spent their utmost power.
> – Author Unknown

29:7. Good men, especially good rulers, are concerned about the plight of the poor. Others shut their eyes to such need. The Apostle John says that care for the poor is a proof that we love God (1 Jn. 3:17). *"The wicked do not understand such knowledge"* in the sense that they do not see the importance of caring for the poor.

Here again we are impressed with God's concern for the poor. His Son was born in poverty. He lived in poverty. He died in poverty.

As we go through life, sometimes the Lord appears to us in the guise of a poor person. The way we treat that person is the way we treat the Savior. It is true of a church also. If it treats a poor believer with cold indifference, that is the way it welcomes Jesus. We must not choose believers with whom to fellowship based on their rank or riches.

In his book *My Utmost for His Highest*, Oswald Chambers wrote:

> In the spiritual life, beware of walking according to natural affinities. Everyone has natural affinities; some people we like and some people we do not like. We must never let those likes and dislikes rule in our Christian life. If we 'walk in the light' as God is in the light, God will give us communion with people for whom we have no natural affinity.[36]

Along the same line, missionary David Croudace reminds us:

---

36 Quoted in *Our Daily Bread*, reading for December 2004.

"Like the Jewish believers in the early church, we are in danger of only reaching out to people of the same social strata as ourselves and forgetting those *"other sheep"* (John 10:16) for whom Christ died. They may be down in the inner city or out in some village across the sea. As the Lord lays the finishing touches to His church, He still says, *"other sheep...I must bring."* Will we be part of His work or will we sail along on a bed of ease with our social peers?"

29:8. Government officials, who mock at sin as if it weren't serious, mislead a city and bring trouble on it. Wise rulers act as stabilizers and peacemakers, dealing with all lawlessness. They save their city from punishment.

Think how the world scoffs at sin today. Men are loud in their defense of abortion, same-sex marriage, homosexuality and live-in partners. They are against family values, the idea of absolute truth, and evangelical Christianity. Any other religion is tolerated. By all this they are inviting divine punishment, and it will come.

If the Lord had found ten righteous men in Sodom, He would have spared the city (Gen. 18:32). Instead He found scoffers. They doomed Sodom to destruction (Gen. 19:24).

29:9. A wise man may try to help a fool, but no matter how the latter responds, nothing changes. The fool may become angry or he may consider it a joke and try to laugh it off. Either way, he continues as he has always been – a fool.

29:10. Bloodthirsty criminals hate an upright person and seek his life (RV). Cain illustrates the first part of the verse; he killed righteous Abel. King Saul sought to kill David, but David had men who were willing to die for him.

29:11. A fool shows no restraint in expressing himself (27:3-4), whereas a wise person holds back from venting his passions. In today's lingo, the fool "runs off at the mouth." A sensible person thinks before he speaks.

29:12. If a ruler listens to liars, soon his whole court will be full of them. They will think that that is the best way of gaining his favor. This shows the importance of choosing courtiers carefully.

29:13. This world is a class society. There are oppressors and oppressed; rich and poor; bond and free. But in one respect we are all on the same level. God has given us life and light. What do the poor man and the oppressor have in common? They have life, intelligence, emotions, and speech. They have sight, hearing, touch, taste, and can smell. In this proverb light to the eyes could mean eyesight but more probably it is a figurative expression for knowledge of God's existence, responsibility to Him, and knowledge of the difference between right and wrong.

29:14. A ruler who treats the poor with equity has an enduring kingdom. Everlasting here means long lasting. David was promised an everlasting kingdom, a promise that is fulfilled in Christ, David's descendant.

29:15. Parents should train their children to obey; they should not allow them to do as they please. An uncorrected child, one who does whatever he wants, or who gets his own way when there is a conflict with his parents, will bring shame to his mother. Among those who qualify for this dubious distinction are Samson (Jud. 14:1-3); Hophni and Phinehas, the sons of Eli (1 Sam. 2:12-17; 3:13); and the sons of Samuel (1 Sam. 8:1-5).

There are parents who refuse to discipline children, as if the young ones can do no wrong. Even if their son is arrested for some crime, they take sides with him against the police. By their ungodly permissiveness, they raise a rebellious monster.

29:16. As a wicked population increases, there is an inevitable increase in crimes. However, good people will see the downfall of transgressors. Sodom is an example. Isaiah 66:24 gives another.

29:17. Parents who faithfully correct their son are assured that he will give them rest, and they will be proud of him. Modern psychology often disagrees, but God's Word is true.

29:18. Where there is no revelation from the Lord, no prophetic ministry, the people practice lawlessness. When Samuel began to minister, *"The word of the Lord was rare; there was no widespread revelation"* (1 Sam. 3:1). The result was that everyone did that which was right in his own eyes. It was a sad time in the history of Israel.

Yet even in such times of anarchy, there is a blessing for the remnant who know the law and obey it. Prophetic ministry teaches and exhorts people to obey the Lord (1 Cor. 14:3). God always preserves a faithful remnant.

29:19. A servant (employee) doesn't always respond to a mere verbal rebuke. He understands what is said, but is unwilling to change. It might help him to change if you dock his pay, put him on report, or fire him.

29:20. If a man's tongue outruns his thought, he is more hopeless than a fool. The man says things that are wild and grossly unreasonable. In the heat of anger he may say something that lands him in jail. The average fool is more restrained.

29:21. Don't pamper a slave from his childhood. Otherwise he may claim an inheritance as if he were a son. God suits people for their position in life. We should recognize differences in mentality and levels of competence in work.

29:22. Anger and strife go together. So do furious outbursts and transgression. Think of the trouble that anger produces in families, neighborhoods, business, and governments.

29:23. Pride doesn't exalt a person. Humility does. *"Therefore humble yourself under the mighty hand of God, that He may exalt you in due time"* (Jas. 5:6).

29:24. A thief's partner is sure to fail. He swears to tell the truth in court but does not reveal it. If he tells the truth, he incurs the wrath and possible revenge of the thief. If he doesn't tell the truth and is caught, he bears the penalty of the law.

> O what a tangled web we weave
> When first we practice to deceive!
> – Sir Walter Scott

29:25. It is foolish to fear man; it brings a trap. It keeps us from witnessing for the Lord Jesus. It prevents us from taking a bold stand for what is right. The trap is our lips. They snap shut when we fear man. Better to trust the Lord and say or do what is right (Ps. 34:4; 118:6; Isa. 51:12). Someone said that the fear of the Lord delivers us from the fear of men.

29:26. A ruler may have many courtiers, but don't look for justice from these yes-men. Justice comes from the Lord. A law professor said, "If you want law, go to law school; if you want justice, go to seminary."

29:27. Decent people and disreputable ones are repulsive to each other. A truly wicked person is repugnant to Christians, but that has to be moderated by New Testament standards. When a person becomes a believer, he no longer looks on the unsaved as disgusting sinners (2 Cor. 5:1). Rather he sees them as people whom God loves and for whom Christ died. He sees them as potential worshipers of the Lord Jesus for all eternity, and seeks to win them to faith in Him. Christians are an abomination to the wicked. People of the world *"think it very strange that* [Christians] *no longer join with them in their riotous excess, and accordingly say all kinds of abusive things about* [them]" (1 Pet. 4:4, JBP). The contrast between them proves convicting. They call believers hypocrites, holier-than-thou, narrow minded, and out of touch with modern culture and scholarship. It is a privilege to be scorned for Christ's sake.

Proverbs 30

1 *The words of Agur the son of Jakeh, his utterance.*
This man declared to Ithiel—to Ithiel and Ucal:

2 *Surely I am more stupid than any man,*
And do not have the understanding of a man.

3 *I neither learned wisdom*
Nor have knowledge of the Holy One.

4 *Who has ascended into heaven, or descended?*
Who has gathered the wind in His fists?
Who has bound the waters in a garment?
Who has established all the ends of the earth?
What is His name, and what is His Son's name,
If you know?

5 *Every word of God is pure;*
He is a shield to those who put their trust in Him.

6 *Do not add to His words,*
Lest He rebuke you, and you be found a liar.

7 *Two things I request of You*
(Deprive me not before I die):

8 *Remove falsehood and lies far from me;*
Give me neither poverty nor riches—
Feed me with the food allotted to me;

9 *Lest I be full and deny You,*
And say, "Who is the LORD?"
Or lest I be poor and steal,
And profane the name of my God.

10 *Do not malign a servant to his master,*
Lest he curse you, and you be found guilty.

11 *There is a generation that curses its father,*
And does not bless its mother.

12 There is a generation that is pure in its own eyes,
Yet is not washed from its filthiness.

13 There is a generation—oh, how lofty are their eyes!
And their eyelids are lifted up.

14 There is a generation whose teeth are like swords,
And whose fangs are like knives,
To devour the poor from off the earth,
And the needy from among men.

15 The leech has two daughters—
Give and Give!
There are three things that are never satisfied,
Four never say, "Enough!":

16 The grave,
The barren womb,
The earth that is not satisfied with water—
And the fire never says, "Enough!"

17 The eye that mocks his father,
And scorns obedience to his mother,
The ravens of the valley will pick it out,
And the young eagles will eat it.

18 There are three things which are too wonderful for me,
Yes, four which I do not understand:

19 The way of an eagle in the air,
The way of a serpent on a rock,
The way of a ship in the midst of the sea,
And the way of a man with a virgin.

20 This is the way of an adulterous woman:
She eats and wipes her mouth,
And says, "I have done no wickedness."

21 For three things the earth is perturbed,
Yes, for four it cannot bear up:

22 For a servant when he reigns,
A fool when he is filled with food,

23 A hateful woman when she is married,
And a maidservant who succeeds her mistress.

24 There are four things which are little on the earth,
But they are exceedingly wise:

25 The ants are a people not strong,
Yet they prepare their food in the summer;

26 The rock badgers are a feeble folk,
Yet they make their homes in the crags;

27 The locusts have no king,
Yet they all advance in ranks;

28 The spider skillfully grasps with its hands,
And it is in kings' palaces.

29 There are three things which are majestic in pace,
Yes, four which are stately in walk:

30 A lion, which is mighty among beasts
And does not turn away from any;

31 A greyhound,
A male goat also,
And a king whose troops are with him.

32 If you have been foolish in exalting yourself,
Or if you have devised evil, put your hand on
your mouth.

33 For as the churning of milk produces butter,
And wringing the nose produces blood,
So the forcing of wrath produces strife.

Chapter 30

The wisdom of Agur

30:1. Here we are introduced to Agur, another author. All that we know about him is that he was the son of Jakeh, and that he declared these precepts to Ithiel and Ucal. The identity of these people is also unknown. Speculation is useless.

30:2-3. Agur introduces himself with unusual humility. He confesses that he is the most ignorant of any man as far as the knowledge of God is concerned. All the questions that follow have to do with God. Agur can be excused for his ignorance. He did not have a Bible.

30:4. There are five things that puzzle him. The first question may be related to Deuteronomy 30:12 where it refers to the law. You don't have to travel to heaven to get it. It is readily accessible. Paul also quoted this question in Romans 10:6-7 where it refers to the gospel. You don't have to bring Christ down. That would be impossible and unnecessary because He already came down in incarnation. You don't have to descend to the abyss to bring Christ up. That, too, would be impossible. And it would be unnecessary because Christ has risen from the dead. All you have to do is confess Jesus as Lord and believe that God raised Him from the dead and you will be saved.

So the answer to the first question is God. God is also the answer to the second question. Only He can gather the wind in His fists. He is the one who bound the waters in a garment of clouds (Gen. 9:14) and bound the oceans with land masses (Gen. 1:9-10).

He is the one who established the ends of the earth (Gen. 1:10).

The question *"What is His name, and what is His Son's name?"* means, "Who is He, and who is His Son?"

This is a surprising reference to God's Son. There is no other Old Testament reference to His Son until later in the time of Daniel. One like the Son of God appeared to Shadrach,

Meshach and Abed-Nego in the fiery furnace, and was seen by Nebuchadnezzar (Dan. 3:25).

30:5-6. Every word of God is true and trustworthy. The Bible is inspired by God (2 Tim. 3:16). Inspiration extends to the very words (1 Cor. 2:13). The Bible contains the faith once-for-all delivered to the saints (Jude 3). It is complete, and a curse rests on those who add to it or take away from it (Deut. 4:2; Rev. 22:18-19).

30:7-9. Agur has only two requests on his prayer list. First, he asks that he be saved from every form of falsehood. Then he asks that his daily needs be supplied. If he had more than enough, he might become self-sufficient and forget the Lord. If he didn't have enough, he might steal and thus blame God for his poverty.

As Agur grew spiritually, his prayers should have included worship, confession, God's interests, needs of others, and thanksgiving.

30:10. As an example of falsehood, Agur warns against falsely accusing a servant to his master. He might take the case to court and the accuser might be found guilty. A New Testament verse similar to this proverb is Romans 14:4. *"Who are you to judge another's servant? To his own master he stands or falls."* There is a chain of command in every segment of society. To interfere in a segment that is not your own is unacceptable.

Slander is an old-fashioned weapon out of the armory of hell, and is still in plentiful use. No matter how holy a man may be, there will be some who will defame him. "Give a dog an ill name, and hang him;" but glory be to God, the Lord's people are not dogs, and their ill names do not injure them. "And such as breathe out cruelty." It is their vital breath to hate the good; they cannot speak without cursing them; such was Paul before conversion. They who breathe out cruelty may well expect to be sent to breathe their native air in hell; let persecutors beware![37]

30:11. In the rest of the chapter, Agur seems to describe some dominant features of the age in which he lived. His age was life as he found it, his world view. It is guilty of abuse of

---

37   C.H. Spurgeon, *Treasury of David*, Vol. II, Grand Rapids:Baker Book House, 1983, p. 5

parents and ingratitude to them, boasting of moral purity when actually filthy, full of unjustified pride and violent oppression of the poor.

The prevalence of sin was conspicuous. Notice that he first mentions parental abuse. It is not limited to our generation as we might think. Even in Agur's day it was widely practiced.

To illustrate the generation that is pure in its own eyes, consider the story of the ruler who decided to visit a prison and examine the conditions there. As he came to each inmate, he asked, "And why are you here?"

One after another answered that he was innocent. His trial was unjust. The witnesses were prejudiced against his race. His public defender was incompetent. To put it bluntly, he was getting a bum rap. It was late in the day when the ruler asked yet another prisoner why he was there. The man replied, "I am guilty of the crime for which I was tried. I am serving time because I committed armed robbery. I pled guilty as charged."

The ruler turned to the jailer and said, "Get this man out of the prison before he corrupts all the good people who are here." And the man was released.

30:12. Then there was no conviction of sin. People denied that they had done anything wrong. Perhaps they argued that sin is a sickness. Or they might have insisted that there are no absolutes. They may have excused their behavior by pleading that "everyone's doing it." Claiming purity, their filthiness clung to them.

30:13. Agur observed that pride was endemic. It characterized the generation. Though their thought-life was impure, their eyes were lifted up in self-worship.

30:14. The same generation violently plunders the poor so that they find it impossible to cope. The result is that the rich grow richer and the poor grow poorer.

30:15. Leeches have a seemingly inexhaustible thirst for blood. In that respect they are like the spirit of the world. It always wants more. Only when we have Christ can we say:

Now none but Christ can satisfy;
None other name for me;
There's love and life and lasting joy,
Lord Jesus, found in Thee.
— B.D. Arr. 19th Century

At the beginning of this book, Solomon mentioned that he would help us to understand enigmas and riddles (v.6). We have already mentioned Proverbs 11:24 as an enigma but where are the riddles? Verses 15 through 33 may not be the riddles, but they certainly are perplexing. On the face of them they are quite understandable, but we keep suspecting that there is a deeper meaning and connection below the surface.

30:16. This continues the thought from verse 15. It is not only bloodsuckers that want more. It is true of four inanimate things that are never satisfied. The grave never tires of accepting the dead. The barren woman never loses her desire for a baby. The land seems to have an endless ability to absorb rain. Fire never refuses fuel.

A labor union official was asked what he wanted for his men. He replied, "More."

30:17. It was a mark of lasting disgrace for a Jew if he did not have a decent burial, that is, if his corpse was exposed to the elements, only to be eaten by scavenger birds.

The proverb says that this would be a fitting reward for sons and daughters who treat their parents with contempt.

Actually there is no record in the Bible for this sentence being carried out on those who were guilty. But the warning is there. If you treat your parents shamefully, you will suffer enduring shame.

30:18. No description of life as it is would be complete without mentioning the marvels that are around us.

30:19. An eagle in the air deals with the wonder of flight. It introduces the whole subject of aeronautics. The serpent on a rock is able to move without legs or wings. What locomotive powers make this possible? A sailing ship moves majestically through the sea, driven by the invisible hand of the wind. The way of a man with a maid – we don't know if this refers to courtship or marriage. In the absence of such knowledge the best we can say is that love is often a mystery.

All four wonders function without leaving a trace.

30:20. Also amazing but morally evil is the ability of an adulterous woman to sin, then wipe her mouth and disclaim having done anything wrong. This verse may be linked to the previous verse. The seductress leaves no trace. It is the last mention of the immoral woman in the book.

30:21. Now Agur mentions four misfits in our world.

30:22. A servant doesn't know how to be an effective leader. When a fool has overeaten, he becomes a bigger fool.

30:23. When a mean-spirited woman finally succeeds in getting married, she behaves without class or grace. So it is that when a maid succeeds her mistress, she is a misfit. She is overbearing and vain.

30:24. Agur's world view includes the observation that there are creatures that are wise beyond their size. He mentions:

30:25. Ants are small and weak, yet they prepare their food before winter comes. Not all ants hibernate, but they have the sense to store food for the time when they can't gather it.

This of course does not justify Christians in laying up treasure on earth, which the Lord has specifically prohibited (Matt. 6:19). The thought here is the simple supply of current needs.

30:26. Rock badgers are also feeble but wise. Making their home in the crags, they are safe from predators. Christians find safety in the cleft Rock of Ages. (Badgers here may refer to the coney. Exact identification is unsure.)

30:27. Locusts move with military precision yet without any visible commander. When guided by the Holy Spirit, believers may do likewise.

30:28. The spider mentioned is the Hebrew word *semamiyth*, and may actually be a gecko or lizard. At any rate, it finds its way into unlikely places such as a royal palace. Agur was probably surprised to see this happen to wise people. The Apostle Paul was able to reach people in Caesar's household (Phil. 4:22).

30:29. Agur closes his description of life in this world with mention of four creatures who walk with stately majesty.

30:30. There is the lion, the king of beasts. It walks with confident stateliness, fearing no attack.

30:31. The so-called greyhound's exact identity is unknown, being a composite of 2 Hebrew words meaning literally slender or girded, and hips or loins. It may refer to an animal now extinct or unknown. The greyhound is tall, slender, and stately. It has grace that is not common to alley dogs.

Then there is the mountain goat, first silhouetted on a lofty mountain precipice, then descending with surefooted precision.

Finally there is a king, marching at the head of his loyal troops. He can be confidently serene because he knows there is no plot to overthrow him.

30:32. The last two verses seem to be totally disconnected to what has gone before. They describe a proud person who is concocting some evil plot. He should hinder it from ever escaping his mouth.

Here the culprit is one who is forever singing his own praises, trying to exalt himself, and advocating some evil project. His suggestions are not welcome but that doesn't stop him. He is a constant irritation to those around him. They endure his persistence and pushiness but nerves become frayed. The atmosphere grows tense. He ought to shut his mouth.

God's advice to Baruch, Jeremiah's servant, was as follows, *"And seekest thou great things for thyself? Seek them not"* (Jer. 45:5).

30:33. Continued agitation will act like the churning of cream and twisting or continued hard blowing of the nose. The one produces butter and the other a nosebleed. The forcing of wrath, that is, badgering another person with arguments, criticisms and threats, will result in anger and strife.

If he doesn't cease and desist, the people will feel that they are being churned like butter and wrung out like a bleeding nose. Eventually the result will be that the constant agitation breaks out in strife.

Proverbs 31

1 *The words of King Lemuel,*
the utterance which his mother taught him:

2 *What, my son?*
And what, son of my womb?
And what, son of my vows?

3 *Do not give your strength to women,*
Nor your ways to that which destroys kings.

4 *It is not for kings, O Lemuel,*
It is not for kings to drink wine,
Nor for princes intoxicating drink;

5 *Lest they drink and forget the law,*
And pervert the justice of all the afflicted.

6 *Give strong drink to him who is perishing,*
And wine to those who are bitter of heart.

7 *Let him drink and forget his poverty,*
And remember his misery no more.

8 *Open your mouth for the speechless,*
In the cause of all who are appointed to die.

9 *Open your mouth, judge righteously,*
And plead the cause of the poor and needy.

10 *Who can find a virtuous wife?*
For her worth is far above rubies.

11 *The heart of her husband safely trusts her;*
So he will have no lack of gain.

12 *She does him good and not evil*
All the days of her life.

13 *She seeks wool and flax,*
And willingly works with her hands.

14 *She is like the merchant ships,*
She brings her food from afar.

15 *She also rises while it is yet night,*
And provides food for her household,
And a portion for her maidservants.

16 *She considers a field and buys it;*
From her profits she plants a vineyard.

17 *She girds herself with strength,*
And strengthens her arms.

18 *She perceives that her merchandise is good,*
And her lamp does not go out by night.

19 *She stretches out her hands to the distaff,*
And her hand holds the spindle.

20 *She extends her hand to the poor,*
Yes, she reaches out her hands to the needy.

21 *She is not afraid of snow for her household,*
For all her household is clothed with scarlet.

22 *She makes tapestry for herself;*
Her clothing is fine linen and purple.

23 *Her husband is known in the gates,*
When he sits among the elders of the land.

24 *She makes linen garments and sells them,*
And supplies sashes for the merchants.

25 *Strength and honor are her clothing;*
She shall rejoice in time to come.

26 *She opens her mouth with wisdom,*
And on her tongue is the law of kindness.

27 *She watches over the ways of her household,*
And does not eat the bread of idleness.

28 *Her children rise up and call her blessed;*
Her husband also, and he praises her:

29 *"Many daughters have done well,*
But you excel them all."

30 *Charm is deceitful and beauty is passing,*
But a woman who fears the LORD,
she shall be praised.

31 *Give her of the fruit of her hands,*
And let her own works praise her in the gates.

Chapter 31

The words of King Lemuel's mother (31:1-9)

31:1. We do not know who King Lemuel was, but we are indebted to his mother for this chapter containing some of the best advice she could give him.

31:2. The three *"what's"* in this verse mean, "What is the best advice I can give to you, the son of my vows to God?" Apparently she had dedicated him to the Lord when he was born. Who can estimate the power of a mother's prayers?

31:3. The first is a warning against sexual immorality, a sin that destroys kings as well as men in all other walks of life. David and Solomon come to mind here.

31:4-7. The second bit of counsel is to avoid excessive use of wine. Kings should practice moderation. They need clear minds in order to make intelligent decisions.

Wine is prescribed here for a dying person or one who is depressed. Let him drink and forget his poverty and gloom. Obviously wine does not mean grape juice as some insist.

31:8-9. Lemuel should speak up for those who can't defend themselves, whether they are condemned to die or are poor and needy. He should be impartial in his judgments.

The excellent wife (31:10-31)

We are not sure who wrote the rest of the chapter. Perhaps it was the queen mother. Some think it was Solomon, but it hardly fits his harem existence with 700 wives and 300 concubines. Maybe it was some other sage. To most readers it doesn't matter. They just accept it in simple faith as the Word of God.

Someone has pointed out that the church should behave as a virtuous woman towards her Lord.

31:10.Verses 10-31 are an acrostic, with each verse beginning with the consecutive letters of the Hebrew alphabet. Verse 10 asks a sort of rhetorical question. A virtuous woman is a real find. There are many stones, but not all are precious. There are many women, but not all are virtuous. Ruth was called a virtuous woman in Ruth 3:11. Remember, the word is *"virtuous,"* not cute, rich, famous, from an important family, highly educated, etc. None of these things can make up for a lack of virtue.

One lesson to take from this section is that a man should choose a wife carefully and base his choice on something deeper than beauty, social position or family name. The writer here may be giving a portrait of an ideal wife, or describing someone he knows. Hopefully the author doesn't mean that the wife has to have all these virtues. Otherwise there might be fewer women who could qualify. For many women, it may be exhausting just to read of this virtuous woman's daily schedule. She really is a jewel.

31:11-12. Her husband has reason to be utterly confident in her as a virtuous woman. In the world they say, "Never give a woman your credit card or checkbook." But this godly woman is completely trustworthy. Rather than spending all his money, she increases the family income. She does him good all the days of her life. Her goodness is constant.

31:13-14. She purchases wool and flax, happily working with her hands to make clothing and accessories. She shops around for food like a merchant ship.

31:15. While it is still dark, she rises to prepare food for her family and for any helpers she may have. Here she rises early and in verse 18 she stays up late. She reminds us of the Lord Jesus, who came not to be served, but to serve (Mark 10:45).

31:16. Now she is carefully considering the purchase of a property to add to her farm. With some of her profit, she buys grapevine plants for a vineyard.

31:17-18. The harder she works, the stronger she gets. She looks over her property and realizes that she is prospering. So what does she do? She continues working on into the night.

31:19. As in verse 13, she works with her hands. She is expert in using the spinning wheel and loom.

31:20. Her hands also are kind; they minister to the poor and needy. When a beggar comes to the door, she gives him food or clothing, but probably not money which could be misused. None leave disappointed. Some Christian women keep gospel tracts near the door also, and include one with each gift. In Acts 9:36 and 39 we read that Dorcas had a ministry of making coats and garments for widows in her area – to whom doubtless she also witnessed.

31:21. She does not fear the approach of winter because there are warm clothes for the entire household.

31:22. She makes tapestry and clothing of the finest quality. The tapestry is used for heavy drapes, hangings, and upholstery. It is hand-woven. You can be sure that the clothing was appropriate for a woman of spirituality and excellence.

31:23. She is not known in public, because that is not her sphere, but her husband is well known at city hall when he sits with the leading men.

This grand lady manages the household so competently that she is able to carry on a dry goods business (v. 24) from her home and to negotiate a real estate purchase (v. 16). This frees her husband to carry on the work to which he feels called.

31:24. In her home she makes enough linen garments to have extra to sell.

31:25. She is a woman of strong godly character and honor. She will look back on her accomplishments with satisfaction.

31:26. People respect her wise conversation and love her for her kindness in speaking. She does not have a sharp tongue.

31:27. She supervises the work in her busy house, and is never idle.

There was a tea for Christian and professional ladies. The women were sharing information concerning their careers. Charlotte's turn came up. She was the mother of three stalwart sons. Someone asked, "And what do you do, Charlotte?" She looked down and answered quietly, "I raise men for God." It was true.

Thomas a Kempis said, "Never be idle or vacant. Be always reading or writing or praying or meditating or employed in some useful labor for the common good."

This woman deserves the plaudits of her husband and children. So do many housewives today whose lives are a streak of activity from day till late at night. Consider the following modern housewife's daily activities.

- She is up early to get breakfast, help the children dress, prepare a lunch for them to take, then gets them to school (in some cases different schools at different times, and in some cases she home schools them, adding "teacher" to her list of responsibilities).
- She tries to restore a measure of order to the chaos the children have left.
- The dishwasher breaks, flooding the kitchen. She arranges for a repairman to come.
- It's time to start laundering the clothes. Sometimes there are three piles a day.
- Now it's time to do the shopping. She crosses off items on a long list as she places them in the shopping cart.
- She picks up the kids from school. On some days, she takes them for music lessons, athletic activities, or for medical appointments.
- She looks for opportunities to help them memorize Scripture and to teach them social graces. Here is where they learn to be courteous and generous.
- After supper she tries to help them with their lessons when necessary.
- Then it's time to iron the clothes.
- If she home schools, she spends time grading schoolwork and preparing lessons.
- And then there's always the unexpected – a talkative neighbor dropping in for a cup of coffee or a relative arriving to stay for a few days.

Times may have changed, but the work load has not decreased. This is a modern version of the virtuous woman of Proverbs 31. Who says that housewives don't work for a living?

31:28-29. As her children grow up, they begin to realize what a treasure their mother is, and they thank her for all she has done for them. Her husband joins in praising her, saying, "There are many good wives, but you are the best of all."

31:30-31. Favor is deceitful, and beauty is vain. Character is better than beauty. Women who really believe this will invest more in character development than in cosmetics. Men who believe this will not choose a spouse based mainly on outward appearance. Marriage is not to a face but to a person, and life is lived with that person's character, day in and day out. A woman who fears the Lord is a real treasure, and is the one to be admired. Let her works be her reward and be the cause of honoring her in the city. And be sure of this, she will be richly rewarded at the Judgment Seat of Christ.

In his book *John Ploughman Talks*, Spurgeon gives his version of the virtuous wife:

> A true wife is her husband's better half, his [bundle] of delight, his flower of beauty, his guardian angel, and his heart's treasure. He says to her, "I shall in thee most happy be; in thee, my choice I do rejoice. In thee I find content of mind, God's appointment to be my contentment." In her company he finds his earthly heaven; she is the light of his home; the comfort of his soul, and (for this world) the soul of his comfort. Whatever fortune God may send him, he is rich as long as she lives.... [38]

---

38 C. H. Spurgeon, *John Ploughman Talks*, Chicago: Moody Press, n.d., p. 224.

OTHER BOOKS by William MacDonald
Published by GOSPEL FOLIO PRESS

Alone in Majesty with Study Guide

Explores God's characteristics—those unique to Him and those shared with humanity. With this in-depth Bible study, you will gain greater knowledge of God's attributes.
B-9077 | ISBN 1893579077

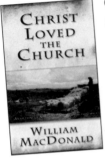

Christ Loved the Church

An outline of New Testament church principles. The Bible itself presents a clear mandate for assembly life where the true authority of the Head at God's right hand is known, loved and served. When you discover the Head of the Church in this way, you will also love His people.
B-17606 | ISBN 1897117606

The Disciple's Manual

For more than half a century, practicing and proclaiming biblical discipleship has been the author's heart-beat. This is that life's ministry captured for you in a book.
B-1860 | ISBN 1882701860

Enjoy Your Bible!

William MacDonald and Arthur Farstad
Studying God's Word should become a delight and a joy. This little volume is to help chart your own early excursions on the limitless seas of adventuring into the written Word of God.
B-EYB | ISBN 1882701585

God Still Speaks

God has spoken to us in varied ways—by creation, conscience and circumstances. This book includes 30 remarkable stories in which the Lord has spoken to people through Scripture.
B-1879 | ISBN 1882701879

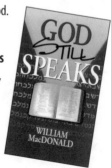

Here's the Difference

This book will bring into clear focus some of the most important teachings in the Word of God. Here's The Difference provides 96 careful biblical distinctions.
B-HTD | ISBN 1882701453

Joseph Makes Me Think of Jesus

A biography of the life of Joseph and commentary which outlines the correspondences between his life and that of the Lord Jesus.
B-1690 | ISBN 1882701690

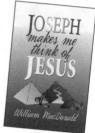

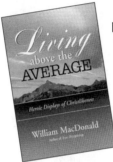

Living Above the Average

This book contains accounts of ordinary people who want God to do extraordinary things through them.
B-1763 | ISBN 1882701763

My Heart, My Life, My All

Love's response to God's ultimate sacrifice ought to be myself—a living sacrifice. This book gives the happy secret of the life on fire for God.
B-HLA | ISBN 1882701445

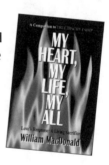

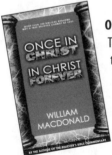

Once in Christ in Christ Forever

There are those who believe they can save themselves and those who believe they need a Saviour. This book offers 100 biblical reasons why a true believer cannot be lost.
B-OIC | ISBN 1882701437

Now That Is Amazing Grace

The well-loved classic, Amazing Grace, has stirred the hearts of millions. William MacDonald takes the reader on a thrilling expedition to discover the breath-taking heights and depths of God's amazing grace.
B-NTI | ISBN 1882701216

Our God Is Wonderful

A devotional which proclaims the wonder of God. The three sections this book covers are: His amazing creation from the vastness of the universe to the marvel of the living cell, His provisions for believers in times of need, and the ends to which He will go to redeem lost sinners.

B-OGW | ISBN 1882701607

The Wonders of God

In this devotional, the author presents an array of evidence—from creation, providence, and redemption—that God is the most wonderful Person in the universe. Know Him better, and love Him more through this stirring real-life drama all around us.

B-GGW | ISBN 1882701259

True Discipleship with Study Guide

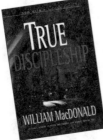

This book clearly explains the principles of New Testament discipleship. The Saviour's terms of discipleship are not only highly practical but will reward in knowing the peace that passes understanding.

B-1917 | ISBN 1882701917

Worlds Apart

A doctrinal book that compares the principles of the kingdom of the world and the kingdom of God. The believer is faced each day with choices which reveal his loyalty to each of these two kingdoms.

B-WA | ISBN 1882701054

One Day at a Time

Each daily meditation is just a page long, but with each Scripture presented in a fresh way. William MacDonald stirs your heart to practical devotedness to the Lord. It is intended to stimulate your thinking in Scripture, and to help you apply the truth to your daily walk.

Hard Cover | B-ODA | ISBN 1882701496

NEW! Paper Back | B-ODAP | ISBN 1882701490

Other Books by William MacDonald
Available at GOSPEL FOLIO PRESS

TRACT by William MacDonald

Emmaus Bible Courses
by William MacDonald
Available at GOSPEL FOLIO PRESS